PENGUIN

The Penguin Guide to
RETIREMENT HOTSPOTS

Rick Osborn was born in Sydney in 1943. He graduated from the University of NSW with a Commerce Degree in Economics, and went on to spend thirty years in the advertising industry. During his career, Rick was the managing director and subsequently chairman of George Patterson Sydney, Australia's largest advertising company at the time.

Rick currently enjoys a very active retirement, travelling extensively within Australia and overseas. He divides his time between the Eastern Suburbs of Sydney and Hervey Bay on Queensland's Fraser Coast.

The **PENGUIN** Guide to

Retirement

HOTSPOTS

The best **100** places to live in Australia & New Zealand

Rick Osborn

PENGUIN BOOKS

PENGUIN BOOKS

Published by the Penguin Group
Penguin Group (Australia)
250 Camberwell Road, Camberwell, Victoria 3124, Australia
(a division of Pearson Australia Group Pty Ltd)
Penguin Group (USA) Inc.
375 Hudson Street, New York, New York 10014, USA
Penguin Group (Canada)
90 Eglinton Avenue East, Suite 700, Toronto ON M4P 2Y3, Canada
(a division of Pearson Penguin Canada Inc.)
Penguin Books Ltd
80 Strand, London WC2R 0RL, England
Penguin Ireland
25 St Stephen's Green, Dublin 2, Ireland
(a division of Penguin Books Ltd)
Penguin Books India Pvt Ltd
11 Community Centre, Panchsheel Park, New Delhi – 110 017, India
Penguin Group (NZ)
Cnr Airborne and Rosedale Roads, Albany, Auckland, New Zealand
(a division of Pearson New Zealand Ltd)
Penguin Books (South Africa) (Pty) Ltd
24 Sturdee Avenue, Rosebank, Johannesburg 2196, South Africa

Penguin Books Ltd, Registered Offices: 80 Strand, London WC2R 0RL, England

First published by Penguin Group (Australia),
a division of Pearson Australia Group Pty Ltd, 2006

10 9 8 7 6 5 4 3 2 1

Cover and text design by Elizabeth Dias © Penguin Group (Australia)
Map design by Damien Demaj © Demaj
Typeset in ITC Galliard by Post Pre-press Group, Brisbane, Queensland
Printed in Australia by McPherson's Printing Group, Maryborough, Victoria

National Library of Australia
Cataloguing-in-Publication data:

  Osborn, Rick.
  The Penguin guide to retirement hotspots: the 100 best places to live in Australia and
  New Zealand.

  ISBN 0 14 300339 9.

  1. Retirement, Places of – Australia. 2. Retirement, Places of – New Zealand.
  3. Retirement – Planning. I. Title.

  646.790994

www.penguin.com.au

This book is dedicated to
Matilda, Tristan, Hamish and Coco,
Retirees of 2060

contents

Introduction *1*

Queensland

Gulf of Carpentaria *11*
  Karumba *11*
Far North Queensland *14*
  Port Douglas/Cairns *14*
  Atherton *17*
  Cassowary Coast *20*
  Townsville *24*
Capricorn Coast *27*
Agnes Water/1770 *31*
Coral Coast *34*
Hervey Bay *37*
Sunshine Coast *42*
  Noosa *42*
  Coolum Beach *45*
  Nambour/Buderim *46*
  Maroochydore *48*
  Caloundra *51*
Bribie Island *54*
Caboolture *57*
Redcliffe *60*
Toowoomba *63*
North Stradbroke Island *66*
Gold Coast *70*
  Security Living *75*
  Broadwater *77*
  Canal Living *78*
  Hinterland *80*

High-rise   *81*
Beach Living   *83*
Queensland's Top 10   *85*

New South Wales   Tweed Valley   *89*
Byron Bay   *93*
Ballina   *97*
Yamba   *100*
Grafton   *103*
Coffs Harbour   *106*
Nambucca Heads   *110*
South West Rocks   *113*
Port Macquarie   *115*
Taree   *119*
Forster & Great Lakes   *123*
Port Stephens   *127*
Lake Macquarie   *131*
Central Coast   *135*
Wyong   *135*
Gosford   *139*
Sydney   *144*
Upper North Shore   *144*
Northern Beaches   *147*
Northern Harbour Suburbs   *150*
Eastern Harbour Suburbs   *153*
Kiama   *156*
Shoalhaven   *159*
Jervis Bay   *163*
Ulladulla   *167*
Sussex Inlet   *171*
Batemans Bay   *171*
Sapphire Coast   *175*
Tamworth   *179*
Mudgee   *182*
Blue Mountains   *185*

Southern Highlands   *189*
New South Wales' Top 10   *194*

Victoria   Mallacoota   *199*
Lakes Entrance   *201*
Inverloch   *205*
Phillip Island   *208*
Mornington Peninsula   *210*
Melbourne   *216*
　　By the Bay   *216*
　　Toorak   *219*
Bellarine Peninsula/Queenscliff   *221*
Apollo Bay/Lorne   *225*
Colac & District   *228*
Hepburn Springs/Daylesford   *230*
Wangaratta to Yarrawonga   *234*
Horsham   *237*
Mildura   *239*
Victoria's Top 10   *243*

Tasmania   Wynyard   *248*
Port Sorell   *251*
Bridport   *254*
St Helens   *258*
Launceston   *261*
Hobart   *264*
Tasmania's Top 10   *269*

South Australia   Robe/Kingston   *273*
Murray Bridge   *276*
Adelaide   *279*
　　Eastern Suburbs   *279*
　　Beach Suburbs   *281*
McLaren Vale   *285*
Strathalbyn   *287*

Victor Harbor   *289*
Barossa Valley   *293*
Copper Coast   *296*
South Australia's Top 10   *299*

Western Australia   Albany   *303*
Augusta   *306*
Busselton   *309*
Mandurah   *312*
Fremantle   *316*
Perth   *319*
Yanchep   *322*
Kalbarri   *324*
Denham   *327*
Carnarvon   *330*
Exmouth   *333*
Western Australia's Top 10   *336*

New Zealand   **North Island**   *341*
Bay of Plenty   *341*
Kapiti Coast   *345*
South Island   *349*
Marlborough Region   *349*
Nelson   *352*
Christchurch   *355*
New Zealand's Top 10   *359*

Appendix 1   The statistics   *360*

Appendix 2   Tips for selecting your ideal
retirement location   *361*

Appendix 3   Notes   *368*

Acknowledgements   *369*

introduction

Most of us spend our lives dancing to the beat of someone else's drum, usually that of an employer or our children. When retirement comes along, we are given choices that we may never have been offered before. There is little forewarning and many people fail to take full advantage of these new opportunities.

Retirement is *our* time. For many of us, it's the first time we have had the freedom to make choices about what to do with our lives. It's important to explore the various options as early as possible, preferably before retirement. Whatever you do, don't leave it too late.

One of the most important options, and the one which can affect every other decision, is where you choose to live in your retirement. This book will help you to explore the many potential locations in Australia and New Zealand from the comfort of your armchair. It is the result of my own personal experience, for like you, I too have been searching for the best possible retirement lifestyle.

Baby Boomers will be familiar with the U2 hit 'I Still Haven't Found What I'm Looking For'. The song sums up the restlessness which has driven me to think hard about retirement and query whether I might be living in the wrong place. For me, trying to find peace in retirement seems akin to selecting a new religion – everyone else appears to be happy with their choice, but I'm not sure.

Standing on the sand at Sydney's Balmoral Beach on an azure-blue autumn morning, breathing in the fresh, crisp air, it's hard to think of a better place to be retired. Only a kilometre away it's a different story, with the traffic gridlocked on Military Road. Maybe I was listening to that song by U2 when I wondered whether there was a better place to spend my retirement years. I could choose to do pretty much whatever I pleased, and live wherever I wanted, but I had no plan. I'd spent most of my working life in the city, but whenever I took holidays I went elsewhere. Now that I was no longer working, I wondered if I should be living somewhere else.

Few cities are more geared for the worker than Sydney. Try getting off a bus with a walking stick in peak hour and you are likely to find yourself in a wheelchair. Anzac Day seems to be the only day that oldies are appreciated en masse, and even then I fear that some of the younger spectators find the marchers too slow for their liking! It's a city where impatience is a virtue and a car without a horn isn't drivable. In the Eastern Suburbs – where cars are double-parked while their drivers run errands or pick up a pre-ordered takeaway – drivers use their horns as a stress-release device.

As a worker, I fitted into Sydney perfectly: I was as impatient as the best of them. That was before my retirement. But as a retired person, did I still fit into the city? Cities are filled with endless annoyances: relentless queues, aggressive motorists, ubiquitous street charity collectors, traffic snarls, roadworks, new one-way streets that were two-way yesterday, blocked-off streets that weren't blocked off yesterday, unintelligible parking signs and voracious parking meters.

I still liked lots of things about Sydney. The harbour and beaches, the restaurants and shops, the weather . . . but the city was rapidly turning me into the stereotypical Grumpy Old Man! Other Aussies seemed to have it sussed. The entire population of Victoria migrates north the day they reach the age of sixty, flying over New South Wales to nest on the Gold Coast. And unlike the short-tailed shearwater and the humpback whale, they don't return. Well, that's what the Gold Coast real estate propaganda would have you believe. My panic buttons were being pushed. I needed to explore the opportunities. But what were they? And how would I tear myself away from Balmoral Beach and my dysfunctional and multi-dimensional family?

The numerous relationships which hold many people firmly rooted in their home town can render thoughts of retiring elsewhere purely hypothetical, but the more you examine the subject, the more you come to realise that anything is achievable for a retired person. After all, you can be anywhere in the world within twenty-four hours, so how easy would it be to commute to visit your family and friends from anywhere in Australia? Suppose you chose to leave Sydney to retire to a small rural property outside Launceston. The flight time between the two cities is under two hours, and with a little planning it is possible to buy a one-way fare for around $100. There are numerous retirees who have made the move and kept a small bolthole in their home city to return to when things get too hot up north or too cold down south.

I was pondering this new information in a coffee shop when a mobile phone at the table next to me burst into 'La Cucaracha'. Almost instantly, another mobile phone began to crow like a rooster. Patrons who had previously been talking in conversational tones raised their voices and yelled into their mobiles. I could feel the Grump returning. I resolved to start taking this exercise more seriously. It soon became an all-consuming project.

In my thirty years in advertising and marketing, I spent countless hours analysing research about markets, products, brands and consumer patterns. This preparatory work was essential before any attempt could be made to put together a marketing strategy or advertising campaign.

One of my clients was the NSW Tourism Authority, and the first questions we would ask about a city or region were: 'What makes this place unique?', 'Why would people want to come here?' and 'What other locations are competing with this place?'. I approached the task of analysing the retirement options in

Australia and New Zealand in the same way. I used the many websites that are out there and the available census data to provide the necessary quantitative information, but the qualitative input could only be gained by my personal observations from visiting and talking to locals.

Speak to your family and friends about where to live in retirement and a far-away look comes into their eyes as they picture an imaginary place or recall a scene from holidays past. This is the stuff of dreams and good times. But to make it work in the long term you need to delve deeper than holiday resorts, which are great for a two-week respite from the rat race but fall short of the mark in providing the stimulus you need for the rest of your life.

Fortunately, there's no shortage of choices in Australia from which to choose. There aren't too many other places in the world where you're faced with such an extraordinary range of potential retirement locations.

Start with climate. We have cold climes, with snow if you like, log fires and colourful autumns; temperate climates with mild winters and warm summers; subtropical regions, where there is virtually no winter; and the tropics, where the seasons are either wet or dry. And within each climate zone there is the choice of seaside, lakes, hill country, city living, country towns, tiny villages and rural farmland.

You'll soon come to realise that the job of identifying your retirement Mecca is enormous, and that to make the project more manageable you'll need to create some guidelines. My first rule was taken from the old advertising catch cry, 'thousands of people can't be wrong'. They can be, of course, as history has proven time and again, but I rationalised that if a lot of other old buggers had decided to live somewhere then it must have something going for it (admittedly, as I came to discover, in some places it wasn't too much more than an RSL and a bowls club!).

And so I had my starting point, and after many weeks spent studying various websites and Australian Bureau of Statistics census data, I was able to identify what I came to refer to as 'the

Retirement Magnets'. They were the locations where the over-sixties tended to congregate, and were therefore home to a higher proportion of over-sixties than the national average. I chose places whose overall population was growing rather than decreasing, as so many places in rural Australia are getting smaller by the month. Some of them have a very high proportion of over-sixties but their total population is contracting at a rate of knots. I didn't want to end up in a place like that.

As I worked on the project, I discovered that a retirement magnet could be a village, town, city, suburb or a number of locations grouped together. The list of potential retirement magnets was taking shape.

When I began to research each location, I found that photographs and tourist information can be misleading. Websites and printed material are produced by parties who are interested in promoting a location. Photographs in particular can conjure up an idyllic image, taken at a certain moment in time, but the lens can't capture the reality of a harsh climate, a lack of infrastructure or the inaccessibility of a location.

I needed to get out there to see these places for myself. I went ahead and visited as many locations as possible in order to make an informed decision. I ended up making twenty trips around the country – some with my partner, Judy; others with my son Antony; and many times by myself. Queensland is so big, measuring almost 2000 kilometres from the Gold Coast to Port Douglas, that it took five trips to cover it properly!

I have chosen 100 retirement magnets, but my book also covers many additional locations. For example, the entry for Port Macquarie also covers nearby options such as Lighthouse Beach, Bonny Hills, Lake Cathie, North Haven and Laurieton.

Although many Australians retire to the country, the biggest retirement populations are found in the capital cities. In 2001, when the last census was taken, 3.3 million of our population were aged sixty years and over, and of these well over half lived in our capital cities. Within each capital city there are a number of different retirement choices and I have identified the more interesting options which have large clusters of over-sixties; for example, Adelaide's beach suburbs and Bayside Melbourne.

Some entries are household names, such as Noosa Heads, Cairns, Port Macquarie, Albany, the Gold Coast and the Southern Highlands. Other retirement magnets – such as Mallacoota and Horsham (Victoria), Yamba and Iluka (New South Wales), and the Copper Coast (South Australia) – are not well known throughout Australia, although they are populated by a high proportion of over-sixties.

My selection has not been ranked or short-listed – that's up to you to decide, depending on your interests, lifestyle and other preferences. Each entry should provide you with enough information to decide whether the location deserves further investigation.

The entries are introduced by an overview, which describes the location and includes first-person observations from my visit. Detailed information on the area follows, including population figures, climate patterns, location and transport, infrastructure, shopping and dining facilities, opportunities for social stimulation and real estate prices. The entries end with a brief summary of the location's pros and cons as a potential place to live in retirement. The rest is up to you.

The 100 retirement magnets listed in this book are organised state by state, beginning with Queensland and the Gulf of Carpentaria and moving clockwise through New South Wales, Victoria, Tasmania, South Australia and Western Australia, followed by New Zealand. There were no retirement magnets identified within the Northern Territory or the Australian Capital Territory. Locations within each state are also listed in clockwise order.

Your comments about retirement hotspots are most welcome. Please send any suggestions for amendments and future inclusions to rickosborn@optusnet.com.au.

I hope this book will help you decide what you really want from your retirement, and help you choose which corner of this wonderful country will suit you best. Put your dream to the test, right now, before it is too late. Happy planning, and may you make the best of what could be the best years of your life.

queensland

Gulf of Carpentaria 11

　Karumba 11

Far North Queensland 14

　Port Douglas/Cairns 14

　Atherton 17

　Cassowary Coast 20

　Townsville 24

Capricorn Coast 27

Agnes Water/1770 31

Coral Coast 34

Hervey Bay 37

Sunshine Coast 42

　Noosa 42

　Coolum Beach 45

　Nambour/Buderim 46

　Maroochydore 48

　Caloundra 51

Bribie Island 54

Caboolture 57

Redcliffe 60

Toowoomba 63

North Stradbroke Island 66

Gold Coast 70

　Security Living 75

　Broadwater 77

　Canal Living 78

　Hinterland 80

　High-Rise 81

　Beach Living 83

Queensland's Top 10 85

Opposite: The busy marina and waterfront shops at Boat Harbour in Hervey Bay

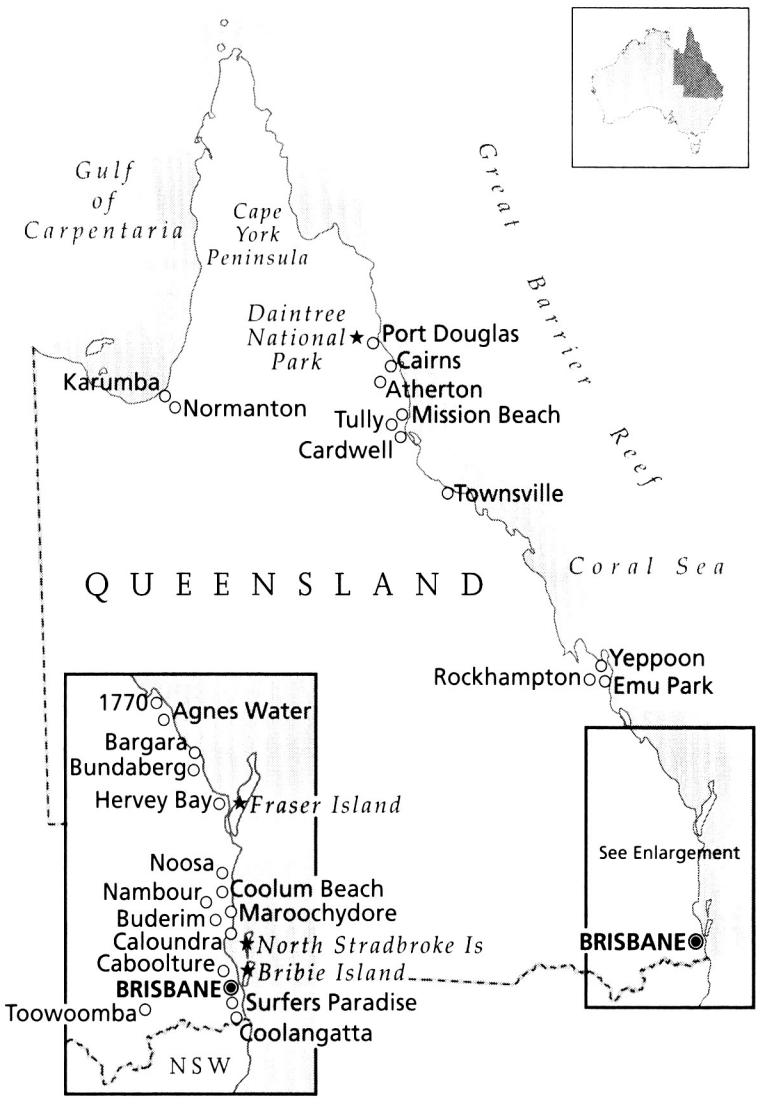

Gulf
of
Carpentaria

Cape
York
Peninsula

Daintree
National ★ ○Port Douglas
Park ○Cairns

Karumba○ ○Atherton
 ○Normanton Tully○ ○Mission Beach
 Cardwell○

 ○Townsville

QUEENSLAND

Great Barrier Reef

Coral Sea

Rockhampton○○ ○Yeppoon
 ○Emu Park

1770○ ○Agnes Water
Bargara○
Bundaberg○
Hervey Bay○ ★Fraser Island

Noosa○
Nambour○○Coolum Beach
Buderim○○Maroochydore
Caloundra○★North Stradbroke Is
Caboolture○★Bribie Island
 BRISBANE◎ ○Surfers Paradise
Toowoomba○ ○Coolangatta

NSW

See Enlargement

BRISBANE◎

gulf of carpentaria

karumba

Where Crocodile Dundee hangs up his hat

Karumba is a remote fishing village at the mouth of the Norman River, 2150 kilometres north-west of Brisbane. Normanton, its nearest neighbour, is 70 kilometres inland on the edge of the Savannah-region grasslands. This is a spectacular part of Australia, with stunning sunsets year-round and the little-known Morning Glory in spring – it's a unique cloud formation which occasionally rolls in across the gulf and is an awesome sight.

Karumba is a centre for prawning and barramundi fishing. The wetlands between here and Normanton are a habitat for many bird species, and Burke and Wills' most northerly camp site is nearby. This is a growth area, driven by tourism.

POPULATION

- 3000
- 25% over sixty

In the winter months the population jumps by 6000 as tourists head north to escape the cooler climes of the south. They leave before it gets too hot.

CLIMATE

Summer 24.4°C to 32.6°C
Winter 14°C to 27.5°C
Sunshine 145 days
Rain 60 days
Rainfall 911 mm
The wet (monsoon) season runs from December to March.

LOCATION & GETTING AROUND

Karumba is seriously remote. It's a 25-hour car trip to Brisbane (2150 kilometres) and nine hours to Cairns (760 kilometres). Flying is the best way to get around up here.

Roads Sealed. The romantically named Matilda Highway links Karumba and Normanton.

Nearest airports There's a small red-earth airport at Karumba and a commercial airport at Normanton, with services to Cairns and Mount Isa.

Nearest train The Gulflander at Normanton, but it won't take you far as it is now a tourist attraction.

Buses Cairns–Karumba–Normanton

Taxis ✓

INFRASTRUCTURE

Hospitals Karumba has a clinic, which a doctor attends twice per week, and it also has an ambulance. Normanton has a small hospital which can take X-rays and has beds for acute and long-term patients. The Royal Flying Doctor Service has a clinic on Tuesdays and Fridays at Normanton.

Retirement villages ✗

Police stations Karumba and Normanton

Television stations Four stations including ABC. Amazing!

Radio Mount Isa radio, plus ABC

Local newspaper None – if you want today's Queensland papers you will have to come back tomorrow.

Communications The area now has access to mobile phones as well as the Internet.

RECREATION

Beaches Kurumba Point is the only stretch of beach in the area that can be accessed by road – but don't think of swimming there, due to the crocs! Five local fishermen are one-legged.

Coastguard ✓

Cycleways Too hot in summer, but anywhere you want to go in the dry season.

Bushwalking & National Parks A winter pastime as it's too hot in the wet season; early-morning or evening beach walks can be pleasant year-round.

Dogs Allowed anywhere, but they don't all return home.

SHOPPING

Karumba has two supermarkets, a butcher, bakery, post office and bank. Normanton is slightly bigger and has a little more of everything plus the Carpentaria Council Chambers and Courthouse.

DINING

Karumba has a seafood restaurant, hotel, tavern and café.

SOCIAL ACTIVITY

Fishing is a popular activity in Karumba, and barramundi are found here in abundance. Locals regularly catch fish in excess of five kilograms, and the annual barramundi fishing contest is one of the year's highlights. Another popular pastime is croc-spotting on the Norman River. The historic Gulflander railway runs from Normanton to Croydon for tourist jaunts rather than commuting purposes.

• Fishing • Golf • Lawn bowls • Library
• Sports centre • Swimming pool • Tennis

REAL ESTATE

• Median house price: $150 000
The prices are higher than they would normally be, due to the lack of available land releases which are controlled by council.

WHY LIVE HERE?

Karumba offers a taste of the outback by the sea. It is a very friendly town and undoubtedly beautiful, in a rugged Australian outback kind of way. Neil, the owner of the local supermarket, said to me, 'It's God's own country, but it helps if you like fishing.'

far north queensland

port douglas / cairns

Sun, sand and stingers

Port Douglas (often referred to as 'Port') looks like a tropical island. The main thoroughfare, Macrossan Street, is to Port Douglas what Hastings Street is to Noosa, only it's more lush, more tropical, more humid and even more picturesque, but with the same emphasis on outdoor cafés, upmarket restaurants and boutiques. At one end of the main street is the beach, at the other there are mangroves. Tourists flock to Port Douglas from May to November when the water is clear of stingers, the cyclone season is over and the mozzies are less threatening. Houses are tucked in behind the foliage in the quiet backstreets, and some of them have water views from the hill above Macrossan.

Cairns lies 70 kilometres to the south. Retirees are more numerous here, but it is a young people's city and the overall percentage of over-sixties is low, whereas in Port Douglas it is high. Cairns is picturesque and busy, and it even has dreaded parking meters, which are seemingly everywhere. The terrain is flat and ideal for mobility scooters, an increasingly popular mode of transport for older folk. The streets are canopied with colourful flowering trees, which protect pedestrians and al fresco diners from the frequent showers in the wet season, when everything seems to be constantly damp.

POPULATION

Port Douglas	Cairns
• 3500	• 100 000
• 22% over sixty	• 12% over sixty

Port Douglas' population rises by at least 2500 in the dry season. The population there grew by 61 per cent between the last two censuses, whereas Cairns' population grew by only 7 per cent.

CLIMATE

Summer 23.7°C to 30.3°C
Winter 16.8°C to 24.6°C

Sunshine 80 days

Rain 121 days

Rainfall 2013 mm

This area isn't known as the 'wet tropics' for nothing – when I was there in January it rained without pause for three days with threats of a cyclone forming!

LOCATION & GETTING AROUND

Cairns is a long way up the coast from Brisbane – it's a 20-hour drive (1700 kilometres). Flying is the only practical way to commute.

Roads The Captain Cook Highway runs from Port Douglas to Cairns, from where the Bruce Highway runs south and the Kennedy Highway heads inland. The roads in the area flow reasonably well, even though they are narrow and single file, and many semi-trailers use them.

Nearest airports Cairns Airport has domestic and international flights. A direct flight to Sydney takes 2.5 hours. Port Douglas has a helicopter service.

Nearest train Cairns–Brisbane

Buses Cairns–Port Douglas

Taxis There are taxi and limousine services.

INFRASTRUCTURE

Hospitals Port Douglas has no hospitals. Cairns Base Hospital has more than 300 beds, and Calgary Private is also quite large. The Royal Flying Doctor is based at Cairns Airport.

Retirement villages One in Port Douglas (Port Haven) and five in Cairns (the Parks, Coral Sea Gardens, Heritage Gardens, Masonic Care and Nazareth Village).

Police stations Cairns and Port Douglas

Local newspaper *Cairns Post*

RECREATION

Beaches Cairns has no beaches, but there are beautiful golden-sand beaches just north of Cairns, including Yorkeys Knob and

Palm Cove, the latter being a large resort. The beaches stretch all the way up to Four Mile Beach at Port Douglas, which is fringed with coconut palms. Surf is kept to a half-metre swell due to the nearby Great Barrier Reef. Stingers are a major problem between November and May – and they can be lethal. Some beaches have stinger nets that stop box jellyfish, but the smaller Irukandji jellyfish can penetrate the nets. Cairns has a very large and attractive free public swimming pool on the Esplanade.

Coastguard ✓

Cycleways Port Douglas has extensive flat areas and the roads are quiet. Cairns is also flat and there are numerous cycle tracks around the beaches of North Cairns.

Bushwalking & National Parks The world-famous Daintree National Park is only 15 kilometres north of Port Douglas; it's accessible on foot and by 4WD. The Harbour Walk on the Cairns waterfront extends along a wooden boardwalk to Trinity Inlet.

Dogs Must be kept on a lead.

SHOPPING

Port Douglas has a mix of exotic and more useful shops, including many boutiques and an adequate Coles supermarket. Being a large city, Cairns has plenty of everything.

DINING

Port Douglas is the dining capital of the north, thanks to its roaring tourist trade. There are some really great restaurants – with prices to match – and many relaxing outdoor cafés. Cairns has less fine dining and plenty of cheaper options.

SOCIAL ACTIVITY

There are plenty of outdoor pursuits to enjoy in Port Douglas, dominated by boating and golf. There are three golf courses in Port Douglas, an excellent one at the Mirage, several in Cairns (Paradise Palms is ranked ninth in Australia), one at Palm Cove, and courses in nearby towns. Fishing for barramundi and snorkelling off the reefs are other popular activities. There are large marinas at Cairns, Yorkeys Knob and Palm Cove, plus a slipway at Port Douglas. For further education, there's James Cook University in Cairns.

• Boating • Fishing • Golf • Most community organisations
• Most religions • Snorkelling

REAL ESTATE

Port Douglas
• Median house price: $310 000
• Median price of bedsitter resort apartments: $200 000

Cairns
• Median house price: $287 000
• Median unit price: $155 000

Executive homes with views cost from $500 000, while a home on the Cairns Esplanade could cost anything between $1 million and $2 million.

WHY LIVE HERE?

Whether you are a romantic who yearns to act out *South Pacific*, or a more rugged type who missed out on being selected to join *Survivor*, FNQ may suit you. Retirement in this part of the world is even better if you can afford to fly up from your home in the south to spend only the winter months here.

atherton
Highland living in the tropics

Atherton is 1200 metres above sea level (the highest point in Queensland), on the tableland inland from Cairns. The plateau was formed by volcanic activity, and many former volcanoes are now picturesque lakes. It's quite amazing to emerge from the lush rainforests to find bucolic pastures that are home to grazing cattle and crops.

Atherton is a typical country town with quite a lot to keep the locals amused. The outback, also known as Savannah Country, is only a two-hour drive to the west, where the lush countryside abruptly ends and the desert begins. Also nearby are a number of attractive villages. Yungaburra, fifteen minutes away by car, is one of the prettiest and has numerous heritage-listed buildings. There are plenty of other tourist attractions in the region, including the Crystal Caves, the Crater, the 500-year-old Curtain Fig and the Skyrail Rainforest Cableway, which runs from Atherton to Kuranda and has views of Barron Falls.

POPULATION

- 5900
- 25% over sixty

The population of the district as a whole exceeds 10 000.

CLIMATE

Summer 18.3°C to 29°C
Winter 9.9°C to 22.9°C
Rain 125 days
Rainfall 1413 mm
Atherton has a mild tropical climate without the high coastal humidity. By the time cyclones reach here, they have usually been downgraded to storms.

LOCATION & GETTING AROUND

Atherton is 80 kilometres inland from Cairns, a drive of 1.5 hours via the Kennedy Highway (depending on the weather – you often have to drive through clouds – and the number of semi-trailers).
Roads Four good major access roads run through Atherton. The main route is the Kennedy Highway linking Cairns to Atherton and Ravenshoe.
Nearest airports Cairns
Nearest train Cairns. The railway station at Atherton is used by tourist steam trains.
Buses Coaches run daily to and from Cairns
Taxis ✓

INFRASTRUCTURE

Hospitals Atherton Hospital has two specialist physicians. There's also a health centre at Atherton and another hospital at Herberton (18 kilometres from Atherton).

Retirement villages Atherton and Yungaburra

Police station Atherton

Local newspaper *Atherton Tablelander*

RECREATION

Cycleways Plenty of quiet back roads for safe cycling.

Bushwalking & National Parks Halloran's Hill walking track winds through rainforest and provides views of the Seven Sisters and Lake Tinaroo. Mount Hypipamee National Park is 25 kilometres away, with a walking track to Dinner Falls and various swimming holes. Hasties Swamp is popular for birdwatching and has a bird hide; there are many different species of waterbirds to be found here. The Wongabel Botanical Walk, nine kilometres from Atherton, is also excellent for birdwatching.

Dogs Regulations are pretty relaxed; Ravenshoe has a dog exercise area.

SHOPPING

Atherton has two supermarkets (IGA and Woolworths) plus a Big W. Occasional trips to Cairns would be necessary. Speciality shops include art and craft stores and antique shops. Weekend markets are held on a rotating basis throughout the district.

DINING

Dining options are somewhat limited but there are reasonable cafés in Atherton and Yungaburra.

SOCIAL ACTIVITY

Unlike the coast, which has a limited barramundi season, fishing for barra is a year-round activity on nearby Lake Tinaroo – in fact, the world record for the largest barra ever caught was on this lake. Tinaroo is also a centre for water-based activities and Lake Eacham is a popular swimming spot. Clubs include sailing, turf and walking activities. There's a TAFE at Mareeba, 30 kilometres from Atherton.

• Arts and crafts • Bushwalking • Fishing • Galleries
• Library • Lawn bowls • Most community organisations
• Most religions • Museums • Swimming
• Tennis • Walking • Waterskiing

REAL ESTATE

• Median house price: $205 000
• Median unit price: $165 000
• Land: from $50 000

Real estate prices have risen significantly over the last year in the Atherton area.

WHY LIVE HERE?

In the words of a local retired woman who works on a part-time basis in the Tourist Information Centre, 'I used to live in Cairns but there's more for retirees to do here – every craft imaginable – and it's a lot cooler.'

cassowary coast
Wet & tropo

Mission Beach is the best-known section of the Cassowary Coast, encompassing the following villages linked by palm-fringed stretches of golden sand: Bingal Bay, Mission Beach, Wongaling Beach and South Mission Beach. Houses are sprinkled behind the foliage and coconut palms, some of them overlooking the beach. Mission Beach itself is where you'll find the majority of shops and cafés. For typical timber Queenslanders fronted by well-ordered, nicely mown lawns, head to South Mission Beach. You won't find any shops here but there's plenty of beach, including the Horizons and Bedarra resorts. South Mission Beach gets my vote as the best spot to retire to in this area of the coast.

It can be uncomfortable up here in the wet season, as the warm and damp environment brings out lots of biting bugs at night. The dry season is the best time here, and many of the residents are part-timers who spend the wet months south in better summer climes. This is the spot to choose if you can afford two homes, though there are a few other problems to consider. They include cyclones, crocodiles (sighted in the ocean as well as the estuaries), stingers and cassowaries, which can attack humans if provoked. My son and I had a brief encounter with an agitated two-metre cassowary. We hastily retreated, as they have sharp claws which could make quite a mess of you.

Further down the Cassowary Coast are the small towns of Tully and Cardwell. Tully is inland of Tully Heads and has the highest rainfall in Australia. Cardwell is a small seaside town opposite Hinchinbrook Island. Houses here are older style and could offer good renovation opportunities. Port Hinchinbrook (attached to Cardwell) is the new hotspot and has been developed by Keith Williams as a planned integrated resort township, with underground services, wide roads and landscaping – quite an improvement on the housing in this area.

POPULATION

Mission Beach	Innisfail	Ingham	Cardwell	Tully
• 2000	• 8000	• 4700	• 1500	• 3000

One third of the populations of both Mission Beach and Cardwell are aged over sixty. Tully, Mission Beach and Port Hinchinbrook are the growth areas.

CLIMATE

Summer 22.8°C to 31.5°C
Winter 13.5°C to 24.9°C
Sunshine 123 days
Rain 127 days
Rainfall 2118 mm

It's humid year-round in the wet tropics. Tully wins the rubber gumboot with an average annual rainfall of 4490 mm, almost all of which falls between January and mid-April.

LOCATION & GETTING AROUND

It's a two-hour drive heading north from Mission Beach to Cairns (140 kilometres) and 20 hours to Brisbane (1600 kilometres). Cardwell is 70 kilometres south of Mission Beach and Tully is 30 kilometres inland.

Roads Mission Beach is 16 kilometres off the Bruce Highway. The roads around here are sealed but narrow.

Nearest airports Cairns and Townsville

Nearest train Cardwell (2.5 hours to Townsville)

Buses Bingal Bay–South Mission Beach

Taxis There are taxi and limousine services.

INFRASTRUCTURE

Hospitals Tully, Innisfail, Babinda and Gordonvale

Retirement villages Cardwell, Tully and Innisfail

Police stations Cardwell and Innisfail

Local newspapers *Cardwell Advertiser* and *Tully Times*

RECREATION

Beaches The beaches are scenic but don't invite swimming because of mud from the mangrove rivers emptying into the Hinchinbrook Channel. Crocodiles and poisonous box jellyfish can be a problem in summer, although the council has erected stinger nets on some beaches. There are a number of freshwater swimming holes heading inland – I'm not sure how they keep the crocs out!

Coastguard ✓

Cycleways Roads are flat and the traffic is light

Bushwalking & National Parks The area is well known for its national parks, stunning waterfalls, spectacular tropical rainforest and crystal-clear creeks. The Misty Mountains network of long-distance walking trails was the first in Australia to be established in a high-altitude rainforest environment. The Edmund Kennedy National Park is four kilometres north of Cardwell and has two walking tracks which pass through tropical rainforest and woodland. The tracks have a system of boardwalks and bridges over the mangrove swamps because of the presence of estuarine crocodiles. The Murray Falls have smooth rock pools for swimming and the Blencoe Falls have a spectacular drop of 90 metres. Hinchinbrook Island is Australia's largest island national park, with sandy beaches and tropical rainforest. It's accessible only by boat, and is mainly frequented by walkers.

Dogs Must be kept on a lead at all times – after all, if you let them roam free, you might end up with just the collar!

SHOPPING

The pedestrianised shopping strip at Mission Beach looks appealing but apart from a mini IGA supermarket, a couple of boutiques and a few café/restaurants there's not a lot there. Monthly local produce markets are held in Cardwell, which also has a supermarket and grocery stores. Port Hinchinbrook has a central shopping complex and grocery outlets. Innisfail has a larger choice, including Coles and Woolworths, and Tully has a reasonable number of shops.

DINING

Mission Beach has only a limited number of cafés but they're quite good, and know how to make a good cappuccino. Quite a few of FNQ's café proprietors are refugees from southern capitals who have introduced a higher standard of catering to the area.

SOCIAL ACTIVITY

Social activities are sporty and active in these parts – you need to drive 75 kilometres to the Cardwell Country Club for golf or lawn bowls. Mission Beach is a popular jumping-off point for the Great Barrier Reef, where you can snorkel and scuba dive, and the beach itself is popular for long walks – in fact, locals often get around from place to place by walking along the beach rather than taking the road.

• Bushwalking • Birdwatching • Fishing • Sailing • Walking

REAL ESTATE

Mission Beach Area

- Median house price: $310 000
- Median unit price: $178 000

There's currently not a lot to choose from in Mission Beach, and beachfront homes have been known to fetch around $1 million. The new development at Port Hinchinbrook features homes with ocean, marina or canal frontage from $695 000.

WHY LIVE HERE?

Retirement doesn't get any more tropical than this in Australia. If you want to opt for the Far North this is the place, provided you're not put off by the mozzies or other lurking predators – and, according to Mavis the barmaid, 'you don't mind wet feet'.

townsville
Australia's Côte d'Azur

The most beautiful city in Queensland, Townsville sits on a bay opposite Magnetic Island. Rising out of the middle of the city is an amazing red hill, which looks more like a fort and seems somehow perfectly in keeping with the surrounding mix of historic and modern. Well-maintained old buildings mingle with fresh contemporary architecture, giving the impression that Townsville has been carefully planned. Plenty of lush greenery borders the bay and its golden beaches – it's just a pity you can't swim there when the stingers are in season. You'll see letter boxes at all the main beaches containing bottles of vinegar to remind you of the problem (the vinegar is used to alleviate the pain from stingers). Some stinger nets are provided but there is also a huge, public rock pool to swim in overlooking the sea.

The Strand twists along the seafront beside a wide public reserve. It's a popular stretch to promenade or exercise for locals and tourists alike – unfortunately, bored hoons also like to roam up and down the Strand at night in their cars – and is lined with hotels, restaurants and expensive homes and apartments. Townsville doesn't rely solely on tourism, as it's also a very active commercial port and there's a large military base here. The city is big enough to absorb these various activities and caters to all ages and lifestyles.

POPULATION

- 95 000
- 15% over sixty

The nearby town of Ayr (pop 8500) has 22 per cent over-sixties.

CLIMATE

Summer 24.7°C to 30.9°C
Winter 15.5°C to 24.3°C
Sunshine 123 days
Rain 73 days
Rainfall 1102 mm

Townsville is tropical but without the heavy rainfall of its northern neighbours.

LOCATION & GETTING AROUND

Townsville is 1360 kilometres north of Brisbane, which is a 16-hour drive. The domestic air service is good – it's just over two hours' flight time to Sydney.

Roads Major roads within Townsville are dual lane. Approach roads are single lane each way.

Nearest airport Townsville
Nearest train Townsville
Buses Local and regional services
Ferries Townsville–Magnetic Island
Taxis ✓

INFRASTRUCTURE

Hospitals Townsville Hospital is a large teaching hospital with full services. Mater Misericordiae is a 167-bed private hospital.
Retirement villages Fifteen, many with full aged-care facilities
Police stations ✓
Local newspaper *Townsville Bulletin*

RECREATION

Beaches Townsville is blessed with golden sand but no surf. The water is often murky due to the flow of fresh water from the estuaries nearby.

Coastguard ✓

Cycleways The Strand shared pathway on the ocean shoreline and Ross River Bikeway are excellent.

Bushwalking & National Parks Castle Hill walking track is right in the centre of the city but it's steep. Two national parks are nearby: Bowling Green Bay National Park and Mount Elliot.

Dogs The city has several exercise areas.

SHOPPING

Townsville has good facilities, as you'd expect, with 12 major shopping centres.

DINING

There are many fine restaurants along the marina and harbour strips as well as on the foreshore and in the various shopping malls.

SOCIAL ACTIVITY

Every activity is available in Townsville, from bellydancing, herpetology and flower-arranging to martial arts and yoga – plus there's a drive-in cinema and five cinema complexes. There are 10 lawn bowls clubs and six world-class golf courses, plus an active theatre programme with many touring performances by groups from further south.

- Cinema • Cricket • Croquet • Dancing • Darts • Golf
- Horse racing • Lawn bowls • Most community organisations
- Most religions • Sailing • Theatre
- University of the Third Age

REAL ESTATE

- Median house price: $281 000

• Median unit price: $190 000

Properties on the foreshore are more expensive, of course. I priced a new two-bedroom apartment in a small block of six on the Strand opposite the rock pool and the asking price was $695 000. There are no bargains on the foreshore, I am afraid, but I am sure such property would only appreciate in value.

WHY LIVE HERE?

Townsville is a beautiful city with much to offer. There may be stingers and mosquitoes to contend with (the Ross River is close by), but there's less of the oppressive humidity and constant rain of the wet season which is so prevalent further up the road.

capricorn coast
Hot and humid

Yeppoon and Emu Park are the Capricorn Coast's retirement magnets, supported by the large, often stiflingly hot city of Rockhampton, slightly inland on the mighty, muddy Fitzroy River, which has the odd croc or two. Rockhampton is a city of tropical vegetation and wide streets with a backdrop of green hills. Numerous statues of bulls remind you that this is Australia's beef capital. Many of the houses around here are classic weatherboard Queenslanders, which have great character and appeal.

Rockhampton is smaller than Cairns or Townsville and lacks the emphasis on tourism, yet it has more fine heritage buildings than I can recall seeing in any other rural centre and they are impeccably maintained. Yeppoon, Capricorn Resort and Emu Park are an easy drive away and all are located on beaches. The turquoise sea backed by the region's green hills creates a very pretty picture. Emu Park is small and its houses aren't modern, but housing developments are under construction and the prices promise to be hefty. And yes, there really are emus there. The locals claim there are more millionaires per head of population in Emu Park than anywhere else in Australia, but I didn't see any evidence of their presence in the quality of the housing to date. Yeppoon is a bigger centre and has a larger, better infrastructure.

The housing in Yeppoon varies but there are many fine architect-designed homes, some of them elevated on the hills with magnificent water views. Air-conditioning would be a must in either town because of the torrid humidity and the mozzies – you'll also need to keep the air-con turned on 24/7 to keep the condensation at bay.

POPULATION

Rockhampton	Yeppoon	Emu Park
• 59 000	• 10 780	• 2700
• 17.5% over sixty	• 22% over sixty	• 30% over sixty

Yeppoon grew by 22 per cent between censuses.

CLIMATE

Summer 23°C to 29.4°C
Winter 10.6°C to 21°C
Sunshine 92 days
Rain 85 days
Rainfall 1312 mm

Yeppoon and Emu Park are hot and humid but less so than inland Rockhampton. Extreme weather conditions, such as cyclones and floods, sometimes occur.

LOCATION & GETTING AROUND

Rockhampton is 640 kilometres north of Brisbane, a drive of approximately 7.5 hours, and is accessible by daily flights from all capital cities. Yeppoon is 40 kilometres north-east of Rockhampton; Emu Park is 45 kilometres north-east.

Roads The Bruce Highway runs through Rockhampton, and Yeppoon is accessed by an excellent road that's in part dual carriageway. The road servicing Emu Park and from there to Rockhampton is a typical narrow country road.

Nearest airport Rockhampton, with daily services to Brisbane; flight time is approximately one hour.

Nearest train Rockhampton has daily train services to Brisbane (8.5 hours)

Buses Intercity coach services. Local services operate in Rockhampton and around the Capricorn Coast.

Taxis ✓

INFRASTRUCTURE

Hospitals Rockhampton Base Hospital, Rockhampton Private Hospital and Mater Misercordiae Hospital in Rockhampton; Yeppoon Hospital has 26 beds and both public and private facilities and there's also the Mater Hospital in Yeppoon.

Retirement villages There are at least 10 in Rockhampton, ranging from no care to full care. There's also one in Yeppoon, and a full-care home in Emu Park.

Police stations Rockhampton, Yeppoon and Emu Park

Local newspapers *Morning Bulletin*, *Capricorn Coast Mirror* and *Emu Park Chatter*

RECREATION

Beaches There's not much surf here due to the Keppel Islands, the reef and a deep shipping channel. Stingers are present in the waters between November and March. The beach from Yeppoon to Capricorn Resort and onwards is very flat and therefore wide at low tide and used by 4WDs and horses as well as us walkers. I would be careful where I chose to sunbake! The sand is unusually fine grained. Yeppoon main beach has surf lifesaving and sailing clubs. There are numerous unspoiled beaches at Emu Park and other coastal hamlets.

Coastguard ✓

Cycleways In central Rockhampton cycleways are incorporated on the roadways; there are some separate cycleways in North Rockhampton.

Bushwalking & National Parks Byfield National Park is north of Yeppoon and Mount Etna Caves National Park lies between Rockhampton and Yeppoon. The Mount Archer National Park to the north-east has many walking tracks and great views of Rockhampton.

Dogs Exercise and obedience area at Duthie Park in North Rockhampton. Dogs are allowed on beaches without leads before 8 a.m.

SHOPPING

Rockhampton has several shopping streets featuring some excellent stores such as James Stewart, where quality clothing is sold at low prices (for example, good T-shirts for $7.50). Major shopping centres include the Glenmore Shopping Village and Richardson Road Centre. Yeppoon has Keppel Bay Plaza with a large Bi-Lo supermarket. Organic fruit and veg are sold at low prices at the showground in Yeppoon every Saturday. There are no shops to speak of at Emu Park.

DINING

As one would expect, Rockhampton has plenty of bistros and steak houses, and can provide a good steak or two. Restaurants in Yeppoon and Emu Park are limited.

SOCIAL ACTIVITY

Yeppoon's river is a good spot to fish for barramundi, and it also has walking paths. There are three golf courses. The library has a home-delivery service. Rockhampton's Walter Reid Cultural Centre has many art, craft, music and leisure workshops and facilities. The city's art gallery hosts visiting and local exhibitions and the Pilbeam Theatre presents cultural groups and performances. The popular Yeppoon cinema has closed due to a real estate development.
- Cruises • Dancing • Fishing • Galleries • Golf
- Horse racing • Lawn bowls • Library
- Most community organisations • Most religions
- Museums • Swimming • Tennis • Theatre • Waterskiing

REAL ESTATE

Rockhampton
- Median house price: $140 000
- Median unit price: $165 000

Yeppoon
- Median house price: $284 000
- Median unit price: $214 000

Medium-density and high-rise housing is coming to Yeppoon, with at least one eight-storey project approved. The street clairvoyant and tarot card reader predicted that there would be more – a fairly safe prediction. In Emu Park the new Tanby development blocks are priced at $350 000 to $500 000. No bargain!

WHY LIVE HERE?

Because you love the sun and the heat and the laid-back lifestyle.

agnes water / 1770
The latest hotspot

It remains to be seen whether this up-and-coming community will transform itself into a playground for the rich, but it's certainly looking that way. New developments are currently being snapped up off the plan all over Agnes Water – from architect-designed villas to multi-storey apartments. Even the caravan park on the main beach is about to be transformed into a multi-storey development named Sansara.

At nearby 1770, named in honour of Captain Cook's landing here, things are more laid-back and reminiscent of Byron in the old days. There is little in the way of infrastructure here at the moment and the nearest centres are 125 kilometres away at Bundaberg or Gladstone, both just under two hours by car. However, developers claim they are working with council to introduce an airport and hospital, and additional shopping facilities are part of their development plans. The rustic Saltwater Café at 1770 doubles as an outdoor pub and the fresh juices and food here are first-rate (I tried the 'pot of prawns', butterflied with lime and very tasty) – plus Alex the proprietor makes a great cappuccino to boot! It's a start, but you'd need both vision and guts if you are punting on 1770 becoming another Noosa.

POPULATION

Agnes Water	1770
• 1262	• 228

• 17.5% over sixty

These figures are a little misleading as they relate to 2001 and both communities have grown significantly since then.

CLIMATE

Summer 22.5°C to 28.4°C

Winter 13.1°C to 20.2°C

Sunshine 131 days

Rain 113 days

Rainfall 1155 mm

Climate figures taken at Bustard Head.

LOCATION & GETTING AROUND

Agnes Water and 1770 are six kilometres apart, and both are around 500 kilometres (a six-hour drive) from Brisbane.

Roads Traffic is light

Nearest airport Bundaberg

Buses The pub has a bus which runs patrons home at night

Taxis ✓

INFRASTRUCTURE

Hospitals ✗ – just a small clinic out of town.

Retirement villages ✗

Police station ✓

Local newspaper ✗

RECREATION

Beaches There are quite good beaches here, especially at 1770, and they're patrolled during the summer holiday season. There's surf here, too. The locals say there are no stingers in the water unless the northerly blows solidly. It was blowing quite solidly when Judy and I were there.

Coastguard ✓

Cycleways Anywhere you want to go, as it is mostly flat.

Bushwalking & National Parks There are two national parks: Eurimbula, with mangroves and rainforest; and Deepwater, with freshwater wetlands. Both parks offer fishing and walking.

Dogs What regulations?

SHOPPING

There are two small shopping centres in Agnes Water, including an IGA supermarket.

DINING

There's not a lot of choice yet – just the main hotel in Agnes Water and the Saltwater Café in 1770.

SOCIAL ACTIVITY

There's a protected boat anchorage at 1770, plus a nine-hole golf course.

• Boating • Fishing • Golf • Lawn bowls
• Surfing • Swimming

REAL ESTATE

• Median house price: $297 000
• Median unit price: $268 000
• New developments: from $650 000 to $1 million

A real estate agent claimed that the introduction of the vendor tax and land tax changes in New South Wales (now reversed) had benefited his business, although there was also significant demand coming from Asia.

WHY LIVE HERE?

Partly because of the climate, partly because you can see the potential and want to be part of an exciting and growing community. You could even run for office and have your say on how the area should develop.

coral coast
Appealing coastal hamlets

Level with the southern tip of the Great Barrier Reef, the popular retirement beaches of Bargara, Elliott Heads, Burnett Heads and Moore Park make up the Coral Coast. The settlements are supported by Bundaberg, which is around 15 kilometres inland through the cane fields on the muddy Burnett River (good news: there are no crocs in this river; bad news: there's no swimming because of the sharks).

Bargara is the largest of the coastal villages, and it has one of the highest older-population skews in Queensland. It's very appealing except for the volcanic rocks strewn over most of the beach. The village is attractive, with open-air cafés and dining among the greenery opposite the sea. Older-style houses are making way for medium-rise apartment developments along the beachfront. The other villages are not as contemporary as Bargara but no doubt will become so as development continues in this popular area. Some observers believe that Bargara is in its infancy, with new residents coming from the Gold and Sunshine Coasts seeking a less-cluttered environment.

Bundaberg is similar to Rockhampton but smaller. It is flat and well ordered with a main shopping street canopied by trees and lined with a number of fine, well-maintained old buildings. The Bundaberg Rum distillery is a local icon, as is Bert Hinkler, the aviator who was born here. In the hinterland is the historic town of Childers, locked in time with magnificent weatherboard buildings and homes. It deserves to win the Tidy Town Award for the whole of Australia.

POPULATION

Bundaberg	Bargara	Moore Park
• 45 000 Est. June 2003	• 5170 Est. June 2003	• 1300 Est. June 2003
• 22% over sixty	• 33% over sixty	• 26% over sixty

Bargara is growing at a faster rate than Bundaberg, and Moore Park doubled its population between censuses.

CLIMATE

Summer 21.3°C to 30.3°C
Winter 9.9°C to 22°C

Sunshine 131 days
Rain 96 days
Rainfall 1141 mm

There are no climate figures for Bargara. These figures are for Bundaberg, which is inland with higher maximums and lower minimums, so they are difficult to compare with coastal locations. I suspect that Bargara would be more pleasant, similar to Agnes Water.

LOCATION & GETTING AROUND

Bundaberg is 370 kilometres from Brisbane, a driving time of 4.5 hours.

Roads The Bruce and Isis Highways run through Bundaberg, and within the town the streets are wide.

Nearest airport Bundaberg's Hinkler Airport has regular Qantas Dash 8 services to Brisbane (40 minutes), plus there's a local helicopter company.

Nearest train Bundaberg. The main Brisbane–Cairns line operates services daily (just over 5.5 hours).

Buses Intercity coaches. Local buses service Bundaberg city and beaches.

Taxis ✓

INFRASTRUCTURE

Hospitals Bundaberg Base Hospital, Mater Hospital Bundaberg

Retirement villages Eight in Bundaberg. Coral Gardens Estate lies between Bundaberg and Bargara.

Police stations Bundaberg and Bargara

Local newspapers *Bundaberg Guardian*, *News-Mail* and *Coastline Bundaberg*

RECREATION

Beaches There is a succession of beaches along the Coral Coast, and most are free of the volcanic rock which covers Bargara Beach. Appealing beaches include Moore Park (a remote 16 kilometres of pristine sand), Kelly's, Nielson Park and the largely undiscovered

Woodgate. Most beaches are patrolled as there is surf here. Elliott Heads and Riverview offer both surf and calm-water swimming and fishing. There are two coral cays off the coast – Lady Elliot and Lady Musgrave.

Coastguard ✓

Cycleways There is a shared pathway along the Burnett River in Bundaberg. Any street in Bundaberg is wide enough to cycle and there are quite a few cyclists about.

Bushwalking & National Parks Bundaberg is surrounded by 15 national parks with many walking tracks. The Woodgate National Park to the south has a boardwalk through tea-tree swamp. Mount Walsh National Park is undeveloped and suitable for keen bushwalkers, as is Coalstoun Lakes with its twin volcanic crater lakes. Auburn Park is particularly scenic with a river, rock pools and caves.

Dogs Regulations are apparently not too restrictive.

SHOPPING

Bundaberg has shopping streets as well as several air-conditioned malls such as Sugarland, Hinkler and Olsen's Corner. Bargara is small but has an IGA supermarket.

DINING

Bundaberg has at least one excellent restaurant with an open-air veranda by the river, and no bugs – just an uninvited cane toad visitor, under our table. There is plenty of casual dining in both Bundaberg and Bargara.

SOCIAL ACTIVITY

Bundaberg has a library and cinema/theatre complex and at Burnett Heads there's the Over-Fifties' Social Club, Historical and Museum Society and galleries. Water activities are popular in the stinger-free ocean. There are golf courses at both Bundaberg and Bargara.

• Boating • Bushwalking • Cinema • Diving • Golf

- Lawn bowls • Library • Most community organisations
- Most religions • Snorkelling • Surfing • Swimming
- Tennis • Theatre

REAL ESTATE

- Median house price: $214 000
- Median unit price: $219 000

The CBagara complex of apartments facing the sea is priced between $460 000 and $935 000.

WHY LIVE HERE?

The Coral Coast offers value for money, good infrastructure and access, as well as a peaceful environment. Plus the climate is less humid than further north. 'I wouldn't leave here for quids,' a retired lady said to me when I was there. 'It's a close-knit community and we have a lot of fun.'

hervey bay
Position perfect in nature's playground

At the southern tip of the Great Barrier Reef, Hervey Bay is perfectly positioned opposite Fraser Island, which provides a huge protected waterway for boating and fishing enthusiasts. It is possible to catch barramundi from the 800-metre Urangan Pier here. Hervey Bay has two faces: apart from being home to many retirees it also has a thriving eco-tourism industry. Tourists flock to unique Fraser Island and also to watch the migrating whales, which don't just pass by but stop over to enjoy the protected waters.

However, my first impression was one of disappointment at the urban sprawl. The drive down the extremely long Boat Harbour Drive takes you past an endless strip of vertically challenged, boring, blond-brick housing built for low-income retirees. It is only when you reach Boat Harbour and the 16-kilometre Esplanade that you see the potential of this location. Fraser Island frames the horizon, while in-between ply boats, ferries and barges (which carry 4WD vehicles to Fraser Island). There is a tree-lined public reserve between the Esplanade and the golden sandy beaches, and the water here is turquoise blue and rich in marine and bird life. Add to this a favourable climate, modern facilities, a relaxed pace and friendly people. The beachside suburbs here are Urangan, Torquay, Scarness, Pialba, Point Vernon and Gatakers Bay.

This is a city in transition and it's well under way. Major developers such as Outrigger and Peppers have recently discovered Hervey Bay, and the Esplanade has the potential to outdo Hastings Street in Noosa or Macrossan in Port Douglas. The airport here only opened to the major carriers in mid-2005, providing much improved access. No doubt Hervey Bay will become increasingly popular, with more-expensive real estate.

And, as one local put it, this is about as far up as you can go in Queensland without the four nasties of the north: stingers, crocs, cyclones and humidity.

POPULATION

- 47 000 Est. June 2003
- 30% over sixty

This is one of the top ten Queensland retirement locations and growing rapidly. My guess is it will top 60 000 in the 2006 census. To the south are the villages of Tin Can Bay and Rainbow Beach; in 2001 their total population was 3000, with one in three aged over sixty.

CLIMATE

Summer 22.4°C to 29.4°C
Winter 14.3°C to 21.1°C
Sunshine 111 days
Rain 118 days
Rainfall 1269 mm
Climate averages are not recorded at Hervey Bay, and the above figures were taken at Fraser Island, which is more exposed.

LOCATION & GETTING AROUND

Hervey Bay is 300 kilometres north of Brisbane, a driving time of approximately four hours.

Roads The Bruce Highway is single file but in good condition. Major internal roads are dual carriageway.

Nearest airport Hervey Bay, with daily flights to Sydney. Virgin Blue and Jetstar commenced flights in 2005, with direct services from Sydney and Melbourne.

Nearest train Maryborough, 40 kilometres away. The rail time to Brisbane is anything between 3.5 to five hours, depending on the type of train.

Buses Local bus service plus two intrastate coach terminals

Taxis There are taxi and limousine services.

INFRASTRUCTURE

Hospitals Hervey Bay Hospital has 125 beds. Also St Stephens Private Hospital.

Retirement villages Fairhaven, Fraser Shores, Golden Shores, Haselmere, Hervey Bay and RSL Homes. These range from independent living to full care.

Police stations Two in Hervey Bay plus water police, one on Fraser Island.

Local newspapers *Fraser Coast Chronicle*, *Heritage Herald*, *Hervey Bay Independent* and *Hervey Bay Observer*

RECREATION

Beaches A strip of bayside beaches along the Esplanade provide calm waters for safe swimming, although at low tide it is very shallow. Many beaches are patrolled in season, even though there is no surf. Torquay Beach is popular for catamarans and canoes, and Scarness has an underwater reef not far from shore which attracts divers and snorkellers.

Coastguard ✓

Cycleways An excellent shared cycleway runs almost 20 kilometres along the foreshore past all the beaches. What's more, it's flat!

Bushwalking & National Parks Fraser Island is absolutely the largest natural playground that any city could have on its doorstep. The sand island is famous for its dingoes and marine wildlife, 4WD driving on the beach, crystal-clear freshwater lakes for swimming and drinking, and old-growth forests for bushwalking. This World Heritage site – measuring 120 kilometres long and 30 kilometres across – is a wonderful gift enjoyed by both residents and tourists, and is accessed by car ferries (the locals call them barges).

Dogs Dog friendly, with off-leash areas on the bay and in reserves.

SHOPPING

Hervey Bay has extensive shopping in a number of centres. Bay Central includes a Franklins and Target, Pialba Shopping Centre has a Coles and Woolworths and the Urangan Central Shopping Centre also has a Woolworths. Boat Harbour Drive passes through warehouse-style retail outlets such as the ubiquitous Bunnings hardware chain.

DINING

There are many casual restaurants and cafés along the Esplanade and a contemporary dockside café precinct at Boat Harbour. These are well positioned but the quality needs to improve and it probably will, as more affluent retirees discover Hervey Bay. Of course, all the usual club restaurants are here as well.

SOCIAL ACTIVITY

The calm waters of the bay are perfect for water sports, and there's estuary, beach and reef fishing. Hervey Bay has a cinema and theatre complex, a historical museum, botanic gardens and various clubs.

- Boating • Cinema • Croquet • Diving • Fishing • Golf
- Lawn bowls • Most community organisations
- Most religions • Museum • Sailing • Snorkelling
- Swimming • Tennis • Theatre

REAL ESTATE

- Median house price: $280 000
- Median unit price: $232 000

It is possible to have sea glimpses and live several kilometres from the coast in Hervey Bay, such is the lay of the land. The long Esplanade running from Boat Harbour to Point Vernon will offer new apartment developments for years to come. The new Peppers development across the road from the waterfront sold large two-bedders off the plan from $550 000 and penthouses for over $1.5 million. On Boat Harbour, which has the only actual waterfront properties, two-bed waterfront apartments are available from $425 000 with 1000-year leases.

I met a forty-ish female executive from Sydney who had just purchased an investment unit in the new Peppers development because, 'I bought here at the time of that draconian exit tax in New South Wales. I'm still glad I did, because I avoid land tax and even stamp duty is cheaper here.'

WHY LIVE HERE?

Of all the locations I have visited around Australia and New Zealand, Hervey Bay has to be one of the best retirement spots due to value for money, climate, infrastructure, access and sheer beauty – and there are plenty of new developments under way.

sunshine coast

noosa
Rodeo Drive by the sea

Noosa is a truly unique part of the world. For most people, Noosa is Noosa Heads, Hastings Street and the adjacent beach. This 300-metre strip caters for everyone, with fabulous restaurants, great boutiques and expensive real estate. Popular retirement areas nearby include Noosaville and Tewantin, both on the banks of the Noosa River. To the south are Sunshine, Sunrise and Peregian beaches, where expensive modern homes overlook the bush bordering the beach and ocean.

Homes in Noosaville and Tewantin tend to be older. Tewantin is a small country town on a wide stretch of the Noosa River – it feels like you're a million miles from the international hubbub of Noosa Heads, but in fact you're only ten minutes away. Not a bad option for some retirees. The lush green forests have been preserved and one third of the area around Noosa is national parkland. The sheer beauty of the forest, powder-white beaches and secluded bays and coves in this part of the world is particularly striking when viewed from the Laguna Lookout on Noosa Hill in Noosa National Park. There are no high-rise developments in the vicinity – nothing over four storeys – which adds to the natural appeal. There is a wide choice of homes on the river, as well as slightly inland, and lots of very stylish homes tucked into the forest near the coast.

POPULATION

Noosa Shire
- **46 000** Est. June 2003
- **25%** over sixty

In Noosaville 29 per cent are over sixty and in Noosa Heads the percentage falls a little to 23 per cent.

CLIMATE

Summer 20.1°C to 29°C
Winter 8.7°C to 20.9°C

Sunshine 111 days
Rain 121 days
Rainfall 1696 mm

LOCATION & GETTING AROUND

Noosa is 135 kilometres north of Brisbane, a driving time of approximately 2.5 hours. Some of the roads are good; others are one-lane only and becoming more congested, especially north of Caloundra.

Roads There are motorways for only part of the way from Brisbane. As already mentioned, the roads are showing signs of saturation and local road-signage is poor.

Nearest airports Maroochydore (approximately 30 minutes away) or Brisbane (two hours). Noosa has its own small airport for charter flights.

Nearest train Nambour. The Brisbane to Nambour train takes two hours; you'll then need to transfer by bus to Noosa Heads, which takes another 45 minutes.

Buses Intercity coach services plus a local service, which doesn't serve the hinterland areas

Taxis ✓

INFRASTRUCTURE

Hospitals Noosa Private Hospital, Noosa Surgical and Endos-copy Centre, Noosaville and Nambour Hospital

Retirement villages Two at Noosaville, one at Peregian Beach

Police stations Noosa Heads and Nambour

Local newspapers *Sunshine Coast Daily*, *Noosa Citizen* and *Noosa News*

RECREATION

Beaches There is plenty of surf here. Noosa Heads Main Beach is fantastic, protected by the headland and featuring boardwalks backed by riverfront parklands. Peregian Beach and Sunshine Beach are patrolled. There are many other beaches near Noosa, such as Sunrise and Alexander; the latter has become a nudist beach.

Coastguard ✓

Cycleways There are six scenic cycle routes around Noosa and Tewantin

Bushwalking & National Parks Noosa Heads is the main entrance to Noosa National Park, which has miles of well-kept trails through bush to beaches. Thirty minutes north of Noosa are the Noosa Everglades, part of the Great Sandy National Park, combining deep and mysterious waterways, clear lakes, golden beaches, sand dunes and rocky headlands, with plenty of opportunities for whale watching.

Dogs Designated leash-free areas.

SHOPPING

There's no shortage of shops in Noosa. Shady Hastings Streets is awash with designer labels and boutique shops, open-air cafés and restaurants. Noosa Junction and Noosaville have large shopping centres with Woolworths and Coles supermarkets. Tewantin has several shopping streets and Sunshine Beach has a cosy cluster of cafés and stores. Craft markets are held regularly at Noosa Harbour and Peregian Beach.

DINING

There's everything from five-star dining to plain fish and chips. Go al fresco in Hastings Street or catch a ferry to the cafés and restaurants along the river. The entire area is full of culinary delights.

SOCIAL ACTIVITY

Most of Noosa's leisure activities are outdoor-based, from surfing and swimming to beach, reef and river fishing. The Noosa Leisure Centre has 25- and 50-metre swimming pools and offers indoor badminton, basketball, futsal (five-a-side indoor soccer), gymnastics, indoor rock climbing, netball and volleyball. There are plenty of clubs, including a photographic society. Tewantin has a local library, cinema and a gallery that holds regular exhibitions. Craft shops abound, particularly in the hinterland.

- Aquatic centre • Boating • Bushwalking • Fishing • Golf
- Lawn bowls • Leisure centre • Most community organisations
- Most religions • Rowing • Sailing • Snorkelling • Surfing
- Swimming • Tennis

REAL ESTATE

- Median house price: $675 000
- Median unit price: $590 000

Areas such as Noosaville and Tewantin are much cheaper than Noosa. There is also canal living with private jetties in Noosaville, although of course homes and apartments on the river, canals or overlooking the ocean have hefty price tags. If you like the buzz of Noosa there is plenty of choice and a range of prices.

WHY LIVE HERE?

To be part of a very cosmopolitan crowd. I met a couple who live in Melbourne and fly up to their apartment in Noosa at least twice a year. One day, they claim, they will move here permanently: 'There's so much more to do here, and there are so many people here from Sydney, Melbourne and Brisbane.'

Simon and Anne have settled beside the golf course at Noosa Springs: 'We didn't like the Gold Coast because it's too hectic, and the kids love coming up to Noosa for their holidays.'

coolum beach
A haven between two icons

Unspoilt Coolum Beach is twenty minutes south of Noosa and twenty minutes north of Maroochydore, with a hilltop position overlooking a terrific stretch of sand. Many of Coolum's houses are elevated and have water views. The beach is patrolled and ideal for long morning or evening walks. Some of the housing is high-rise but a feeling of space and freedom remains (unlike in neighbouring Maroochydore to the south). There are shops next to the beach and a shopping complex set a few streets back from the water which includes an IGA supermarket. Some nice eateries are located on the beach strip and there are more not far up or down the road. A mobile library serves the area. Plans for further development are afoot, with new luxury residences under construction opposite the beach. The infrastructure is as for Maroochydore and Noosa.

POPULATION

Coolum and Peregian
- 15 500
- 21.1% over sixty

REAL ESTATE
- Median house price: $445 000
- Median unit price: $337 000
Prices are somewhat higher in the beachfront developments.

WHY LIVE HERE?

To be just far enough away from the fun to be able to enjoy it whenever you want to without living it all the time.

nambour / buderim
Peaceful country life on the fringe of excitement

In a valley surrounded by luxuriant green hills, Nambour is a large centre with plenty of shops and activity. There is no river, just a few creeks running through town, but there is an Olympic Swim Centre if you want to get your feet wet. Nambour is home to the Maroochy Council but there is no longer any tourist information here as the volunteer force manning the centre lost interest (and so did the tourists, no doubt). Tourists are attracted instead to Maroochydore (15 kilometres away) or to Buderim (17 kilometres).

Buderim is a colourful town in the hills and is known for its ginger factory. It has nice solid homes, some of them typical Queenslanders. Buderim and

Nambour are good locations for retirees who don't want to be in the thick of it and don't yearn for the sea breeze, but like the rural lifestyle. The infrastructure is as for Maroochydore, and along with the usual religions represented there are also Baha'i Faith, Baptist Union, Lutheran and Church of Jesus Christ of Latter-Day Saints.

POPULATION

Nambour
- 13 000
- 24% over sixty

Buderim
- 27 250
- 23% over sixty

The population of both Buderim and Nambour grew slowly between the censuses.

CLIMATE

Summer 19.7°C to 29.2°C
Winter 7.5°C to 21.1°C
Sunshine 75 days
Rain 147 days
Rainfall 1709 mm

LOCATION & GETTING AROUND

The Bruce Highway runs past both towns. Brisbane is 100 kilometres south, a 1.5-hour drive.

REAL ESTATE

Nambour
- Median house price: $293 000
- Median unit price: $187 000

Buderim
- Median house price: $399 000
- Median unit price: $276 000

WHY LIVE HERE?

Because you like to live in a largish rural environment, very close to everything the Sunshine Coast has to offer.

maroochydore

A chip off the Gold Coast

Maroochydore is located in the centre of the Sunshine Coast, on the estuary of the Maroochy River and fronting a long stretch of beach. Swimmers have a choice of river, lagoon or surf. The southern bank of the river is a tourist destination of parkland and picnic spots, and hosts major sporting carnivals. There is a lot of high-rise unit development along the beach, but some older-style housing remains. South is Alexandra Headland and a five-minute drive away, at the mouth of a river, is Maroochydore's small sister, Mooloolaba, with its share of high-rise development.

I doubt there ever was a plan to develop Maroochydore; it looks like it exploded with little or no thought. Development runs right to the river's edge, high-rise development abounds unchecked and pedestrians have to dodge the cars in a chaotic tangle of streets. You have to explore to find the beach and it's easy to end up on the river instead.

POPULATION

Maroochy Shire

- 136 500 Est. June 2003
- 16.8% over sixty

In the 2001 census, 30 per cent of Maroochydore's population was aged over sixty; the figure for Mooloolaba was 20.6 per cent.

CLIMATE

Summer 20.8°C to 29.1°C
Winter 6.9°C to 21.2°C
Sunshine 101 days
Rain 133 days
Rainfall 1634 mm

LOCATION & GETTING AROUND

Maroochydore is 100 kilometres from Brisbane, a travelling time of approximately one hour and 45 minutes on busy roads. It has its own busy regional airport.

Roads The roads here are only just coping with the increasing traffic.

Nearest airport Maroochydore, with regular services to all capital cities

Nearest train Nambour. From Brisbane the trip takes just under two hours, followed by a bus trip of 16 kilometres to Maroochydore, which takes about 20 minutes.

Buses Intercity coach services and local scheduled services

Taxis ✓

INFRASTRUCTURE

Hospitals Nambour Hospital, Selangor Private Hospital in Nambour, Nambour Day Surgery, Sunshine Coast Private Hospital in Buderim

Retirement villages Several in Maroochydore

Police stations Maroochydore, Mooloolaba Police Beat (this means they visit, but do not reside in Mooloolaba; many rural areas complain of the problem of understaffing)

Local newspaper *Sunshine Coast Daily*

RECREATION

Beaches Maroochydore's main beach is patrolled and has a large surf club. Mooloolaba (the Spit) is also patrolled and has parkland and picnic areas. Alexandra Headland is patrolled, and there are a number of sheltered beaches along the Cotton Tree Esplanade near the river.

Coastguard ✓

Cycleways On- and off-road cycleways to Mooloolaba and Buderim as well as on Aerodrome Road and in some parks

Bushwalking & National Parks In the hinterland is Mount Coolum National Park, with spectacular views of the coast from the top of Mount Coolum. The track to the top, although not a great distance, is steep and rocky. There is also Mooloolah River National Park, south-west of Mooloolaba. This is an undeveloped park with plenty of bird life. Most of the access is from the river.

Dogs There are nine leash-free areas in the Maroochy Shire.

SHOPPING

There's an abundance of shopping opportunities. Maroochydore's Sunshine Plaza Shopping Centre contains over 200 speciality shops, cinemas and cafés, as well as Myer, Target, Kmart, Best & Less, Coles and Woolworths. There's also the Big Top Shopping Centre. Two weekly markets provide fresh fruit, vegetables, arts and crafts. Mooloolaba is also well known for its small boutique shops.

DINING

Mooloolaba has numerous restaurants and cafés on the Wharf and Esplanade. Maroochydore has a similar range of places to eat on the River Walk. There's plenty of diversity here.

SOCIAL ACTIVITY

All the expected clubs are here, including an RSL, a yacht club at Mooloolaba harbour and golf courses at Maroochydore, Buderim and Nambour. Local artists display their work at Mooloolaba and in the hinterland galleries and the craft town of Montville. There are numerous walking tracks through rainforest.

• All religions • Boating • Bushwalking • Cinema • Fishing
• Galleries • Golf • Lawn bowls • Library
• Most community organisations • Sailing • Scuba diving
• Snorkelling • Surfing • Swimming • Tennis • Theatre
• Walking • Waterskiing

REAL ESTATE

• Median house price: $350 000
• Median unit price: $299 000

WHY LIVE HERE?

Because you like the Gold Coast lifestyle but on a slightly more manageable scale.

caloundra

Beachside living without the tourist crush

Caloundra is north of Bribie Island and south of Maroochydore. It has long been a classic retirement town, but more recently it has experienced a commercial and population explosion which includes young commuters. The area is noted for its excellent surf beaches and attracts a number of tourists.

Caloundra has both high-rise and low-rise developments and a canopy of trees covering the main street, which is well served by shops of every nature. The Glasshouse Mountains and Blackall Range tower over the town like a theatrical backdrop. The sea breezes caress the branches of the Norfolk Island pines which overlook the lovely beach on the estuary. It is a truly beautiful spot, and you have the choice of swimming in the calm lagoon waters or in the surf. The hinterland is known for its art and craft galleries.

POPULATION

- **34 000** Est. June 2003
- **30%** over sixty

The population of the entire Caloundra LGA ('local government area') was estimated at 83 000 in June 2003; one quarter of these residents were aged over sixty, making it a very significant retirement area.

CLIMATE

Summer 21.5°C to 27.6°C
Winter 10.8°C to 19.3°C
Sunshine 101 days
Rain 120 days
Rainfall 1575 mm

LOCATION & GETTING AROUND

Caloundra is 90 kilometres north of Brisbane, a driving time of just over 1.5 hours.

Roads A dual-lane highway runs from Brisbane to Caloundra

Nearest airports Caloundra has a small airport; Brisbane's international and domestic airports are 87 kilometres away (an hour's drive) and Maroochydore is 30 kilometres (20 minutes).

Nearest train Landsborough Station is 20 kilometres from Caloundra and a 20-minute drive. Rail time from here to Brisbane is 80 minutes.

Buses Local and interstate, plus a free community bus service

Taxis ✓

Water taxis ✓

INFRASTRUCTURE

Hospitals Caloundra Hospital and Caloundra Private Hospital

Retirement villages There are three retirement villages within Caloundra

Police stations Caloundra

Local newspaper *Caloundra City News*

RECREATION

Beaches There are 30 kilometres of beaches extending south from Buddina Beach through Kings and Bulcock Beach in Caloundra's city centre, south to Pelican Waters in the Pumicestone Channel. This continuous strip of beach is backed by parkland which extends through to Lake Currimundi, popular for canoeing, fishing and swimming. The majority of beaches are patrolled year-round. Kings is particularly popular for surfing and swimming, and fishing is popular at Moffat and Shelly Beaches.

Coastguard ✓

Cycleways There are five kilometres of coastal cycleways from Bulcock Beach to Diamond Head.

Bushwalking & National Parks The Glasshouse Mountains are only 30 kilometres away with many walks of varying difficulty and good views.

Dogs This is a dog-friendly area with numerous parks and beaches designated as off-leash areas.

SHOPPING

Caloundra and its beachside villages have many large shopping centres with supermarkets and trendy boutiques to satisfy most people's needs. There are also markets every Sunday with fresh local produce such as pineapples, strawberries, avocados and macadamias, as well as arts and crafts.

DINING

As with most coastal towns, seafood is always on the menu and many of the restaurants are on the beachfront. There are also Thai, Mediterranean, Italian and an abundance of Chinese restaurants. The Surf Club at Kings Beach and the Golf Club and Lawn Bowls Club also have good bistros.

SOCIAL ACTIVITY

The Civic Cultural Centre includes a theatre and playhouse, the Regional Art Gallery with continuous exhibitions and the Queensland Air Museum. For those who love walking there are coastal walks along the beachfront and tracks near the Glasshouse Mountains in the hinterland.
- All religions • Aquatic centre • Bushwalking
- Lifestyle centre • Boating • Fishing • Galleries • Golf
- Horse racing • Indoor Sports Stadium • Lawn bowls
- Library • Most community organisations • Museum
- Surfing • Swimming • Theatre

REAL ESTATE

- Median house price: $385 000
- Median unit price: $320 000

WHY LIVE HERE?

Because you love the beach and sunshine but you don't want to live in a tourist Mecca.

bribie island

Different lifestyles on one island

Bribie Island is changing, as an increasing number of younger families are discovering Pacific Harbour, an adventurous new development of around 2500 houses with canals winding through luxury home sites. Most retirees wouldn't be able to afford to buy here, unless they were fortunate enough to get in during the cheaper first release of land. However, Bribie is big enough to accommodate a variety of demographics and lifestyles, and the current development can only improve the facilities for all. In fact, the island is so big that even with this development most of the island remains a nature reserve.

Bribie Island is connected to the mainland by a long, narrow bridge over the Pumicestone Passage, a marine park and home for dugongs, turtles and dolphins. This relaxing and beautiful spot has attracted many retirees as well as tourists. Retirees are mostly located at Bongaree and Woorim, older areas with less-expensive housing that's close to the clubs. Bongaree is on the Passage whilst Woorim is on the eastern side of the island on a beach which, although claiming to be a surf beach, is pretty flat thanks to Moreton Island. From Bongaree you can enjoy magnificent sunsets over the Glasshouse Mountains, while Woorim looks onto Moreton Island. Sandstone Point, another popular retirement location, is on the mainland next to the bridge to the island; it has a newish retirement village. I suspect that in the 2006 census we will see a younger age profile for Bribie but this won't mean that there aren't heaps of older folk still romping around the sand dunes.

POPULATION

- 15 500
- 39% over sixty

The ratio of over-sixties is likely to change with the Pacific Harbour development. Bongaree grew by 1860 people to 13 000 between censuses, and Sandstone Point grew by 755 to 2150.

CLIMATE

Summer 21.9°C to 26.8°C
Winter 13.2°C to 18.8°C

Sunshine 114 days
Rain 144 days
Rainfall 1567 mm
Climate figures taken at Cape Moreton Lighthouse.

LOCATION & GETTING AROUND

Bribie Island is located about midway between Brisbane and the Sunshine Coast. The island measures 34 kilometres long and eight kilometres wide, stretching along the northern end of Moreton Bay. Brisbane to Bribie Island is 65 kilometres, travelling time approximately one and a quarter hours.

Roads A bridge connects the island to the mainland – Bribie is the only offshore island to have this convenient link. Driving conditions from Brisbane to Caboolture are good via the Gateway Motorway and Bruce Highway. The drive into Bribie is quite long and only one lane each way.

Nearest airports Brisbane is 70 kilometres away. Caloundra is 65 kilometres, a driving time of one hour.

Nearest train If travelling from Brisbane, you'll need to take a train to Caboolture, then a coach to Bribie. This will take about one hour and 45 minutes – not very practical.

Buses Local buses service the island. Intercity coaches travel only to the Bribie Island turnoff at Caboolture.

Taxis ✓

INFRASTRUCTURE

Hospitals Caboolture Hospital, Caboolture Private Hospital and Redcliffe Hospital
Retirement villages Three on Bribie Island
Police stations Bribie Island and Caboolture
Local newspapers Brisbane newspapers

RECREATION

Beaches There are beaches on the calm side of the island as well as on the ocean side. One of the popular patrolled beaches on the ocean side of the island is Woorim, and other safe swimming beaches that are also suitable for fishing and picnicking are Red Beach, Bongaree, Sylvan, Banksia and Pebble Beach. There's no shortage to choose from. Some of the beaches, particularly on the ocean side, are isolated and accessible only by 4WD or on foot.

Coastguard In addition to the Coastguard, there is also a Volunteer Marine Rescue group on the island.

Cycleways A network of bike tracks extends from the calm side of Pumicestone Passage to Woorim Beach

Bushwalking & National Parks Over 80 per cent of the island is national park, with 350 different species of birds, kangaroos, emus and dingoes. There are seemingly endless stretches of sandy white beaches, and 4WD is allowed provided you buy a permit. Bushwalking tracks are abundant through various types of vegetation such as eucalypt forests, melaleuca swamp and heath. So there's plenty of opportunities for getting close to nature.

Dogs There are five on-leash areas and two off-leash areas on the island, plus two on-leash areas at Sandstone Point on the mainland.

SHOPPING

The main shopping centre is at Bellara, immediately after you cross the bridge from the mainland, with a Woolworths as well as other stores. A reasonable shopping centre is located at Bongaree. There are also many local arts and crafts shops. Caboolture and Redcliffe on the mainland have markets with fresh produce.

DINING

Bribie has many restaurants, and meals are also served at the local pubs and clubs. A lot of them specialise in seafood since this comes directly from the trawlers. Bongaree, on the calm side of the island, has become a hub for restaurants and cafés, many of them with outdoor tables.

SOCIAL ACTIVITY

The weather and the natural beauty of the island tend to mean that most of the activity is outdoors. Bribie is an absolute haven for anglers; sailing and scuba diving are also popular, and there is a large marina and many boat ramps. Many of the island's facilities are set up for retirees, such as a sports centre with tennis and croquet facilities, the Aquatic Leisure Complex with heated and hydrotherapy pools and the Recreation Centre with indoor bowls and tennis. There are two golf clubs, three lawn bowls clubs, an orchid society, quilters club, gardeners club and handicraft club. Banksia Beach also has a large community arts centre.

- Aquatic centre • Arts & crafts • Boating
- Bushwalking • Cinema • Croquet • Fishing • Indoor bowls
- Lawn bowls • Library • Most community organisations
- Most religions • Sailing • Scuba diving • Sports centre
- Swimming • Tennis

REAL ESTATE

- Median house price: $345 000
- Median unit price: $290 000

Many homes have water views or waterfrontage. Expect to pay a minimum of $600 000 to live in Pacific Harbour, and that would be in the backblocks, more for a canal berth.

WHY LIVE HERE?

Because you like the exclusivity of living on an island with nature all around.

caboolture
Country life close to the seaside action

Once they let you into Caboolture they really want you to stay. It took me several attempts to find my way north as the sign posting is nonexistent, but I guess that doesn't worry the locals.

Caboolture Shire extends to the beaches of Deception Bay and Bribie Island, while the town of Caboolture is inland and considered the fruit bowl of the south-east for bananas, pineapples, pawpaws, avocados and strawberries. Caboolture is also the seat of government for the shire. It is an appealing and friendly town, large enough not to be claustrophobic, and many of its houses are attractive older-style homes on large blocks. The wide streets in the town centre are lined with red flowering trees and look over a large botanic garden, complete with fountain and artificial lake.

POPULATION

- 30 000
- 18% over sixty

CLIMATE

Summer 20.6°C to 29°C
Winter 10.6°C to 21.8°C
Sunshine 142 days
Rain 125 days
Rainfall 1094 mm

LOCATION & GETTING AROUND

Caboolture is 47 kilometres from Brisbane, a travelling time of around one hour by road. The town is also accessible by train from Brisbane (50 minutes).

Roads Spacious divided main roads with bugger-all meaningful sign posting, so you can easily get to where you don't want to be.
Nearest airports Brisbane. There is an airfield at Caboolture used predominantly for hot-air ballooning.
Nearest train Caboolture
Buses Local and intercity buses
Taxis ✓

INFRASTRUCTURE

Hospitals Caboolture Public Hospital and Caboolture Private Hospital are adjacent

Retirement villages Three in the area

Police stations Caboolture. Media reports claim the station is under-staffed, resulting in an increase in petty crime from visiting hoons.

Local newspapers *Caboolture Shire Herald* and *Northern Times*

RECREATION

Cycleways There are some existing cycleways radiating out from the town and a number of proposed extensions

Bushwalking & National Parks Mount Mee State Forest Park on the northern end of D'Aguilar Range has four different walks and views of Moreton Bay and the Glasshouse Mountains. The tracks lead to mountain streams and swimming holes.

Dogs This is a dog-friendly area, with three on-leash areas and two off-leash areas.

SHOPPING

Kmart, Woolworths and Coles are all here and the shopping area is extensive. Caboolture markets are held weekly.

DINING

There is a large range of eateries, from casual bistros and clubs to cafés, serving a good variety of food. The charming hinterland villages of Woodford and Wamuran offer Devonshire teas, and of course the coast with its extensive list of eateries is only a stone's throw away.

SOCIAL ACTIVITY

There are golf courses at Caboolture, Bribie Island and Wood-ford, as well as numerous lawn bowls clubs throughout the area. There are many museums, including the Art and Archaeology Museum which houses a collection of antiques and fine art, a Steam Train Museum, Agricultural Museum and Warplane and Flight Museum. There are many hobby groups, from pigeon fanciers to folk dancing, horticulture to handicrafts, gliding to gem collecting, woodcrafting to writing. The Urban Country Music Festival has become an annual event.

- Aquatic Leisure Centre • Boating • Cinema • Dancing
- Fishing • Golf • Hot-air ballooning • Lawn bowls • Library
- Most community organisations • Most religions • Museums
- Theatre

REAL ESTATE

- Median house price: $242 000
- Median unit price: $140 000

WHY LIVE HERE?

Because it's uncluttered and unhurried, with the opportunity to live in town or on a small rural holding, only 20 kilometres from the Queensland coast and one hour from Brisbane.

redcliffe
Holidaying in the city

Redcliffe is like being on a beach holiday while living in Brisbane. Its sandy beaches are the closest to the capital, so it attracts many daytrippers, and the public pool by the water's edge at Settlement Cove is something you would expect to find in a five-star resort. It's a pity more public pools aren't like Redcliffe's – it's up there with those at Cairns and Townsville.

Redcliffe was the site of the first European settlement in Queensland and consequently has a number of heritage sites. Places with views are limited here, as this is flat country, but there are some water views and views of the Glasshouse Mountains to the west. There is a lot to explore in this area, including the peninsula's wetlands and Moreton Island, a ferry ride away. The housing is a mix of old and new, incorporating some classic Queenslanders.

POPULATION

Redcliffe and Scarborough

- 18 500
- 27% over sixty

CLIMATE

Summer 21.8°C to 28.9°C
Winter 10.6°C to 20.6°C
Sunshine 142 days
Rain 125 days
Rainfall 1089 mm

LOCATION & GETTING AROUND

Situated on a peninsula overlooking Moreton Bay, Redcliffe is 33 kilometres from Brisbane, an easy 45-minute drive via the Gateway Motorway.

Roads The local roads are wide and mostly flow smoothly
Nearest airport Brisbane
Nearest train ✗
Buses Coach and local services
Taxis ✓

INFRASTRUCTURE

Hospitals Redcliffe Hospital, Caboolture Hospital and Pine Rivers Private
Retirement villages Redcliffe and Deception Bay
Police stations Redcliffe
Local newspapers *Redcliffe & Bayside Herald*, plus Brisbane newspapers

RECREATION

Beaches There are a number of beaches and bays on this coastline, but don't expect surf due to the barrier provided by Moreton Island. Suttons Beach is patrolled, and other beaches include Margate Beach (popular for windsurfing and fishing), Pelican Park, Bells Beach, Queens Beach and Scarborough Beach. The Settlement Cove Lagoon Pool is a favourite for swimming.
Coastguard ✓
Cycleways 35 kilometres of scenic bikeways

Bushwalking & National Parks Moreton Bay Marine Park and Moreton Island National Park

Dogs Dogs are generally not allowed on the beaches, with the exception of Bells Beach. Some foreshore and park areas have been set aside for exercising dogs.

SHOPPING

Kippa-Ring Shopping Village and Peninsula Fair Shopping Centre are the main shopping areas. Smaller shops line the street on the foreshore and weekly markets are held on the peninsula.

DINING

Redcliffe is known for its succulent seafood, particularly at Scarborough Harbour, and there are many first-class dining options. Cuisines are varied, from international to modern, and many of the restaurants and outdoor cafés are on the foreshore with views of Moreton Bay.

SOCIAL ACTIVITY

Annual festivals include the Festival of Sails and First Settlement Festival. The Cultural Centre caters for local and touring theatre groups, and the Redcliffe City Gallery hosts exhibitions. There are many picnic and barbeque areas, plus the botanic gardens. An extensive network of walking tracks runs along the foreshore and the interesting Heritage Walk takes you past the site of the original penal colony.

- All community organisations • All religions • Boating
- Cinema • Galleries • Fishing • Golf • Horse racing
- Lawn bowls • Library • Major community organisations
- Major religions • Museum • Squash • Swimming • Tennis
- Walking

REAL ESTATE

- Median house price: $315 000
- Median unit price: $328 000

Many of the units have been recently built and are within large estates.

WHY LIVE HERE?

Retirement life with sea breezes yet it's such an easy trip into the city. A tradesman who used to live in Sydney told me: 'There's less stress up here. People have time to talk. That's why I'm here.'

toowoomba
Garden paradise

Toowoomba is appropriately named the Garden City. It is also Queensland's largest inland city, conveniently positioned adjacent to Brisbane on the Great Dividing Range. To its west are the fertile agricultural plains of the Darling Downs.

Despite Toowoomba's size there is a definite feeling of being in the country. This is a relaxed and appealing city, with wide streets and limited high-rise buildings. There are 150 parks and public gardens within the metropolitan area, many with creeks running through them and feeding into nearby lakes. The infrastructure here is good and the air is unpolluted. Overall, it's a very appealing and pretty place.

POPULATION

- **92 555** Est. June 2003
- 17.6% over sixty

The population of Toowoomba grew by 7 per cent between censuses. Many retirees are farmers from the Darling Downs.

CLIMATE

Summer 16.6°C to 27.6°C
Winter 5.3°C to 16.3°C
Sunshine 114 days
Rain 106 days
Rainfall 950 mm

Located on the slopes of the Great Dividing Range, Toowoomba is less hot and humid than the coast.

LOCATION & GETTING AROUND

Toowoomba is 125 kilometres inland from Brisbane, under a two-hour drive. The Warrego Highway links Toowoomba with Brisbane and the Gold Coast.

Roads The Warrego, New England and Gore Highways all meet in Toowoomba. The local byroads are smooth but narrow. The Warrego Highway climbs the Great Dividing Range and has excellent views.

Nearest airport Dash 8 aircraft operate from Toowoomba Airport; there are no regular commercial flights at the moment, but this may change. The Airport Flyer offers direct ground service transport between Brisbane and Toowoomba airports.

Nearest train Toowoomba, with regular services to Brisbane

Buses Regular services between Brisbane and Toowoomba. A local city bus service operates within Toowoomba.

Taxis ✓

INFRASTRUCTURE

Hospitals Toowoomba Base Hospital (public). St Andrew's Hospital is a large private hospital and St Vincent's Hospital is the largest acute private hospital on the Darling Downs. Others are Baillie Henderson, Gatton and Oakey Hospitals, plus day surgeries. Toowoomba claims to have more medical specialists per head of population than any other non-capital city in Australia.

Retirement villages At least 15 aged-care homes and villages

Police stations Toowoomba and Drayton, which now adjoins Toowoomba

Local newspapers *Toowoomba Chronicle* and *Toowoomba Mail*

RECREATION

Cycleways A cycleway follows East Creek through Lake Annand to Queens Park near the centre of the city.

Bushwalking & National Parks The 293-hectare Jubilee Park has graded walking trails shared by walkers and horse riders. Redwood Park (197 hectares) adjoins, with a shared walking and riding trail, and there are several other parks with extensive walking trails.

There are also a dozen national parks nearby in the Great Dividing Range, including Bunya Mountains National Park with walking trails through rainforest, Crows Nest with displays of wild flowers and Lake Broadwater Conservation Park, whose lake and wetlands are an important habitat for birds on the Darling Downs. Several bushwalking tracks have been developed in the area, and boating and skiing are permitted on the main body of the lake. Main Range National Park has impressive peaks and views, while Sundown has water holes for fishing and canoeing.

Dogs Dogs are not permitted at some of the lakes as they are fauna conservation areas. There are off-leash parks throughout the city.

SHOPPING

Toowoomba's main shopping district centres on Ruthven Street and Margaret Street, which includes a wide pedestrian mall. There are also large shopping centres at Wilsonton, Clifford Gardens, Kmart Plaza and Grand Central Shopping Centre, which is large and undercover. Malls have off-street parking and all the major stores and supermarkets are represented.

DINING

Toowoomba offers a variety of restaurants, some of which are very good indeed.

SOCIAL ACTIVITY

Toowoomba has many leisure and craft groups and all kinds of clubs and activities, from lawn bowls for the blind to yoga and bellydancing. There are at least three golf courses and lawn bowls clubs, and the Milne Bay Aquatic Centre has several pools (indoor and outdoor), including a hydrotherapy pool used by arthritis and other degenerative-disease sufferers. The annual Festival of the Flowers attracts many visitors. Some of Toowoomba's many lakes have restrictions on boating and waterskiing.

• Aquatic centre • Boating • Bushwalking • Dancing • Fishing
• Lawn bowls • Most community organisations
• Most religions • Sailing • Swimming • Windsurfing
• Waterskiing

REAL ESTATE

• Median house price: $235 000
• Median unit price: $182 000

WHY LIVE HERE?

This is a good choice if you like to live close to the earth and not too far away from the big smoke, as well as enjoying the pleasures and comforts of a large town, with a mild climate.

north stradbroke island
Stranded on your own desert island

North Stradbroke Island, known by all as 'Straddie', is one of the world's largest sand islands. It's south-east of Brisbane, and shields much of Moreton Bay from the ocean swells. The main villages on the Island are Dunwich, Amity Point and Point Lookout, and there are also sizable retired populations on neighbouring Russell and Macleay Islands. These two islands are in the top 200 communities of over-65s in Australia, and all three islands are accessible only by ferry or water taxi.

   The islands include mangrove habitats, bays and beaches, but North Stradbroke in particular has contrasting scenery, from rugged headlands to pristine stretches of beach and dunes and tranquil inland lakes. Dunwich is the island's largest village but it's still not very big; Amity Point has excellent views of Moreton Bay; and Point Lookout, on the island's most easterly point, is more exposed to the weather. Although inhabited and a tourist destination, these islands remain very much unspoiled and secluded.

POPULATION

Dunwich
• 1000

Amity Point
• 450

Point Lookout
• 900

Russell & Macleay Islands
• 3800

All the islands are experiencing a growth in population, although the village of Point Lookout declined slightly between censuses. On Russell and Macleay Islands, 30 per cent of the population are over sixty, whilst 18 per cent are over sixty on Stradbroke.

CLIMATE

Summer 20°C to 28.9°C

Winter 8.1°C to 20.4°C

Sunshine 81 days

Rain 60 days

Rainfall 1284 mm

LOCATION & GETTING AROUND

The drive from Brisbane to the mainland jumping-off point of Cleveland takes around 40 minutes. There is also a Citytrain service from Brisbane to Cleveland. Access from Cleveland is by car ferry (one hour) or water taxi (30 minutes).

Roads All townships on the island are linked by sealed roads. Only 4WDs are allowed on the beaches.

Nearest airport Brisbane, approximately 90 minutes by car including the ferry trip

Nearest train Cleveland (one hour to Brisbane)

Buses Buses meet the ferry on Stradbroke

Ferries Cleveland–Stradbroke

Taxis ✓

Water taxis ✓

INFRASTRUCTURE

Hospitals   There are ambulance and medical facilities on the islands, but the nearest hospital is Redland Hospital on the mainland in Cleveland, with 144 beds

Retirement villages   On the mainland at Cleveland, Redland Bay, Ormiston, Alexandra Hills, Birkdale and Victoria Point

Police stations   North Stradbroke

Local newspapers   Brisbane newspapers

RECREATION

Beaches   The beaches stretch for 32 kilometres of surf and dunes. Main Beach at Point Lookout is popular for surfing, with big swells and big views and with extensive Aboriginal shell middens. This beach, along with Cylinder Beach which is a picturesque cove, is patrolled. There are numerous other beaches such as Alder Rock Beach, Home Beach, Deadman's Beach, Flinders Beach and Frenchman's Beach, some of which are only accessible by 4WD or on foot. Amity Point and Dunwich on the sheltered side of the island offer calm-water swimming and fishing.

Coastguard ✓

Cycleways   The islands are fabulous places to ride bikes, even on the beaches at low tide (but watch out for 4WD vehicles).

Bushwalking & National Parks   The Blue Lake National Park, accessed by road from Dunwich and then walking track, has an intense blue lake set amongst sand dunes. There's a variety of fauna in the area, which incorporates heath, swamps and marshes. Brown Lake is also very attractive, with tropical rainforest, barbeque facilities and swimming holes. Walking tracks run from Dunwich all the way to Point Lookout via Myora Springs.

Dogs   Dogs are banned from almost all beaches and camping grounds. They must be kept on a leash in all other areas.

SHOPPING

Stradbroke Island has a bakery, supermarket, hotel, chemist, butchery, bottle shop, convenience stores and takeaway food outlets. Russell and Macleay Islands have similar shops.

DINING

There are a number of restaurants and outdoor cafés on Stradbroke serving seafood, Modern Australian and Italian dishes. The lawn bowls club and Masonic Club also serve meals. Restaurants are very limited on the other islands.

SOCIAL ACTIVITY

Most activities involve the outdoors, of course, and fishing in particular is very popular – on the beach, from a jetty or from boats around Dunwich and the other islands. There is a lawn bowls club at Point Lookout, a spot well known for whale watching and headland walks. Swimming is popular in the inland freshwater lakes. Macleay Island has a nine-hole golf course.
- Boating • Bushwalking • Fishing • Gallery • Golf
- Lawn bowls • Museum • Sailing • Scuba diving • Surfing
- Swimming • Tennis

REAL ESTATE

- Median house price: $678 000
- Median unit price: $315 000

Homes are often older style and modest; a modern unit with a great view is likely to fetch over $600 000. On Russell and Macleay Islands bush blocks start at $35 000 and those with water views from $100 000. You could pick up a neat weekender there for $150 000.

WHY LIVE HERE?

It is as isolated from the world as you can get yet still only a hop, step and a ferry ride away from Brisbane.

gold coast

Growing pains

The Gold Coast stretches along 57 kilometres of coastline but it also includes a maze of inland waterways and a hinterland of rainforest, the Nerang River and towns. The residential areas tend to cluster around the rivers, beaches and canal estates, as well as the newer inland retail hubs. Is it a city or a sprawl of townships which have joined together?

Either way, it is bursting at the seams, and no-one quite knows what the future holds. The locals say they would live nowhere else but in the same breath they bemoan the fact that the Gold Coast is not what it used to be. It has become too big, they say. They add that the infrastructure is not coping, although they are yet to experience the blackouts suffered by their neighbours on the Sunshine Coast. They worry that the entire Gold Coast coastal strip from Coolangatta to Paradise Point will become high-rise like Surfers, which would certainly change the style of living in the low- to medium-rise areas. Perhaps it's inevitable. The Gold Coast Council certainly appears to be pro high-rise.

The Gold Coast is many things to many people, and in my travels around the area I identified six different retirement lifestyles:

SECURITY LIVING

American-style gated communities are a relatively new phenomenon. There are three huge resort/estates, locked to all but residents, in close proximity at Sovereign Islands, Sanctuary Cove and Hope Island. And there are more on the way.

BROADWATER

The area north of Southport along the Gold Coast Highway is separated from the sea by a spit of land which creates the Broadwater. This is an older area, encompassing the suburbs of Labrador through to Biggera Waters, Runaway Bay, Hollywell and Paradise Point.

CANAL LIVING

Many tourists would not be aware of the maze of waterways and canals which divert the flow of the Nerang River and are mostly artificially created. The canals are largely hidden behind homes, taking the place of back lanes, and every home backing onto a canal has its own private jetty.

HINTERLAND

Inland from the coast are large towns which offer both infrastructure and residential living. These include Robina, a hub of the future; Nerang; and various suburbs including Varsity Lakes, home to the very impressive Bond University.

HIGH-RISE

This is the famous strip, from Broadbeach through Surfers Paradise, Main Beach and Southport. High-rise apartment blocks define the boundaries and defy gravity. They all face the ocean but as an increasing number of new, bigger skyscrapers have popped up between them and the beach, many of them now have varying degrees of views.

BEACH LIVING

This is the stretch from Coolangatta through Currumbin, Palm Beach, Burleigh Heads, Miami and Mermaid Beach. There is a small amount of high-rise development but it's mostly medium-density housing, with the focus on the beaches.

POPULATION

- 455 000 Est. June 2003
- 18.2% over sixty

The Gold Coast is Australia's sixth-largest city and it's growing rapidly. The population is expected to increase to 700 000 residents by the year 2021.

The Gold Coast has one of the most mobile populations in Australia. Many people who live here have lived somewhere else in the not so distant past and quite likely will live somewhere else in the future. The ever-increasing influx comes first and foremost from elsewhere in Queensland and secondly from New South Wales; the number of people who hail from New South Wales is double that of those from Victoria.

CLIMATE

Summer 20.5°C to 28.5°C
Winter 9.2°C to 20.6°C
Sunshine 111 days
Rain 82 days
Rainfall 1439 mm

LOCATION & GETTING AROUND

Surfers Paradise is 78 kilometres south of Brisbane, a driving time of approximately 75 minutes. It's 850 kilometres from Sydney, a drive of 11.5 hours.

Roads The roads up here are good – if you're approaching from New South Wales, you will appreciate the improvement as you proceed north. The Pacific Highway has four lanes each way, and it becomes the Pacific Motorway near Nerang and all the way to Brisbane. Unheard of in New South Wales! Even the Gold Coast Highway through Surfers Paradise is two lanes each way and the absence of potholes is noticeable. The only bottleneck is where the Pacific Highway and the Gold Coast highway join up, which is often a bit slow going. The question is: will these roads be able to handle the increased traffic flows that are predicted for the future?

Nearest airports Gold Coast Airport, Coolangatta (25 kilometres, 30 minutes by car from Surfers Paradise) or Brisbane Airport (90 kilometres, 80 minutes by car). Trains run twice every hour to Brisbane Airport.

Nearest train Nerang and Robina. Brisbane to Nerang by train takes approximately 70 minutes, followed by the bus transfer to Surfers, which takes another 30 minutes.

Buses Intercity and local coach services

Taxis ✓
Water taxis ✓

INFRASTRUCTURE

Hospitals Gold Coast Hospital at Southport and Robina, All-amanda Private Hospital at Southport, John Flynn Hospital at Tugun, Pindara Private Hospital and 24-hour emergency centre at Bundall, Vision Centre Day Surgery at Southport, Southport Surgicentre

Retirement villages More than 20 on the Gold Coast at Ashmore, Banora Point, Robina, Runaway Bay, Nerang, Mount Gravatt, Currumbin Waters, Miami, Benowa, Elanora, Hope Island, Southport and Helensvale.

Police stations Surfers Paradise, Broadbeach, Burleigh Heads, Canungra, Coolangatta, Coomera, Mudgeeraba, Nerang, Palm Beach, Runaway Bay, Southport and Tamborine, plus Water Police

Local newspaper *Gold Coast Bulletin*

RECREATION

Beaches A strip of beaches runs all along the Gold Coast. The major beaches are the Central Surfers Paradise Beach, Main Beach, Mermaid Beach, Miami, Burleigh Heads, Palm Beach, Tugun and Coolangatta. Most of the beaches are patrolled, and Main Beach has water sports equipment for hire. The beach is almost entirely continuous and lacks definition or vantage points. Burleigh Beach is the exception and is the preferred beach for many surfers, swimmers, walkers and spectators.

Coastguard ✓

Cycleways There are shared bike paths along the coast line. At some points they can get a little congested with pedestrian traffic but they are relatively free of traffic on the Spit. At Burleigh Heads cyclists are separated from pedestrians by dual pathways. Cycleways can also be found in other areas of the Gold Coast and hinterland; for example, at Hinze Dam.

Bushwalking & National Parks There are a number of national parks in the hinterland, including the Springbrook National Park which has walks, twilight tours, glow-worm caves and an astronomy observatory. There are even galleries, shops and coffee shops in this lush rainforest.

Hinze Dam is good for freshwater fishing, bike tracks, barbeques and picnicking. Lamington Park has over 150 kilometres of walking tracks and many waterfalls, and Mount Tamborine is also popular for walking.

It's hard to beat the coastal walks though: there are 36 kilometres of pathways along the beaches, including the large nature reserve on the hills and foreshore at Burleigh Heads which has panoramic ocean and beach views.

Dogs Dogs can be walked on most beaches on leashes. Exercise areas tend to centre around the Nerang River, Southport, Broadbeach and the islands just behind Surfers such as Chevron and Capri.

SHOPPING

The Gold Coast is somewhere you really could shop til you drop. Surfers Paradise has plenty of boutique shops within a block of the beach, particularly on Cavill Avenue, and on Orchid and Elkhorn Avenues. There are Friday-night craft markets along the beach esplanade and the shops in this area are open until nine every night. The Marina Mirage shopping complex at Main Beach has exclusive boutiques, an art gallery and restaurants. Pacific Fair, behind Broadbeach, is Queensland's largest shopping complex with arcades, department stores and cobbled streets. A large Asian supermarket is nearby. There are major shopping centres at Robina, which is very contemporary, Harbour Town at Biggera Waters, Runaway Bay, Nerang River, Southport (Australia Fair) and Burleigh. The shopping centres are smaller at Hope Island, Paradise Point and Elanora.

DINING

As it's the number one tourist destination for Australian and overseas visitors, the Gold Coast is crowded with restaurants and cafés. They vary hugely in terms of cuisine, price range and quality. A particularly trendy dining area is at Main Beach on Marina Mirage with its waterfront restaurants and cafés.

SOCIAL ACTIVITY

Almost every type of association, group and hobby is catered for here, but the focus is definitely on the outdoors. Locals can choose from a host of water sports, cruises, game fishing or whale watching. There are numerous world-standard golf courses, and no doubt many keen golfers retire here partly because of that factor alone. Many locals have their own boats and jetties, but there is no shortage of marinas. Power boating rules over sail – perhaps there are so many areas to explore from the Broadwater to the islands in Moreton Bay, there's just not enough time to spend sailing.

The area is well known for its nightclubs, theatres and cabaret restaurants. Jupiters Casino is in Broadbeach, with gaming, restaurants, bars, a nightclub and entertainment venues. Six-screen cinemas are located in Robina, Coolangatta and Surfers. There are also the many theme parks in this area, notably Water World, Sea World and Movie World.

Mount Tamborine in the hinterland has art and craft galleries, wineries, antique shops, cafés and restaurants. For further education, there are four universities in the area (Bond University has the most impressive architecture) and a large TAFE campus.

• All community organisations • All religions • Arts & crafts
• Boating • Cinema • Fishing • Galleries • Golf • Library
• Museum • Surfing • Swimming • Theatre

security living
Do not disturb

The American concept of gated communities has caught on in parts of the Gold Coast, and three standout gated communities are Sanctuary Cove, Hope Island and Sovereign Island. These communities represent a totally different lifestyle concept, and although they are not especially for retirees or older people, they do include many over-sixties.

These are very wealthy areas, where the homes are large, although perhaps a bit close together, often with swimming pools, tennis courts and private marinas. The gardens are carefully manicured and I didn't see a veggie patch anywhere, or a kid's tree house or a swing. At least one new development claims not to allow families with children. The cars are mostly prestigious European types and those that aren't probably belong to the housekeepers.

They are also isolated communities, where it is virtually impossible to walk anywhere. A trip to the shops, a cup of coffee or a chat with a friend is a car ride away. Sanctuary Cove and Hope Island resorts are built around perfectly maintained golf courses and have shopping villages which are open to the general public. Sanctuary Cove also has an extensive marina complex. The canals and waterways around the Broadwater provide ample opportunity for relaxation, fishing and fun.

Gated communities don't necessarily provide a sense of community – sometimes quite the opposite in fact, as residents feel cut off and alone. You would need to experience life in these resorts to find out whether you like it or not. Personally, I find these neighbourhoods too carefully manicured and clinical. They are somewhere to visit rather than to live.

POPULATION

These communities are not skewed to the over-sixties; rather, they represent a cross-section of ages conforming with the national average.

LOCATION & GETTING AROUND

Although these communities are somewhat isolated, the roads are good and in parts paved with red bricks, accentuating the upmarket nature of these resorts. The roads are single lane but not congested. It's a 25-kilometre drive to the major shopping centres, which takes about 30 minutes. The airport at Coolangatta is 50 kilometres away, about a 45-minute drive.

SHOPPING

Hope Island has a medium-sized shopping mall. The shops at Paradise Point are pleasantly situated overlooking parkland and the Broadwater. Runaway Bay and Harbour Town are the nearest major centres.

REAL ESTATE

Hope Island and Sanctuary Cove

• Median apartment price: $530 000

There are plenty of homes for sale within these communities, both new and not so new. The price range can vary greatly, however; for example, a five-bedroom home with tennis court, pool and marina on Hope Island could be $850 000 or $1 850 000, with quite a few choices in between. A block of land on the waterfront at any one of these communities is likely to be $1 million plus. Prices on Sovereign Island start from $2.8 million and are frequently over $3 million. There are numerous beautiful luxury homes for sale along the Sovereign Mile, some brand-new and others slightly used.

WHY LIVE HERE?

For those retirees who do not want to be disturbed.

broadwater
Woy Woy on the Gold Coast

The real estate here is not inspiring for the most part. Only the more expensive homes looking onto the Broadwater have views, as housing is low rise. It's a relaxed neighbourhood though, where residents can walk to shops and restaurants. Some very expensive neighbours are creeping in; for example, in parts of Paradise Point, Hollywell and Biggera Bay on the water. The likelihood is that as the Gold Coast continues to expand, the older homes will gradually be bought up and new developments will take place. In fact, one development is already well under way on Ephraim Island.

POPULATION

- 38 000
- 27% over sixty

Includes the suburbs of Labrador, Runaway Bay, Hollywell, Coombabah and part of Paradise Point, which are home to 10 000 over-sixties. In Paradise Point one in every three residents is over sixty.

SHOPPING

Paradise Point's popular strip of shops has a pleasant aspect overlooking the parkland and the Broadwater. Runaway Bay Centre and Harbour Town are close by.

REAL ESTATE

- Median house price: $455 000
- Median unit price: $280 000

Two-bedroom homes, townhouses and units start from $200 000.

WHY LIVE HERE?

These suburbs represent affordable living just a stone's throw from the Gold Coast.

canal living

Venice meets Vegas

An extensive yet little-known system of canals and waterways has been created by reclaiming land or dredging the Nerang River and the Broadwater. In suburb after suburb, the houses back onto water and jetties jut out to pontoons crowded with motor boats of every size. Some of them are now considered older areas while others are filled with architect-designed contemporary dwellings. Project home builders won't do so well here.

The canal dwellers are concentrated on the reclaimed islands behind Surfers at Isle of Capri, Rio Vista, Sorrento, Broadbeach Waters, Rialto, Florida

Gardens, Miami Keys, Chevron Island, Cypress Gardens and Paradise Waters. Further south there are canal communities at Currumbin Waters, Elanora, Burleigh Waters, Mermaid Waters and Clear Island Waters. To the north there's Biggera Waters, Runaway Bay and Paradise Point. Imagine the congestion if they all took their boats out at once!

Once out of the canals there is a lot of water to play on. The Broadwater leads to the many islands between the mainland and the very long Stradbroke Island; then there's Moreton Bay and, of course, the Pacific Ocean.

Canal living is an interesting concept and one with a lot of appeal if you use a boat frequently. I didn't see many boats in use in my travels though, and I am reminded of the many boats which sit idle in any harbour. Remember that old adage that the two days you enjoy owning a boat are the day you buy it and the day you sell it. One drawback to living on the canals are the midges (small sand flies), which is something the real estate agents won't tell you about.

POPULATION

- 75 000
- 25% over sixty

REAL ESTATE

- Median house price: $600 000
- Median unit price: $320 000

The homes vary in quality, depending upon the area, and you can expect to pay a lot more for a contemporary home in a prestigious neighbourhood. Houses in these suburbs are very close to the Gold Coast's facilities and services, but none of them have ocean views.

WHY LIVE HERE?

A waterway paradise for boaties.

hinterland
Planned and affordable

Behind the Gold Coast there are many suburbs filled with affordable housing and shops offering residents value for money. There are few high-rise developments here; the houses are mostly newish in leafy residential estates, although some of them are cheek by jowl. A key development has been the expansion of Robina as a major hub for the area. The other hub is Nerang, which is scarred by the Pacific Motorway that slices through it. Both hubs have train stations and bus interchanges.

Nerang is an older centre and hosts one of the two offices for the Gold Coast Council. It has industrial as well as commercial and retail facilities, and gives the appearance of evolution rather than any thoughtful planning. In its centre there's a large permanent-resident caravan park by the river.

In contrast, Robina is a proud example of government planning. Its retail and commercial centre is large and entirely free of traffic. It is meticulously clean and its shops include the major stores as well as a six-screen cinema complex. There's casual dining and undercover pedestrian streets leading to an open-air village square. New residential developments surround the centre and the subdivisions continue to Varsity Lakes, which is home to Bond University. Not surprisingly, it is Robina rather than Nerang which is attracting newcomers, including older people who presumably do not want to live in high-rise apartments or perhaps cannot afford the prices closer to the coast.

POPULATION

Robina
- 3000
- 18% over sixty

REAL ESTATE
- Median house price: $435 000
- Median unit price: $305 000

This is a newish area and the housing is comparatively modern.

Affordable living in good-quality housing and carefully planned streets within driving distance of the Gold Coast. Many retirees would be very happy here.

high-rise
Sun, surf and glitz

Surfers Paradise is in the centre of the Gold Coast, stretching from South-port to Broadbeach. An almost continuous progression of gigantic high-rise developments, shopping arcades, nightclubs, luxury resorts and hotels, it's like nowhere else in Australia. The view looking north from Burleigh Heads gives the impression of a giant staircase of glass, metal and concrete as far as the eye can see – quite a spectacle when you take it in for the first time. This is living in a bird's nest, but chances are another high-rise will grow up in front of you as you watch, and block out your view. There is endless construction as older buildings make way for newer and even taller structures. At eighty-eight storeys, Q1 is the tallest residential tower in Australia and all the apartments were sold off the plan before the building was completed.

The over-sixties who live in these towers enjoy the security, the views and the simplicity of locking the doors and taking off. They travel, sometimes living elsewhere for part of the year. They promenade on the boardwalk and enjoy the pulse and interaction of this international strip. Other retirees find this area is just too frenetic; they might try it out for a while but then move on. The census figures indicate a considerable degree of population mobility. Others keep a small apartment here to escape the winter months elsewhere.

Many locals feel that development has now gone too far and they have real concerns about the ability of the infrastructure to keep pace. They're also concerned that their lifestyle is about to be compromised. One thing is for sure, the hordes keep coming!

Note: In 2005 there were problems with young hoons racing their cars at night on a small section of the roadway adjacent to the beach at Surfers Paradise. The problem was bad enough for some residents to relocate elsewhere within the Gold Coast and according to real estate agents it had a downward effect on market prices. If you're considering moving here you'd need to check whether this situation is continuing before making a final decision.

POPULATION

- 100 000
- 26% over sixty

Although one in four residents is aged over sixty this is not solely a retired person's area, as it offers something for everyone.

LOCATION & GETTING AROUND

Gold Coast Airport at Coolangatta is 24 kilometres away (a 30-minute drive) and Brisbane Airport is 90 kilometres (just under 1.5 hours).

The train stations at Nerang and Robina are 12 kilometres away, about a 20-minute drive.

REAL ESTATE

- Median house price: $600 000
- Median unit price: $320 000

For a two-bed apartment with good views, including distant glimpses of the ocean, you will be looking at over $500 000. For an apartment that's a little more special or overlooking the beach, prices are in excess of $900 000. And for something really special, such as a penthouse apartment, be prepared to spend $2 million and upwards.

WHY LIVE HERE?

If you love the sun, the surf, the glitz and all the comforts of the city, as well as good access to other cities, then you can't do much better than put your feet up in Surfers. As a couple from Melbourne said to me: 'We moved up here fifteen years ago, and we've seen it change a lot. It's getting too congested, too hectic. Still, we couldn't go back now.'

beach living
On the edge of chaos

This strip is less glitzy than its neighbour to the north. Coolangatta lies at the extreme southern end of the Gold Coast, at the mouth of the Tweed River with twin town Tweed Heads. Other popular retirement suburbs following the coast to the north are Tugun, Currumbin, Palm Beach, Burleigh Heads, Miami and Mermaid Beach. From Coolangatta you can see the entire coastline, from Surfers Paradise all the way down to Byron Bay, but the best view is from elevated Burleigh Heads. The view from here is stunning, a panorama of ocean and coast, and the steel and concrete towers of the Surfers strip disappearing into the distance are a constant reminder of the high-rise creep which is likely to spread south as well as north.

Burleigh Heads is an appealing place, with a fabulous nature reserve on the headland adjacent to the beach that's very popular with walkers and joggers. The town has open spaces, with a mix of low- and medium-rise buildings, plus plenty of beachfront cafés and restaurants. The beaches to the north of Burleigh are less appealing as they merge into a long strip of continuous beach that reaches all the way past Surfers to the end of Main Beach.

POPULATION

Coolangatta	Currumbin	Palm Beach	Burleigh Heads
• 8500	• 2750	• 14 000	• 8000

This area is home to a large number of over-sixties; in Coolangatta, for instance, they represent an enormous 44 per cent of the population.

LOCATION & GETTING AROUND

The roads in this part of the strip are some of the most congested on the Gold Coast. The Pacific Highway meets the Gold Coast Highway and bottlenecks occur near the airport. They don't continue for long though, and generally the traffic flows smoothly.

REAL ESTATE

Coolangatta

- Median house price: $545 000
- Median unit price: $335 000

Burleigh Heads and Miami

- Median house price: $432 000
- Median unit price: $300 000

WHY LIVE HERE?

This is like the Gold Coast used to be: medium-rise and low-rise architecture mingling happily together. How long this will remain so is anybody's guess. Burleigh in particular offers open spaces, good surfing, beach walks and cycling and a beautiful nature reserve on the headland. It would be my retirement preference on the Gold Coast.

queensland's top 10

1. BEST RETIREMENT HOTSPOT: Hervey Bay
Excellent climate, beaches, facilities, access to the water and Fraser Island National Park. I've also chosen Hervey Bay because it is still affordable and has plenty of future growth potential.

2. BEST RETIREMENT LIFESTYLE: Noosa
Great food, shopping, beaches, facilities and nature reserves.

3. BEST SMALL LOCATION: Bargara
A picturesque village on the sea, with a comfortable climate and outdoor café culture, and close to the city of Bundaberg.

4. BEST LARGE LOCATION: Townsville
This well-planned city has an impressive infrastructure, and a good arts and culture scene.

5. BEST SHOPPING: Gold Coast

6. BEST DINING: Noosa

7. BEST PLACE TO CURL UP WITH A GOOD BOOK: 1770

8. BEST BEACHES: Noosa, Coolum, Burleigh Heads

9. BEST OUTDOOR ACTIVITIES: Cairns for golf and adventure sports; Gold Coast for golf and water sports.

10. BEST-VALUE REAL ESTATE: Rockhampton

new south wales

Tweed Valley 89

Byron Bay 93

Ballina 97

Yamba 100

Grafton 103

Coffs Harbour 106

Nambucca Heads 110

South West Rocks 113

Port Macquarie 115

Taree 119

Forster & Great Lakes 123

Port Stephens 127

Lake Macquarie 131

Central Coast 135

  Wyong 135

  Gosford 139

Sydney 144

  Upper North Shore 144

  Northern Beaches 147

  Northern Harbour Suburbs 150

  Eastern Harbour Suburbs 153

Kiama 156

Shoalhaven 159

Jervis Bay 163

Ulladulla 167

Sussex Inlet 171

Batemans Bay 171

Sapphire Coast 175

Tamworth 179

Mudgee 182

Blue Mountains 185

Southern Highlands 189

New South Wales' Top 10 194

Opposite: The Ocean Shores golf course and residential development, close to Byron Bay

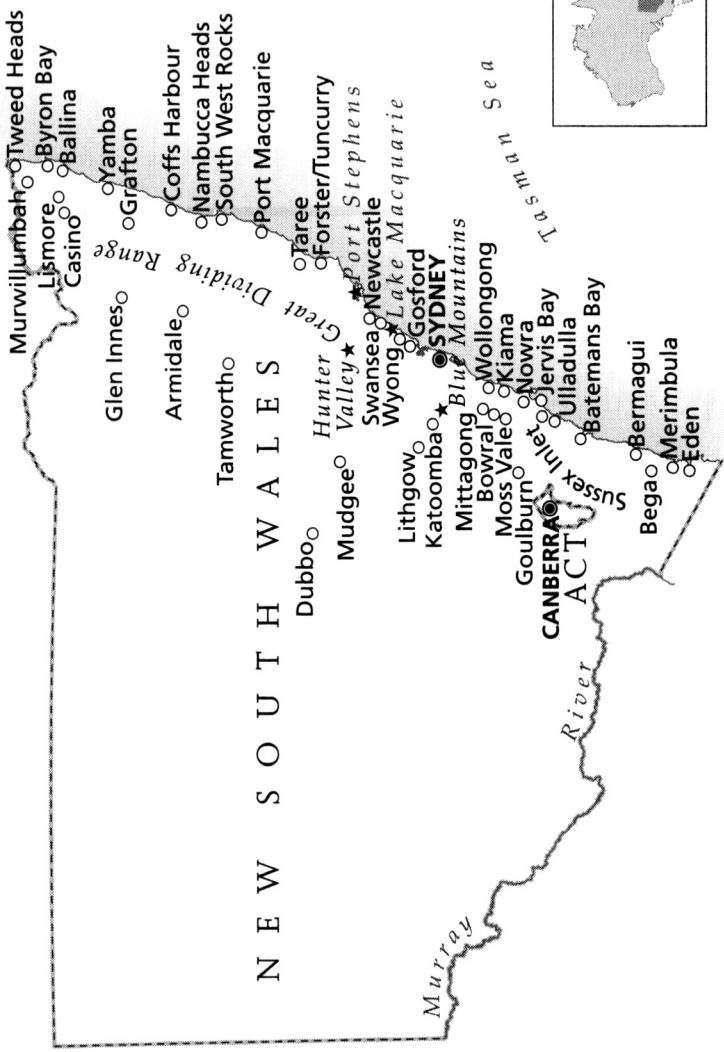

tweed valley
Still like the old days ... for the moment

Tweed Heads is a large coastal centre located right next door to its Queensland twin, Coolangatta. It is a hub of commerce and tourism and has a variety of sporting, recreational and social clubs.

The Tweed Valley takes in 35 kilometres of beaches and estuaries, small villages and headlands. The region runs south from Tweed Heads, Fingal, Kingscliff and Bogangar to Pottsville Beach; it also stretches inland to Murwillumbah, a picturesque town on the western bank of the Tweed River. Kingscliff has a large retired population and is a quaint coastal village with a strip of old-fashioned shops and a permanent-resident caravan park. The beach is hidden by scrub, a common occurrence on the New South Wales coast.

Kingscliff has a sleepy 'yesterday' feel about it, as does a lot of the Tweed Valley, but this would appear to be changing. Just around the corner is Salt, an enormous, state-of-the-art luxury resort and residential development on the beach at Kingscliff. This is the way of the northern New South Wales and Queensland coasts: the old continues to make way for the new. I doubt that Salt will be the last of the new estates in this area as developers are continually searching out new opportunities. The Tweed Valley has banned ultra high-rise developments outside the central district, but you will still need to do your homework and make sure a developer doesn't have big plans for your neighbourhood if you want a quiet hideaway.

POPULATION

Tweed Heads
- 45 000
- 34% over sixty

This is an oldies area. The population of the entire Tweed Valley as at June 2003 was estimated to be 78 000, with a median age of 42.8 and 29 per cent of residents aged over sixty.

CLIMATE

Summer 19.5°C to 29.6°C
Winter 8.5°C to 20.9°C

Sunshine 105 days
Rain 82 days
Rainfall 1588 mm

LOCATION & GETTING AROUND

It's 10 hours by car from Sydney (840 kilometres) and 1.5 hours south of Brisbane (100 kilometres).

Roads The roads are noticeably poorer than those in neighbouring southern Queensland

Nearest airports Coolangatta Airport is a 20-minute drive from Tweed Heads; Ballina Airport is a 1.5-hour drive.

Nearest train The Sydney train terminates at Murwillumbah, which is 15 minutes from Tweed Heads

Buses Numerous coach and scheduled bus services

Taxis ✓

INFRASTRUCTURE

Hospitals Tweed Heads District, John Flynn Private and Murwillumbah District. Community Centres are at Kingscliff, Murwillumbah and Tweed Heads, and there are numerous support groups for the aged.

Retirement villages Pottsville, Murwillumbah, Kingscliff and Tweed Heads, though the number of villages is limited

Police stations Murwillumbah, Tweed Heads and Kingscliff

Local newspapers *Daily News*, *Tweed Sun* and *Tweed Valley Times*

RECREATION

Beaches There are a number of good beaches around here, and they're patrolled from Tweed Heads south to Pottsville. Fingal in particular is excellent for surfing, and visitors frequently watch for dolphins in this area. Other beautiful surfing beaches are close by at Cabarita, Hastings Point, Pottsville and Wooyung. Kingscliff, just south of Fingal, is great for sheltered swimming, boating and fishing.

Coastguard ✓

Cycleways Kingscliff and the coastal area have 25 kilometres of bikeways

Bushwalking & National Parks Six national parks, as well as a koala colony

Dogs Designated leash-free areas.

SHOPPING

There are two major shopping centres in Tweed Heads with a good range of major supermarkets, stores, cinemas and a Medicare branch. South Tweed Heads has a Homemart and speciality shops. Murwillumbah has a Coles supermarket and a host of individual shops. The shopping centres in Pottsville and Kingscliff are smaller, with takeaway outlets, restaurants, a hotel and supermarket. Local vegetable farms sell fresh produce at markets in Kingscliff, Murwillumbah, Tweed Heads and Pottsville Beach.

DINING

A variety of dining options are available, including Mexican cantinas on the beach, bistros, coffee shops, bar and grills, seafood restaurants and buffets, Chinese restaurants and freshly cooked prawns straight off the trawler. In Murwillumbah and Kingscliff there are outdoor cafés and restaurants, pubs and clubs.

SOCIAL ACTIVITY

The Tweed Valley offers plenty of opportunities for outdoor activities and it also has a large artistic community and active theatrical groups. There are a number of festivals in the Tweed area, including the Cultural and Country Harvest Festival and a Music Festival. There are two golf clubs, at Murwillumbah and the Coolangatta and Tweed Heads Golf Club. Toastmasters International is located at Murwillumbah. There are libraries at Kingscliff, Murwillumbah and Tweed Heads. Tweed Heads offers entertainment at Seagulls and the Twin Towns Services Club, which has six floors of entertainment, dining and leisure.

- All community organisations • All religions • Arts & crafts
- Boating • Bushwalking • Fishing • Galleries • Horse riding
- Lawn bowls • Libraries • Picnicking • Sailing • Scuba diving
- Surfing • Swimming • Tennis

REAL ESTATE

Tweed Heads
- Median house price: $380 000
- Median unit price: $261 000

Kingscliff
- Median house price: $465 000
- Median unit price: $351 000

Pottsville
- Median house price: $408 000
- Median unit price: $337 000

Murwillumbah
- Median house price: $275 000
- Median unit price: $190 000

The prices at the Salt residential development are considerably higher.

WHY LIVE HERE?

The Tweed Valley offers the opportunity to find a quiet, unpretentious rural or beach retreat or the contemporary and prestigious lifestyle offered by Salt. The Gold Coast is within easy reach when you feel the need to add a little glamour to your otherwise peaceful existence.

byron bay

A melting pot in the sun for all types and ages

Byron Bay attracts a very eclectic group of residents, with an average age much lower than the population average. Byron is yet to become a retirement magnet but it is evolving because the real estate prices here are forcing out all but the wealthy, and these tend to be older folk.

It is in the hinterland and coastal areas around Byron Bay that you find the over-sixties – and lots of them. Retirees are gravitating to Bangalow, Brunswick Heads, Ocean Shores, Mullumbimby, Federal and Possum Creek (the former home of actor Paul Hogan). The most popular options are beach houses or small farms.

Bangalow is a small inland village, whose main street features historic buildings, cafés, restaurants, a friendly pub and antique, craft and speciality shops. Mullumbimby is a picturesque town which sits at the base of Mount Chincogan. On the coast, Brunswick Heads is an older-style place with modest housing and the choice of calm water or surf, as it is on an inlet. The town has the highest proportion of over-sixties in the Byron Bay area. The Ocean Shores resort and recreation development here is a well-maintained, very comfortable community with lots of space, good views and nice homes, and the additional facilities of a luxury country club and golf course.

Byron Bay is unique but it has a 'passing through' feel about it, which is indeed what most people are doing. There are all types of people in town – don't be surprised if you're approached by someone who looks like they've been involved in a game of paint ball asking you for money. Look beyond Byron, however, and you will find some magic hideaways which are home to people just like yourself. Well, almost.

POPULATION

Byron Bay
- 7000
- 14% over sixty

Mullumbimby
- 3000
- 23% over sixty

Brunswick Heads
- 2000
- 30% over sixty

Ocean Shores
- 3500
- 25% over sixty

The population of the Byron LGA was estimated to be in excess of 30 000 in June 2003, and growing rapidly.

CLIMATE

Summer 20.6°C to 27.5°C
Winter 11.7°C to 19.4°C
Sunshine 107 days
Rain 153 days
Rainfall 1721 mm

LOCATION & GETTING AROUND

Sydney to Byron Bay is 775 kilometres, which takes over 10 hours to drive; from Brisbane to Byron it's only 170 kilometres, taking two and a quarter hours. The road from Brisbane is dual carriageway for most of the journey. The road from Sydney is a nightmare but there are plans for improvement.

Roads The roads around Byron are in a reasonably good condition

Nearest airports Ballina, just 35 minutes to the south. Coolangatta Airport is 60 minutes north and Lismore is 40 minutes west

Nearest train Sydney to Grafton or Casino takes up to 11 hours, then it's a one-hour coach ride to Byron Bay. Brisbane to Casino takes 2.5 hours by rail. There used to be a train station in Byron, but as in so many country towns it is no longer used

Buses Buses connect Byron Bay with Ballina and Coolangatta airports as well as the capital cities

Taxis ✓

INFRASTRUCTURE

Hospitals Byron Bay has a small hospital; services include maternity, palliative care, chemotherapy, general medical procedures and a day surgery. Because Byron Bay is a tourist hub, the hospital's accident and emergency department is open 24/7.

Ballina District Hospital is a larger hospital serving the area (40 kilometres away). A small hospital is also located at Nimbin.

Retirement villages Three in Ballina, one in Bangalow and Lennox Head

Police stations Ballina, Byron Bay, Brunswick Heads and Mullumbimby

Local newspaper *Echo*. The *Echo* leads the charge in 'the battle for Byron' as it is known. Many of the locals are opposed to overdevelopment such as has happened in Surfers Paradise, and not so long ago they prevented Club Med and McDonald's from moving in.

RECREATION

Beaches Byron's main beach is safe and popular, and is also a key pedestrian thoroughfare to Wategos Beach and the lighthouse. If you walk along the beach for long enough you will meet every visitor to Byron Bay. There are also some serious surfing beaches such as the Wreck, the Pass and Wategos (the names say it all!).

Coastguard ✓

Cycleways Cyclists use the streets and often don't wear helmets

Bushwalking & National Parks You would never tire of taking a walk through the bush to the lighthouse. It's the most easterly point in Australia, and has the most amazing ocean views, complete with dolphins and eagles. There are eight nature reserves in the vicinity.

Dogs Several off-leash areas.

SHOPPING

Byron Bay has a large number of shops lining the main streets as well as a large Woolworths supermarket. Health food shops and therapeutic massage clinics front the main streets and many of the shops cater for the alternative lifestyle. If you are into astrology, numerology, any alternative-ology then this is the place.

DINING

There are many restaurants in and around Byron, both casual and fine dining. A remarkable range of cuisine helps city slickers feel at home. What's more, they know how to make a good cappuccino here!

SOCIAL ACTIVITY

Scuba diving is particularly good at Julian Rocks, offshore from Byron. There are seven golf courses in the area, five of them with 18 holes. Libraries are located in Byron Bay, Mullumbimby and Brunswick Heads, and there are council swimming pools in Byron Bay and Mullumbimby. There are yoga schools and numerous health and beauty clinics. Thongs on the feet as well as elsewhere are normal attire.

• Arts & crafts • Fishing • Golf • Libraries
• Most community organisations • Most religions
• Scuba diving • Snorkelling • Surfing • Swimming

REAL ESTATE

Byron Bay
• Median house price: $535 000
• Median unit price: $370 000
Brunswick Heads
• Median house price: $385 000
• Median unit price: $265 000
Mullumbimby
• Median house price: $330 000
Possum Creek
• Median house price: $429 000

Don't expect a view for these prices. Something right on the water at Wategos Beach is likely to be over $4 million. An issue currently dividing Byron is whether short-term rentals should be banned in order to keep the peace for residents.

WHY LIVE HERE?

Because you want to stay young at heart.

ballina

Byron satellite without the price tag

Only thirty minutes south of Byron Bay, Ballina is a flat, easy-to-get-around town situated on an island at the mouth of the Richmond River. The long main street is lined with attractive public buildings and a wide range of retail outlets. Ballina is surrounded by water, in the form of a river and a lake, but there are no sea views or beaches until you cross the bridge to more-expensive East Ballina. The permanent caravan park in Ballina has, as always, one of the best positions on the river.

The Ballina Shire incorporates Lennox Head, a laid-back beach resort ten minutes up the coast at the southern end of Seven Mile Beach. There are great views and opportunities to spot whales and dolphins from the headland. Just metres behind the beach is the freshwater Lake Ainsworth, whose waters are stained a deep red by the tea-trees that line its banks.

In the hinterland there are rainforests and villages, and to the south heathlands. The inland town of Alstonville is like a warmer version of New South Wales' Southern Highlands or Victoria's Dandenongs, with an abundance of gardens, stylish cafés, galleries and antique shops which give it an overall boutique village feel.

POPULATION

Ballina LGA

- **40 000** Est. June 2003
- **25% over sixty**

Ballina, Alstonville and Lennox Head are all growth areas, with large proportions of over-sixties. Lennox Head grew 30 per cent between censuses as farms are increasingly being subdivided for housing. Evans Head, south of Ballina, has a static population of 2600 and a high percentage of over-sixties.

CLIMATE

Summer 19.4°C to 27.1°C
Winter 9.8°C to 18.5°C
Sunshine 107 days

Rain 156 days
Rainfall 1861 mm

LOCATION & GETTING AROUND

Ballina is 195 kilometres from Brisbane, a driving time of approximately 2.5 hours. It's 750 kilometres to Sydney, a driving time of just under nine hours.

Roads The streets in the main centres are wide and well maintained but between villages they tend to be narrow and winding, particularly in the hinterland.

Nearest airport Ballina; it's a 30-minute flight to Brisbane and 75 minutes to Sydney.

Nearest train XPT to Casino then coach to Ballina; the trip takes just under 13 hours from Sydney.

Buses ✓

Taxis ✓

INFRASTRUCTURE

Hospitals Ballina District Hospital. There are Community Health Centres at Ballina and Alstonville.

Retirement villages Three in Ballina and one each in Lennox Head and Alstonville

Police stations Alstonville, Ballina and Wardell

Local newspapers *Northern Star*, *Advocate* and Lismore Northern Rivers *Echo*

RECREATION

Beaches The most popular beaches are those north of Ballina, such as Shelley Beach and Lighthouse, which are patrolled; Angel's and Shaws Bay Lagoon, popular for swimming; and Seven Mile Beach at Lennox Head.

Coastguard ✓

Cycleways There is an extensive network of cycleways around Ballina, which has a flat terrain that's conducive to cycling.

Bushwalking & National Parks Broadwater National Park,

Tuckean Nature reserve, Lennox Head Heathland, Broken Head Nature Reserve, Lake Chickiba and Richmond River Nature Reserve.

Dogs Alstonville, East Ballina and North Ballina all have an off-leash area. Beach off-leash areas include part of Seven Mile Beach and South Ballina Beach.

SHOPPING

Ballina has a very good shopping strip with lots of variety, including major supermarkets and stores. Alstonville has a reasonable retail strip with a Bi-Lo supermarket but Lennox Head has only a small group of shops. There are monthly markets at Ballina and Lake Ainsworth.

DINING

Fine dining is limited in Ballina but there are plenty of cafés and bistros. There are a few good restaurants at Lennox Head and Alstonville.

SOCIAL ACTIVITY

Ballina is a haven for anglers, beach and boat lovers, and there is a protected marina on the river. Canoeing is popular in the wetlands of North Creek or Lake Ainsworth. Outdoor facilities include two golf courses and a large swimming complex. There are libraries at Ballina, Lennox Head and Alstonville, as well as a mobile library. Alstonville Leisure and Entertainment Centre hosts theatre productions by amateur and professional groups.
• Arts & crafts • Boating • Dancing • Fishing • Galleries
• Golf • Library • Most community organisations
• Most religions • Museums • Swimming • Theatre

REAL ESTATE

Ballina and Lennox Head
• Median house price: $393 000
• Median unit price: $300 000

Alstonville

• Median house price: $327 000
• Median unit price: $218 000

More-expensive canal-front homes in Ballina have water access, and homes with good water views at Lennox and East Ballina typically go for around $700 000.

WHY LIVE HERE?

Because it hasn't been 'spoiled' by development (yet) and has all the advantages of living in the sunny north without the crowds and the expensive price tags.

yamba

Going upmarket with a Paddington makeover

To get to Yamba you exit the Pacific Highway at Maclean and wind your way along a narrow road for 20 kilometres. Yamba is divided into the flat part of town, where the long main street is lined with older-style brick-veneer homes on neat blocks of land, and the hillier part of town overlooking the ocean and the mouth of the Clarence River. Atop the hill is where the most expensive housing can be found, although there are two appealing riverfront sub-divisions tucked away on the flat.

Yamba is a town in transition, as major developments have taken up the available land on the headland. The exclusive Paddington-style terraces surrounding a new golf course are the most stylish, and elsewhere on the headland there are expensive individual homes overlooking the sea and a small street with trendy eateries. The Oyster Cove Over-Fifties' Lifestyle Resort is on the inlet and has around 200 lots with water on three sides.

Iluka, on the opposite side of the river, is Yamba's poor cousin. Although it's only a short ferry ride away from Yamba (four times daily), by car it's a good fifty minutes. Iluka is set back from the sea but has river access. It's popular with retirees but the population overall is waning – this could perhaps in part be because Iluka is not yet on sewerage! Maclean, on the Clarence River, is a proud and pretty Scottish town, a bit smaller than Yamba but also growing.

The Clarence River has many tributaries to explore, including the Wooloweyah Estuary, and just west of Maclean is a huge stretch of water called the Broadwater.

During the holiday seasons the influx of holiday-makers in Yamba doubles the population and puts stress on services. A permanent caravan park is located on the river. Just how do they get the best spots?

POPULATION

Yamba	Maclean	Iluka
• 5660	• 3250	• 1850
• 39.6% over sixty		• 47% over sixty

CLIMATE

Summer 20.3°C to 26.7°C
Winter 9.7°C to 19°C
Sunshine 131 days
Rain 134 days
Rainfall 1459 mm

LOCATION & GETTING AROUND

Sydney to Yamba takes nine hours by car (680 kilometres), and it's just under four hours from Brisbane (290 kilometres).
Nearest airports Ballina offers the best choice of flights; it's 95 kilometres away, a drive of 80 minutes. There's also Grafton (65 kilometres, one hour) and Lismore (95 kilometres, 80 minutes). Bus connections are provided by the Yamba Airport Shuttle bus.
Nearest train Grafton, with CountryLink Bus connections
Buses Bus companies travelling along the Pacific Highway have arrangements to stop at Yamba
Taxis ✓

INFRASTRUCTURE

Hospitals There are three doctors' surgeries, and it's a 20-minute drive (20 kilometres) to Maclean District Hospital

Retirement villages Oyster Cove's Over-Fifties' Lifestyle Resort and Caroona

Police station Yamba

Local newspaper *Daily Examiner*, published in Grafton

RECREATION

Beaches Main Beach (with pool) and Pippi, Convent, Whiting (on the estuary) and Turners beaches. Lifeguards patrol some of the beaches during holiday season.

Coastguard ✓

Cycleways Shared pathway along Ford Park on the estuary

Bushwalking The Yuraygir National Park has plenty of opportunities for bushwalking. Hickey Island is connected to the mainland. In Iluka the Rainforest Nature Reserve has wheelchair access.

Dogs Designated leash-free areas.

SHOPPING

Yamba isn't a large place and the shopping precinct is only just adequate. It has a Bi-Lo supermarket, but the closest Woolworths and Coles supermarkets are in Grafton. Maclean has two small supermarkets.

DINING

Yamba has 16 restaurants and 11 cafés, three of which featured in the *Sydney Morning Herald Good Food Guide*.

SOCIAL ACTIVITY

Yamba has three art galleries, a cinema (it's cute but don't expect the range of films you get in metropolitan multi-screen cinemas), a modern lawn bowls club, boating (there is a protected marina), over 20 clubs and associations, two national parks and a nature reserve.

• Boating • Cinema • Cricket • Galleries • Golf • Lawn bowls
• Library • Many community organisations • Some religions
• Swimming • Tennis

REAL ESTATE

- Median house price: $346 000
- Median unit price: $290 000

These prices are a bit misleading as there are clearly two standards of homes here: houses in the backblocks start at $250 000, while the luxurious Sands townhouse estate offers brand-new apartments with water views, with only the road between them and the beach, for $650 000. A waterfront home would cost $1 million plus. The Oyster Cove Over-Fifties' Lifestyle Resort offers home packages from $200 000. There are also some canal-front homes at Crystal Waters behind Yamba. The median price for a house in Iluka is $264 000.

WHY LIVE HERE?

To enjoy the river and the beach, and perhaps live in a stylish townhouse. The shopping currently leaves something to be desired, though this may change with further growth.

grafton
Jacarandas, verandas and lots of charm

This welcoming town, 50 kilometres from the coast on the mighty Clarence River, is known as the 'City of Trees' – specifically, jacarandas. To add to the city's lush foliage, parks are scattered throughout the city. Many of the houses are spacious older-style weatherboards, and the streets are flat, wide and overhung with trees. Grafton was settled in around 1830, as the land around it is particularly fertile, and it has some elegant Victorian heritage buildings. The river is popular for sailing, fishing, kayaking and cruising.

POPULATION

- 17 500 Est. June 2003
- 22% over sixty

Grafton is one of the few inland towns which are growing, increasing by around 1000 people between censuses.

CLIMATE

Summer 19.6°C to 30.1°C
Winter 6.2°C to 20.4°C
Sunshine 118 days
Rain 128 days
Rainfall 1051 mm

LOCATION & GETTING AROUND

Grafton is 620 kilometres north of Sydney, a drive of 7.5 hours. It's a four-hour drive (340 kilometres) south of Brisbane.

Roads The highways to Casino and Glen Innes pass through, but the city is bypassed by the Pacific Highway. Local streets are wide with generous use of roundabouts rather than traffic lights.

Nearest airport Grafton Airport is 16 kilometres out of town, with regular flights to Sydney

Nearest train Grafton Station; from Sydney the XPT takes just under 10 hours

Buses ✓
Taxis ✓

INFRASTRUCTURE

Hospitals Grafton Base Hospital
Retirement villages One in Grafton
Police stations Grafton
Local newspaper *Daily Examiner*

RECREATION

Cycleways Being flat, Grafton encourages cycling and has a cycleway network, both on-road and off-road

Bushwalking & National Parks The nature reserve on Susan Island in the middle of the Clarence River has walking trails through rainforest. There are also the Yuraygir and Bundjalung National Parks on the coast, and Washpool and Gibraltar Range parks to the west (the latter is mainly accessed by 4WD tours).

Dogs Designated leash-free areas.

SHOPPING

This is a major town, with the department stores and major super-markets you'd expect. Key shopping centres are Market Square Shopping Centre and Grafton Shopping World. There's also a range of craft and supply stores, studios, galleries and antique shops in the village of Ulmarra, 12 kilometres to the north.

DINING

There are numerous restaurants, some of them in the hotels, and plenty of choice.

SOCIAL ACTIVITY

The Clarence River is the venue for all kinds of water sports and clubs, including rowing and sailing clubs. Other clubs include golf, lawn bowls and a historical society. There's a TAFE, art gallery and numerous arts and crafts groups, from quilting and woodwork to embroidery, ceramics and photography. The annual Jacaranda Festival takes place in October, with street and arts events.
- All community organisations • All religions • Arts & crafts
- Gallery • Golf • Horse racing • Lawn bowls • Library
- Museum • Rowing • Sailing

REAL ESTATE

- Median house price: $193 000
- Median unit price: $185 000
You can buy a 'golden oldie' with bull-nose verandas and the works for under $400 000.

WHY LIVE HERE?

If you want to live in an inland country centre, this is one of the best. It's not too far from the coast or from Brisbane and it's so beautiful when the jacarandas are in bloom. The only drawback could be the heat, but it's not as bad as in a lot of other inland towns.

offs harbour
Clean and green

Coffs Harbour is a major coastal centre, almost midway between Sydney and Brisbane. The moment you arrive in Coffs, either by air or via the highway, it's easy to see that it's a substantial place indeed. The well-planned city is efficiently run; the streets are wide and green; and there is a general air of prosperity. The highway slices through town, although it's so well managed that you hardly notice it. There are plans to reroute the highway, which some locals say will only add to the noise, due to the amphitheatre nature of the Coffs Valley.

The beautiful beaches are away from the town centre. Diggers in particular is the most perfectly shaped beach I have ever seen, and the headland has an extensive paved walkway. Overall, it is hard to fault Coffs, and the influx of new residents is proof of its appeal. An English couple I met here had visited every location from Adelaide to the north of Brisbane, and they'd picked Coffs for their retirement on the grounds of climate, university campus and access for their overseas visitors. There are many professionals here, both retired and working, some no doubt as a result of the presence of the Southern Cross University.

There is only one high-rise building in town (now how did that one get through?) but as Coffs is built on undulating land many homes have views of either the surrounding hills or the ocean. There are many choices if you want to live out of Coffs but be close enough to shop and dine, including numerous beach enclaves heavy with retirees such as Emerald, Arrawarra, Sapphire, Opal Cove and Korora. Larger towns nearby include dust-blown Woolgoolga, which has a large Indian community, and Sawtell, which is hidden from the sea by a rise of bushland. You could sail past Sawtell and not know it was there, which would be a shame as it's really quite cute, with a tree-lined shopping strip.

The region encompasses golden beaches, rainforest escarpments, quiet country lanes, farms and historic villages such as charming Bellingen.

POPULATION

- 26 000
- 23.7% over sixty

retirement hotspots

The population of Coffs Harbour increased by 4000 between censuses. Around 64 000 people were estimated to live in the Coffs Shire at June 2003, and of these 15 000 were likely to be aged over sixty. Both Woolgoolga (total pop 3795) and Arrawarra (pop 1564) grew only slightly between censuses.

CLIMATE

Summer 19.5°C to 27°C
Winter 7.5°C to 18.8°C
Sunshine 122 days
Rain 141 days
Rainfall 1677 mm
It's warm enough to grow bananas and they do; any further south is too cool.

LOCATION & GETTING AROUND

It's 540 kilometres to Sydney, approximately six hours' driving time. Brisbane is five hours (400 kilometres).
Roads The roads are well maintained and wide in Coffs Harbour, but they can be busy.
Nearest airport Coffs Harbour Airport is only five minutes from town. It's a modern airport with regular daily flights to Sydney (one-hour flight), Brisbane and Melbourne.
Nearest train Coffs Harbour. The XPT from Sydney takes 8.5 hours; from Brisbane it's 5.5 hours.
Buses Three local services and regular intercity coaches
Taxis ✓

INFRASTRUCTURE

Hospitals The modern Coffs Harbour Base Hospital has 200 beds; it looks and claims to be state of the art.
Retirement villages Coffs Harbour, Woolgoolga and Sawtell
Police stations Coffs Harbour, Woolgoolga and Sawtell. Sawtell's station is manned during the daytime only, so there have been some problems with break-ins there at night.

Local newspapers *Coffs Harbour Advocate*, Coffs Harbour and District *Independent Weekly*

RECREATION

Beaches Most beaches are fringed with bush. Park Beach, Diggers Beach and Sawtell Beach in particular are classic beaches, while Jetty Beach is by the marina and protected from ocean swells by a breakwater. All the beaches are good for swimming and some for fishing, and most are patrolled during summer holidays.

Coastguard ✓

Cycleways Sawtell to Coffs Harbour off-road cycle route, and from Coffs' city centre to Muttonbird Island

Bushwalking & National Parks There are over 20 national parks and nature reserves nearby, plus the Solitary Islands marine park. The Boambee Headland walk from Coffs to Sawtell is part of the Solitary Islands Coastal Walk. The Toormina Reserves Walk is a flat, easy walk and the Coffs Creek Walk is a nine-kilometre circuit of bushland tracks and boardwalks.

Dogs Designated leash-free areas

SHOPPING

Shopping opportunities are substantial at Coffs. There are two major shopping districts, one on the main street and the other a large plaza set back from the road. Most of the well-known retailers are represented, although some locals are critical about the lack of a really big department store. Jetty markets are held in Coffs every Sunday and once a month there are markets with fresh produce and crafts in Sawtell and Woolgoolga.

DINING

Dining options offer a choice from a variety of styles, including ethnic cuisines (especially Indian, as there is a large Sikh community in nearby Woolgoolga), outdoor cafés or more formal 'haute cuisine' restaurants which highlight the use of local produce.

SOCIAL ACTIVITY

Coffs has plenty of clubs, including deep-sea fishing and golf (there's another golf club in Sawtell). Outdoor activities run the gamut from canoeing/kayaking, ocean rafting and white water rafting to horse riding, whale and dolphin watching, scuba diving and walking along the foreshore. There are various arts and crafts centres and the City Gallery hosts regular exhibitions. There's also a TAFE and Southern Cross University.

- All community organisations • All religions • Arts & crafts
- Boating • Bushwalking • Fishing • Gallery • Golf
- Horse racing • Horse riding • Lawn bowls • Rafting
- Walking

REAL ESTATE

Coffs Harbour
- Median house price: $310 000
- Median unit price: $215 000

Sawtell
- Median house price: $290 000
- Median unit price: $199 000

WHY LIVE HERE?

Coffs Harbour has everything retirees need: an almost perfect climate, pristine beaches, tracts of natural bushland, good infrastructure and access to capital cities, well-planned streets, a protected harbour, major shopping centres with undercover parking, good restaurants and entertainment.

As a retired couple in their mid-sixties said to me: 'It's nice to know we can get down to Sydney in an hour or so if we need to. Actually we hardly ever need to.' A lady in her early sixties noted: 'The only thing I miss is a decent department store for clothes. But I'm being picky – the shopping here is adequate.'

nambucca heads

Great climate and great views

Nambucca Heads is a busy town on a hill overlooking the spectacular and expansive Nambucca River as it flows into the sea. In general, this is not an affluent area, and many homes are humble weatherboard or brick veneer, but new subdivisions are appearing. Many retirees live in the permanent caravan park which dominates the river foreshore on the flat below the shopping precinct.

Nearby towns include Urunga, a small place on an inlet with only a few shops; it has a large caravan park with both demountables and caravans which appeal to retirees. About the only other landmark here is the Urunga pub, which once played host to Russell Crowe and Tom Cruise who motorbiked into town. Macksville, inland on the Nambucca River, is around half the size of Nambucca Heads. The Pacific Highway slices through the middle of town, and it seems to have a plethora of churches and religious schools.

POPULATION

Nambucca Valley
- **22 000** Est. June 2003
- **31.8%** over sixty

This area is stagnating a little, but there are record proportions of over-sixties living here.

CLIMATE

Summer 19.6°C to 26.8°C
Winter 11.2°C to 18.6°C
Sunshine 117 days
Rain 138 days
Rainfall 1492 mm

A subtropical climate with mild winters and warm summers.

LOCATION & GETTING AROUND

Positioned halfway between Sydney and Brisbane, Nambucca is 500 kilometres north of Sydney, which takes just under 6.5 hours to drive on the dreaded Pacific Highway. It's 470 kilometres south of Brisbane, taking around six hours to drive.

Roads Somewhat neglected and only just adequate

Nearest airports Coffs Harbour is 50 kilometres to the north and 40 minutes away; Kempsey is 70 kilometres south and one hour away.

Nearest train The station is just out of town. It's eight hours from Sydney to Macksville and Nambucca Heads, six hours from Brisbane.

Buses Local and intercity services

Taxis ✓

INFRASTRUCTURE

Hospitals The District Hospital at Macksville has 56 beds. There are two ambulance stations and Wheelchair Commuter Transport.

Retirement villages Several in Nambucca, one in Macksville and one in Bowraville

Police stations Nambucca, Macksville and Bowraville

Local newspaper *Nambucca Guardian News*

RECREATION

Beaches There's 23 kilometres of coastline with beautiful beaches and views, including whale watching (it seems everywhere claims to be ideal for whale watching, but Nambucca does have the advantage of looking down on the whales from the Yarrahapinni Lookout). Good beaches here include Nambucca Heads and Scotts Head.

Coastguard ✓

Cycleways ✗

Bushwalking & National Parks The district is teeming with national parks where you can bushwalk through pristine old-growth forests to cascading waterfalls. Parks include Bindarri National Park, Bongil Bongil National Park, Cathedral Rock National Park and Dorrigo National Park.

Dogs Designated leash-free areas.

SHOPPING

Woolworths, Cut Price and IGA supermarkets are at Nambucca Heads, plus markets are held every second Sunday. There's a Four Square Supermarket in Macksville.

DINING

Nambucca's range of restaurants includes steakhouses and bistros. Macksville offers Modern Australian cuisine and seafood in colonial surroundings.

SOCIAL ACTIVITY

Nambucca has three golf courses (the Island Golf Club is on its very own island), four lawn bowls clubs, a bushwalkers club, a number of cultural clubs (including bridge and a local writers group) and its entertainment centre hosts various artists and a local theatre company. There is a triple cinema complex and limited galleries, plus there are a few museums at Bowraville and Nambucca. A number of organisations specialise in further education for adults, including Macksville's TAFE.

• Arts & culture • Boating • Bushwalking • Cinema • Fishing
• Galleries • Golf • Horse riding • Lawn bowls
• Many community organisations • Most religions • Museums
• Squash • Swimming • Theatre

REAL ESTATE

• Median house price: $298 000
• Median unit price: $202 000

In Nambucca Heads the prices of newish three- or four-bedroom houses with ocean or river views start at around $450 000, more for waterfrontages although they top out below $700 000. Villas start at around $280 000 and townhouses with ocean views are in the low $300 000s. Building blocks commence at $150 000. Macksville's homes are usually between $100 000 and $200 000.

Subtropical climate, low cost of living and good choice of housing.

south west rocks
Historic town amid the pines

South West Rocks is a quaint seaside town complete with Norfolk Island pines and a lighthouse. The place looks like it's been around for some time, and indeed it has; the nineteenth-century Trial Bay Gaol, now a museum, overlooks the village.

To get there, you leave the Pacific Highway to drive along a country lane that twists along the Macleay River for 15 kilometres. The first sign of South West Rocks is a modern but small shopping mall, followed by a neat row of weatherboard houses leading to the village shops and the headland with its rows of Norfolk Island pines. There are several ocean beaches, the Macleay River and bushland – and a high proportion of retirees. The housing is well established but the place feels more like a holiday resort than a place of residence. There's still a lot of bush around here, and not a lot of infrastructure, and it's a long way from any substantial shops.

POPULATION

- 4000
- 37% over sixty

South West Rocks grew by 15 per cent between censuses.

CLIMATE

Summer 19.7°C to 26.8°C
Winter 11.2°C to 18.6°C
Sunshine 118 days
Rain 137 days
Rainfall 1487 mm

LOCATION & GETTING AROUND

Sydney is 460 kilometres south, a drive of around 5.5 hours.

Roads The local roads are narrow

Nearest airport Port Macquarie, 70 minutes by car (85 kilometres), with daily services to Sydney

Nearest train Macksville, a one-hour drive (60 kilometres)

Buses ✓

Taxis ✓

INFRASTRUCTURE

Hospitals The District Hospital at Macksville, with 56 beds.

Retirement villages Nambucca Heads and Macksville

Police station South West Rocks

RECREATION

Beaches Good beaches include Horseshoe Bay, Back Beach, Main Beach, Trial Bay (which faces west, one of the few beaches on the east coast to do so), Little Bay, Gap Beach, North Smoky and Smoky Beach.

Coastguard ✓

Cycleways Shared pathways along Saltwater Creek; it's also easy to cycle around the town's quiet streets

Bushwalking & National Parks Walking trail to Trial Bay Gaol and Smokey Cape Lighthouse. Parks include Arakoon State Recreational Area and Hat Head National Park.

Dogs Relaxed attitude to dogs.

SHOPPING

There are a number of shopping streets and a small mall on the road into town, which isn't too bad for a small town. It's 40 kilometres to Kempsey for the nearest major shopping centre.

DINING

The best choice here is fresh local seafood.

SOCIAL ACTIVITY

The SWR Country Club is a very impressive building and the centre for entertainment.
• Fishing • Golf • Lawn bowls

REAL ESTATE

• Median house price: $340 000
• Median unit price: $240 000
Some nice homes facing Saltwater Creek fetch $600 000 or more.

WHY LIVE HERE?

A secluded but established coastal hideaway with a pleasant climate and lots of water to fish and play in.

port macquarie
Self-sufficient, comfortable and affordable

Port Macquarie is a thriving coastal centre in the Hastings Valley, surrounded by similarly popular retirement satellites that are steadily evolving into suburbs. Those that lie to the south of Port Macquarie are within an area known as Camden Haven, which comprises the villages of North Haven, Laurieton and a few other hamlets. In the 2001 census, Camden Haven had the highest proportion of over-65s in the whole of Australia. North Haven and Laurieton are side by side at the mouth of an estuary which opens onto a lake, having the advantage of sea or still waters, and Lake Cathie is close by. Other popular 'suburbs' of Port are Lighthouse Beach and Bonny Hills.

Port Macquarie is the area's commercial centre, strategically located at the mouth of the Hastings River. It was established as a penal settlement in 1821, and early sandstone buildings such as St Thomas' Church and the Military Surgeon's Residence remain, complementing the beauty of the natural landscape of grassy headlands covered in Norfolk Island pines. There are stretches of pristine beach, ocean and river water views and, in the hinterland, rainforests. The reserve adjacent to the river is beautifully landscaped with open-air restaurants and a mix of architecture old and new, making this area very appealing.

POPULATION

Hastings Valley	Port Macquarie
• 68 500 Est. June 2003	• 38 000
• 29.2% over sixty	• 28.9% over sixty

The median age in the valley is 43.6, well above the national average of around 36 and one of the oldest in Australia. The population of Port Macquarie grew by 4000 between censuses.

CLIMATE

Summer 18.4°C to 25.7°C
Winter 7.2°C to 17.9°C
Sunshine 119 days
Rain 134 days
Rainfall 1541 mm
Temperate and obviously just right for many retirees.

LOCATION & GETTING AROUND

Port Macquarie is 420 kilometres north of Sydney and 500 kilometres south of Brisbane. The drive from Sydney takes about four hours. There are freeway conditions to Newcastle, then dual carriageway on and off to Port Macquarie. Upgrading to full dual carriageway is well under way.

Roads Most of the internal roads are good. The Pacific Highway bypasses Port Macquarie and the 10-kilometre drive into town is via a dual-carriageway avenue of trees.

Nearest airport Port Macquarie, with flights to Sydney several times each day (one hour). There are also daily flights to Brisbane.

Nearest train Wauchope (30 kilometres away) then bus to Port Macquarie

Buses ✓
Taxis ✓

INFRASTRUCTURE

Hospitals The Port Macquarie Base Hospital is very modern and well equipped. There's also Wauchope District Memorial Hospital, plus Community Health Centres at Camden Haven, Port Macquarie and Wauchope, as well as numerous doctors' clinics.

Retirement villages Numerous, concentrated in Port Macquarie and Laurieton

Police stations Port Macquarie and Laurieton

Local newspapers *Port Macquarie News*, *Hastings Gazette*, *Camden Haven Courier* and *Holiday Coast Pictorial*

RECREATION

Beaches There are numerous surfing beaches such as Flynn's (with a surf club), Town Beach, Oxley, Rocky and Nobby's. Shelly Beach has walking tracks along the coast and Lighthouse Beach, also with a surf club, offers camel rides.

Coastguard ✓

Cycleways These are limited with some in North Haven and Laurieton.

Bushwalking & National Parks Sea Acres' 72 hectares of rainforest can be viewed from boardwalks. Limeburners Creek Nature Reserve has bushwalking trails and is popular for fishing, birdwatching, canoeing and swimming. Kooloonbung Creek Nature Park is in the centre of Port Macquarie. The Werrikimbe National Park beyond Wauchope has inviting waterfalls, rivers and rainforests. There are many walking tracks along the coast and it is possible to walk from Settlement City to Windmill Hill south of Oxley Beach, and from Shelly Beach to Miners Beach.

Dogs The Hastings area is dog friendly. Some beaches are off limits to dogs, some permit dogs on leashes and seven allow dogs to run free.

SHOPPING

Port Macquarie's shopping streets are extensive and thronged with pedestrians. Woolworths, Coles, Big W and Target are represented in two large shopping complexes. A free bus operates at Christmas time to the Settlement City shopping complex, which is a large impressive centre. Regular markets around the area offer fresh produce as well as local arts and crafts. Laurieton has a small shopping centre which includes a Bi-Lo supermarket.

DINING

The range includes various cuisines, the choice of indoor or out-door dining and café style to fine dining. The waterfront is a particularly nice spot for a meal, with plenty of ambience.

SOCIAL ACTIVITY

There are many clubs in the Port Macquarie area, including dance, sailing (popular on the Hastings River and on the lakes), golf (Port Macquarie Golf Club and Emerald Downs Public Course) and lawn bowls clubs at Port Macquarie, Lake Cathie and North Haven. There are a number of craft galleries throughout the region plus a regional art gallery. Port Macquarie has a large cinema and there's a minuscule cinema in Laurieton.

• All community organisations • All religions • Arts & crafts
• Birdwatching • Bushwalking • Cinema • Dancing • Fishing
• Galleries • Golf • Lawn bowls • Libraries • Sailing • Surfing
• Swimming • Tennis • Waterskiing

REAL ESTATE

Port Macquarie
• Median house price: $350 000
• Median unit price: $275 000
Laurieton, Camden Haven and Lake Cathie
• Median house price: $358 000
• Median unit price: $275 000

Prices vary considerably, as there is plenty of choice and the quality of homes is generally quite good. For instance, a modern, two-bedroom villa starts at $270 000, and units with river views cost from $330 000. Waterfront settings or expansive water views will cost $490 000 or more. Units in beach resort complexes start at $750 000. A three-bedroom duplex on a waterway with private boat ramp and a sandy beach costs around $650 000. A home on small acreage with mountain views 20 minutes from Port costs around $450000. New real estate developments are under way in the area, notably at Laurieton.

WHY LIVE HERE?

Just look at the number of retirees living here! The weather is fairly consistent, with a narrower range and warmer winters than further south. As one local who moved from Sydney said to me, 'I'm here for the climate: it's never too hot and it rarely gets too cold.' It is also a well-established area, big but without being huge, and with just about all the facilities retirees need. If you don't want to be too close to the tourist action, North Haven and Laurieton are idyllic locations and not too far from Port Macquarie for the major weekly shop or regular outing.

taree
A choice of retirement lifestyles

On the beautiful Manning River, Taree is well laid out with the wide streets typical of many country towns. Fortunately, the highway no longer passes through so the town has reclaimed the streets for the use of its locals – an important point if you live here. Taree has many retail and commercial streets on the gradual slope north of the river, and behind this expansive shopping precinct is the suburban housing, including solid older-style homes with wraparound verandas on large blocks of land. It is hoped that the authorities can address an increase in petty crime which has been reported within the township, as Taree is otherwise a very appealing country city with good infrastructure, just 15 kilometres from the coast.

Many retirees live in town, but many have opted for beachside retirement at the sleepy fishing village of Crowdy Head, the slightly more-populated village of Harrington (with the third-highest proportion of over-65s in Australia), Old Bar (twenty minutes from Taree) or the heritage township of Wingham (13 kilometres inland from Taree, with a population of 3000), with its spacious streets, parks and restored old buildings. A substantial development of 1100 dwellings at Harrington Waters, a kilometre or so before Harrington, is offering a modern retirement alternative of stylish townhouses with waterfrontage on the Manning River, plus shops, pub, marina and golf course. Small and sleepy Crowdy Head offers the opposite: panoramic views from the lighthouse that are not unlike Byron Bay's, but older-style housing and no shops. Old Bar is moderately populated and has few ocean views as it is flat and most housing is set back from the beach. Overall, the architecture in these beach locations is modest and unappealing. The weatherboard homes in Taree and Wingham and the housing in the new Harrington Waters development have much more character.

POPULATION

Greater Taree

• **46 000** Est. June 2003
• 21.7% over sixty

The towns around Taree are growing whilst Taree itself remained fairly static between censuses, with a population of 16 650.

CLIMATE

Summer 17.5°C to 29°C
Winter 5.9°C to 18.5°C
Sunshine 103 days
Rain 113 days
Rainfall 1175 mm

The climate is temperate to warm, but in winter you will need heating; there's plenty of timber for log fires. If you choose to live on the coast, the sea breeze in summer alleviates the need for air-conditioning.

LOCATION & GETTING AROUND

Sydney is 305 kilometres away, a drive of just over 3.5 hours. Newcastle is 170 kilometres, a two-hour drive. The dual-carriage freeway runs for much of the distance and is continually being extended.

Roads Off the freeway the roads are single lane, but the streets of Taree are wide and well laid out. The roads to the neighbouring villages are narrow but quiet.

Nearest airport Taree has its own airport, six kilometres out of town at Cundletown, with daily flights to Sydney (55 minutes) and Newcastle.

Nearest train It takes under six hours in the XPT to travel to Taree from Sydney.

Buses Major bus companies travelling along the Pacific Highway have arrangements to stop at Taree, but the journey takes a long time as there are frequent stops on the way. There are also several local bus companies in the area.

Taxis ✓

INFRASTRUCTURE

Hospitals Taree has a large base hospital providing a full range of services, plus there are various specialist medical services in the town.

Retirement villages Taree, Wingham, Old Bar and Cundletown

Police stations Taree, Wingham, Coopernook and Nabiac

Local newspapers *Manning River Times* and *Manning Great Lakes Extra*

RECREATION

Beaches There are seven surfing beaches nearby to choose from, some of which are patrolled in the summer holiday season.

Coastguard ✓

Cycleways There's a new shared pathway on the water's edge at Harrington Waters, and in Taree there are plenty of opportunities for a quiet cycle on the streets outside the centre of town.

Bushwalking & National Parks There are many national parks in this area, including Crowdy Bay National Park with easy walks and ocean views, and rainforested Wingham Brush Nature Reserve with Moreton Bay figs that are hundreds of years old. Some parks have 4WD access.

Dogs Allowed on beaches but must be on leash between 8 a.m. and 7 p.m.

SHOPPING

Taree's range and variety of shops attracts residents from as far away as Forster, as the main streets are lined with outlets and there's an undercover parking complex with a large Woolworths and other stores. Wingham's main street has small retail stores and there are some shops and cafés at Old Bar and Harrington.

DINING

Taree's casual dining options are substantial and there's also some fine dining.

SOCIAL ACTIVITY

Just about every type of club, association and activity is represented in this area, from amateur drama groups to cake decoration. If you want to keep active there are three public swimming pools, five national parks (all in close proximity) and plenty of water-based activities on the river. Bushwalks are great in this area, taking you past streams and waterfalls. There are lawn bowls clubs in Taree and Harrington, plus golf clubs at Taree, Wingham and a new nine-holer at Harrington Waters with extensive water hazards. And not forgetting the annual Wingham Rodeo.

• All community organisations • All religions • Boating
• Bushwalking • Fishing • Galleries • Golf • Horse riding
• Lawn bowls • Libraries • Sailing • Surfing • Swimming
• Waterskiing

REAL ESTATE

• Median house price: $240 000
• Median unit price: $179 000

It is possible to buy a large older home with wraparound verandas and brick chimney stacks on a quarter-acre block from $350 000. New townhouses at Harrington Waters go for $425 000 and waterfrontage homes start at $675 000.

WHY LIVE HERE?

This could be a good choice if you're looking for variety in country or beach living in a temperate climate, with good health services and ample shopping, but without the bustle and pollution of Sydney or Newcastle. It is largely undiscovered, and the development at Harrington Waters could be the first of several. Certainly the beachside villages could do with an injection of better architecture.

forster & great lakes
Affordable coastal retirement

Forster and its sister town Tuncurry sit on either side of the entrance to the 26-kilometre Wallis Lake. The towns are the cornerstone of the Great Lakes community which encompasses three large lakes (Myall, Smiths and Wallis), numerous beaches and national parks. The tower at Cape Hawke will help you get your bearings, with amazing views extending south to the Seal Rock lighthouse, over Forster Keys on Wallis Lake to the mountains far in the west, north towards Taree and to the expansive view of beaches and Pacific Ocean to the east.

Forster is a typical beach resort town with lots of accommodation, plenty of places to eat local seafood (including Wallis Lake oysters), good fishing and prawning, whale and dolphin watching, surfing and swimming (with a choice of ocean or lake). It's no surprise that many retirees have made Forster their home. However, the remote and beautiful beaches from Blueys to Elizabeth have some of the best beachfront locations in Australia but are too isolated for most retirees to consider.

There are some high-rise apartment blocks in Forster, but not too many, and the main shopping centre is on the edge of town, leaving the town centre uncrowded. Its half-hearted attempt at a pedestrian mall is lined with small shops and cafés but cars are permitted heading one way, which is a pity as the townsfolk would be better served if the strip was completely closed to traffic. Building and renovations are ongoing in the area, but away from the beaches the housing is pretty ordinary.

POPULATION

Forster
- 12 000
- 36% over sixty

Tuncurry
- 6000
- 36% over sixty

The twin towns have the highest proportion of over-sixties in any population in New South Wales. The towns grew by more than 2000 between censuses.

CLIMATE

Summer 17°C to 28°C
Winter 5°C to 18°C
Sunshine 170 days
Rain 130 days
Rainfall 1205 mm

LOCATION & GETTING AROUND

Forster is two hours north of Newcastle (165 kilometres) and 3.5 hours north of Sydney (300 kilometres). There is little alternative but to drive to and from this area, but the good news is that the roads have improved enormously over the last two years (the Karuah Bypass, for example) and the work is ongoing.

Roads Off the dual carriageway the roads are potholed and patched, narrow and dangerous.

Nearest airport Taree Airport is 36 kilometres and a 30-minute drive from Forster – longer if you are in one of the lake or seaside villages. Taree has daily flights to Sydney (55 minutes).

Nearest train Intercity coach (5.5 hours from Sydney)

Buses Major bus companies travelling along the Pacific Highway have arrangements to stop at Forster, but the journey takes a long time as there are frequent stops on the way.

Taxis ✓

INFRASTRUCTURE

Hospitals Most of the medical services are located in South Street, including a private hospital. Taree Base Hospital is large and well equipped. For those living in the Smiths Lakes area there is a clinic with three doctors at Blueys Beach.

Retirement villages Forster is not well serviced; there are only two retirement villages both with long waiting lists, which will present a problem for the Great Lakes area as the population ages.

Police station Forster

Local newspaper *Great Lakes Advocate*

RECREATION

Beaches Other than Forster Main Beach and Elizabeth Beach the beaches are not well patrolled.

Coastguard ✓

Cycleways ✗

Bushwalking & National Parks The three great lakes of Smiths, Myall and Wallis offer some of the best opportunities for exploring the bush, and kayak is the perfect way to explore their tributaries. 4WD is permitted in part of the Myall Lakes National Park.

Dogs Only permitted on beaches before 8 a.m., and council actively enforces this rule.

SHOPPING

The main shopping centre for the Great Lakes is on the edge of Forster, with Woolworths, Coles, Kmart and speciality stores. Plans for an upgrade are under way. Taree, 30 minutes away, offers more shopping diversity. There are small shopping precincts around the Great Lakes, for example at Blueys Beach and Smiths Lake, but other than that there are only general stores. Produce and craft markets are held in the Great Lakes area every weekend, even in winter, and are proof that the cost of living here is significantly cheaper than in capital cities.

DINING

Various casual dining and restaurants can be found in Forster, Smith Lakes, Boomerang and Blueys.

SOCIAL ACTIVITY

There are various clubs and associations, including the 18-hole Forster/Tuncurry Golf Club; there is also a nine-hole fun course in the bush with kangaroos and their joeys for company at Sandbar. Forster has a large indoor Aquatic and Leisure Centre, two bowling clubs and three tennis clubs, and there's a three-screen cinema at Tuncurry. All major religious denominations are represented, plus there's the wonderful nondenominational open-air Green Cathedral by the lake.

• All religions • Aquatic and leisure centre • Bowling • Cinema
• Golf • Lawn bowls • Most community organisations
• Surfing • Tennis

REAL ESTATE

• Median house price: $365 000
• Median unit price: $314 000

The prices in this area vary tremendously, depending upon which part of the Great Lakes you are looking at. There is plenty to choose from: newly built and older houses plus vacant blocks of land.

In Forster it is possible to buy a two-bedroom home from $200 000, with quite a lot of choice over $300 000. New apartments as well as new homes are being built here; some are referred to as 'cluster villas', where four freestanding homes share the same strata plan. Forster Keys offers homes with marina berths but these could be hard to come by.

At Smiths Lake, blocks of land start from around $120 000 and homes from $230 000. A substantial home near the lake can be purchased for under $400 000.

When it comes to beachfront properties, however, it is another story. Prices at Blueys and Boomerang beaches have gone through the roof and are somewhere between $2 million and $3 million. As a local builder put it: 'We were offered $2.6 million for our beachfront, so I retired! It was like winning Lotto.' Away from the beach, homes are selling from $400 000. The whole area has seen an escalation in price which is slowly squeezing out the locals.

WHY LIVE HERE?

The beaches are amazingly varied and largely empty. The air is clear and at night the stars are bright as neon. The picturesque lakes have little marine traffic and the bird life is abundant, as are the dolphins. And as one local lady, formerly from Sydney, told me: 'Everyone talks to you and you get to know everybody. It's like life used to be when I was a child.' The only drawback is that Forster lacks the infrastructure of Port Macquarie or Taree.

port stephens
Beaches, bays and bush

Sixty kilometres north of Newcastle, the beautiful waterway of Port Stephens has unspoilt beaches, numerous bays and lots of bush. Nelson Bay is the area's largest town and commercial centre, and has some medium-rise apartment buildings. Tourists frequent Nelson Bay and Shoal Bay every weekend and at holiday times, which can be bothersome for residents. Parking in Nelson Bay can be a problem at these times and parking meters have been introduced, so it is now a costly problem! The port attracts dolphins and migrating whales, and tourists are attracted by the waterways, sand dunes, boating and fishing (including game fishing) and the many backwaters to explore.

There are many quieter villages for retirees sprinkled throughout the area, including Corlette, Salamander Bay–Soldiers Point, Lemon Tree Passage, Karuah and Fingal Bay, on the ocean side of the Tomaree Peninsula. Tea Gardens and Hawks Nest are both just across the water from Nelsons Bay but quite a long distance by road (85 kilometres). In terms of proportions of over-sixties, all these locations fall in the top 200 Australia wide.

The housing is mostly modest, although Corlette has some better-quality homes. Most of the housing is grouped in tight suburban areas, with the villages separated by bush reserves. If you prefer more solitude Hawks Nest is quiet and isolated. Outside of Nelsons Bay it would be essential to have a car to get to the shops.

POPULATION

Port Stephens Shire	Nelson Bay and Shoal Bay
• 60 000 Est. June 2003	• 8000
• 20% over sixty	• 30% over sixty

Nelson Bay's population grew by 1000 between censuses. Salamander Bay–Soldiers Point grew by 900, Corlette by 475 and Lemon Tree Passage by 200.

At the last census, Corlette's population was 2700, Salamander Bay–Soldiers Point 5000, Lemon Tree Passage 5500, Karuah 1100, Fingal Bay 1600, Tea Gardens 1400 and Hawks Nest 1175.

CLIMATE

Summer 17.6°C to 27.5°C
Winter 7.9°C to 17.6°C
Sunshine 119 days
Rain 128 days
Rainfall 1350 mm

LOCATION & GETTING AROUND

Port Stephens is 200 kilometres from Sydney via the Newcastle Freeway, taking 2.5 hours to drive. Newcastle is one hour away.

Roads The 30 kilometres or so from the turn-off on the Pacific Highway is one lane each way for most of the way (there is some divided road). The road is in good condition but in holiday periods it can be slow going.

Nearest airport Newcastle Airport, 35 kilometres from Nelsons Bay

Nearest train XPT from Sydney to Broadmeadow, then coach to Raymond Terrace and on to Nelson Bay, taking about four hours all up.

Buses ✓
Taxis ✓
Water taxis ✓ (the best way to commute to Hawks Nest)

INFRASTRUCTURE

Hospitals Nelson Bay and District Polyclinic Hospital has 14 beds and three casualty beds; it has a 24-hour emergency ward although the doctor is sometimes on call. The John Hunter Hospital in Newcastle is one hour's drive. There are Community Health Centres in Nelson Bay and Raymond Terrace.

Retirement villages Shoal Bay, Anna Bay, Salamander Bay and Tea Gardens. The quality of housing varies, and there are a number of cheap demountable villages.

Police stations Nelson Bay, Tea Gardens, Karuah, Raymond Terrace

Local newspaper *Port Stephens Examiner*

RECREATION

Beaches Over 20! Fingal Bay is patrolled, Shoal Bay is protected and Little Beach has both sheltered swimming and a marina. Duchies is a favourite for picnics, with shaded lawns and sandy beach. On the ocean side, Anna Bay has numerous surfing beaches and Stockton Beach has massive sand dunes. Samurai Beach allows nude bathing.

Coastguard ✓

Cycleways There is an extensive network of paved tracks all around Port Stephens, many of them providing access to reserves and close to beaches. Well done, council!

Bushwalking & National Parks The Tomaree National Park includes a large bushland reserve as well as 20 kilometres of rocky coastline and beaches, and is a place of serenity and beautiful views. Looking out from Tomaree Head you can see a vast panorama from Seal Rocks to Newcastle.

Dogs Dogs may be exercised off-leash in parks in the shire.

SHOPPING

Nelson Bay has quite a reasonable shopping centre which includes a Bi-Lo supermarket. Most of the villages have small shopping centres. Raymond Terrace, a 45-minute drive away, is home to the shire council as well as to Woolworths.

DINING

Nelson Bay has a variety of good-value restaurants and cafés offering outdoor dining; some of them are on the marina, a modern complex which caters for the tourist trade. Seafood is a speciality of the area, and other cuisines include Thai, Italian, French, Indian, Greek, Chinese and Modern Australian. Local wines are available from the Port Stephens winery or the Hunter Valley vineyards which are not far away.

SOCIAL ACTIVITY

There are five golf courses in the shire, including the prestigious Horizons course complete with on-course villas at Corlette. A Sports and Recreation Club is around the headland at Fingal Bay. Outdoor activities are popular, including dolphin and whale watching, and barbeque and picnic areas are plentiful. There is a cinema complex in Nelson Bay but cultural activities are generally limited.

• Boating • Bushwalking • Cinema • Cycling • Fishing • Golf
• Horse riding • Lawn bowls • Most religions • Sailing
• Scuba diving • Some community organisations • Surfing
• Swimming

REAL ESTATE

• Median house price: $475 000
• Median unit price: $367 000
Waterfront properties are, of course, more expensive.

WHY LIVE HERE?

This is an unspoilt part of Australia even though it's relatively close to the major city of Newcastle. In particular, this area suits retired Novocastrians who want to stay close to their friends and families.

lake macquarie
Lake living close to Sydney and Newcastle

Lake Macquarie is a deceptively large saltwater lake (it's four times the size of Sydney Harbour), just south of Newcastle. A narrow neck of land meets the Pacific Ocean at Swansea, and the lake is dotted with secluded bays, coves and sandy beaches, framed by natural bush. It really is quite spectacular. On any weekend the lake is dotted with colourful sails as yachts compete in races and power boats dart back and forth, and locals promenade along the pathways that run alongside the lake.

Popular retirement towns on the lake include Swansea, Belmont, Warners Bay, Toronto and Speers Point. Much of the housing is older style and in need of a makeover but an increasing number of new developments are emerging with snazzy modern homes in subdivisions such as Valentine, Green Point and Coal Point (on the western side of the lake). Of course, there are some very nice dwellings on the water's edge.

Lake Macquarie is one of the fastest-growing areas in New South Wales. In addition to tourism it is also home to major industries such as coal mining, electricity generation and metal smelting. Visible signs of this are the chimney stacks of Vales Point Power Station and Wangi Power Station, which make parts of the western side of the lake less inviting.

POPULATION

Lake Macquarie LGA
- 190 000 Est. June 2003
- 21% over sixty

CLIMATE

Summer 19.1°C to 25.6°C
Winter 8.4°C to 16.7°C
Sunshine 89 days
Rain 135 days
Rainfall 1102 mm

LOCATION & GETTING AROUND

Sydney via the F3 freeway is 125 kilometres, which takes just over 1.5 hours. From Newcastle it's 40 kilometres, which takes 30 minutes to drive.

Roads The roads are in good condition, and most of the major roads in the area are two lanes each way.

Nearest airports Belmont (30 kilometres from Lake Macquarie) is a 30-minute flight from Sydney. Newcastle Airport is based at Williamtown (60 kilometres from Lake Macquarie); it has regular services from capital cities (Sydney, Melbourne and Brisbane) and Coolangatta is soon to be added.

Nearest train CityRail and country services, with stations at Wyee, Morisset, Dora Creek, Awaba and Fassifern, with a side line to Toronto. The nearest station to the eastern side of Lake Macquarie is Cardiff, a 15-minute drive from Belmont.

Buses Interstate coaches, as well as Newcastle buses. Charlestown is a hub for the area.

Taxis ✓

Water taxis Water taxis run from Wangi Wangi.

INFRASTRUCTURE

Hospitals Belmont Hospital has Accident and Emergency plus standard hospital services such as Radiology and Pathology etc. The John Hunter Hospital is the principal referral centre for both Newcastle and Lake Macquarie. The Toronto Polyclinic serves the western side of Lake Macquarie, with after-hours medical and a range of other services. The Royal Newcastle Hospital specialises in bone and joint disorders. Lake Macquarie Private Hospital, at Gateshead, is an acute surgical hospital.

Retirement villages Belmont, Toronto, Wyee, Swansea and several at Cooranbong. Styles vary; some are demountable villages, which is pretty basic housing. A large retirement complex was recently developed at Jewells, just north of Belmont. Complexes for the over-55s are appearing around Warners Bay and Toronto.

Police stations Charlestown is the area command for Lake

Macquarie and there are other police stations at Morisset, Swansea, Toronto and Belmont. Swansea police station seems to be closed more often than it is open.

Local newspapers *Lake Macquarie News, Newcastle Herald, Newcastle Star* and *Newcastle Post*

RECREATION

Beaches Patrolled ocean beaches in the Lake Macquarie area include Redhead, Blacksmiths, Caves Beach and Catherine Hill Bay.

Coastguard ✓

Cycleways There is an extensive network of at least 11 off-road shared paths providing opportunities for recreational cycling. It is possible to cycle around the entire lake by using some on-road sections.

Bushwalking & National Parks Lake foreshore walks are popular and extensive. For more serious hiking there are walking trails in the Watagan Mountains.

Dogs Dog friendly, with numerous leash-free areas, but no dogs are allowed on the lake path.

SHOPPING

Major malls are at Lake Macquarie Fair at Mount Hutton, Charlestown Square (also the transport hub) and Westfield Kotara Centre. Swansea, Morisset, Toronto and Belmont all have large supermarkets.

DINING

Diverse cuisines are available around the area, from award-winning restaurants to lakeside cafés, accompanied by Hunter Valley wines from up the road. You can pick your view – lake, beach or mountain.

SOCIAL ACTIVITY

There are golf clubs at Belmont, Morisset, Toronto and Charlestown, and yacht clubs at Belmont Bay and Toronto. Activities include water-based sport and leisure pursuits, houseboating on the lake and hiking through the trails of the Watagan Mountains. For something less strenuous the Belmont Library has branches throughout the region and Lake Macquarie Art Gallery is on the shoreline at Booragul, with both local and national exhibits. There is also a historical society and a number of museums, performing arts groups and a music society.

- Boating • Bushwalking • Galleries • Golf • Lawn bowls
- Libraries • Most community organisations • Most religions
- Museums • Sailing • Scuba diving • Swimming • Theatre
- Walking • Waterskiing

REAL ESTATE

Warners Bay
- Median house price: $390 000
- Median unit price: $306 000

Belmont
- Median house price: $370 000
- Median unit price: $292 000

Swansea
- Median house price: $390 000
- Median unit price: $285 000

Morisset and Dora Creek
- Median house price: $320 000

Toronto and Awaba
- Median house price: $320 000
- Median unit price: $280 000

Architecture and prices vary widely, and houses in the south and west are cheaper than those to the east and north. At Coal Point, a renovated waterfront home could cost in excess of $2.25 million.

WHY LIVE HERE?

It's like living on Lake Como, but with better facilities and access! The unspoilt lake is relatively uncrowded even though it's close to the two largest cities in New South Wales – many Sydney residents aren't even aware of its existence.

central coast
wyong
Mixed bag a stone's throw from Sydney

The Central Coast can be divided into two distinct areas: Wyong Shire and Gosford Shire. Wyong Shire is the less industrial of the two, and consists of Tuggerah, Wyong, Gorokan, Toukley, Norah Head, the Entrance, Shelly Beach, Toowoon Bay, Bateau Bay, Yarramalong Valley and Dooralong Valley.

Wyong Shire is like a big wheel: picture a 60-kilometre circuit around Tuggerah Lake with valleys off to one side and plenty of variety along the way. For part of the circuit you have Tuggerah Lake on one side and the blue Pacific on the other. There are quiet lakeside hamlets, busy towns, bays, ocean beaches and rural landscapes to choose from, so if you can't find somewhere you like here you might be considered hard to please.

At the top of the wheel is the gateway to this retirement Mecca, the giant Westfield Tuggerah Shopping Centre, well positioned at the Tuggerah Interchange as you exit the expressway from Sydney. This is one of the best shopping centres you could hope for. Wyong, only 10 kilometres away, is the administration hub where the municipal council is located. The town is well laid out and has a large TAFE if you are considering undertaking further adult education. Light industrial and commercial areas are concentrated near Wyong or just past the Entrance, and the remainder of the wheel is residential, with small shops, restaurants and cafés. Although pollution is low you can see the distant smog from the Munmorah power stacks north of Norah Heads.

It is hard to believe that fifteen minutes away from these bustling centres are the sleepy valleys of Yarramalong and Dooralong, where the only sound is the melodious call of the bellbirds. Small acreages are available and If you like the country but don't want to be too far from civilisation, these valleys could be the spot.

If you prefer living by the water you have the choice of lake or ocean (still or bubbles). The lake meets the sea at the Entrance, which has a pedestrian mall with cafés and casual restaurants offering outdoor dining overlooking the lake. The Entrance is the only place in the vicinity with high-rise apartment living and there are quite a number of new construction sites.

Long Jetty used to consist of cute weatherboard cottages but now the architecture is mostly bland red brick bungalows which leave a lot to be desired. Around the corner in Toowoon Bay and in other pockets some of the old charm remains.

This shire appears to have just about everything a retiree could ask for. The only drawback is that you need a car to enjoy living here as it's quite a large area to get around.

POPULATION

- 140 000 Est. June 2003
- 25% over sixty

Around one quarter of the population is over sixty years old – the over-sixties alone outnumber the entire population of most country towns!

CLIMATE

Summer 17.1°C to 27.4°C
Winter 4.5°C to 17.4°C
Sunshine 96 days
Rain 116 days
Rainfall 1321 mm
The climate is temperate but temperatures no doubt vary between the coast and hinterland.

LOCATION & GETTING AROUND

The drive from Sydney to Tuggerah takes 75 minutes (95 kilometres). Avoid peak hours and Sunday afternoons as the freeway tends to become gridlocked.

Roads The roads are generally in good condition, which comes as a bit of a surprise for those used to New South Wales roads. Some are dual carriageway.

Nearest airports Swansea and Belmont
Nearest train Wyong and Tuggerah are both connected by City-

Rail to Sydney and Newcastle with frequent services.

Buses Two bus companies operate almost hourly schedules, including services to Gosford

Taxis ✓

INFRASTRUCTURE

Hospitals Wyong Hospital (with emergency service), Long Jetty Hospital and Berkeley Vale Private Hospital. Gosford Hospital (with emergency service) is a 20-minute drive (20 kilometres) from Tuggerah. There are numerous doctors' clinics, some catering specifically for older people.

Retirement villages Tuggerawong, Bateau Bay, Berkeley Vale, Tumbi Umbi and Toukley. Aged-care facilities are also at Norah Head, Killarney Vale, Kanwal, Lake Haven, Bateau Bay, Toukley and Wyong.

Police stations The Entrance, Wyong and Toukley

Local newspapers *Central Coast Express*, *Herald* (Central Coast edition) and *Senior Citizens* (Wyong edition)

RECREATION

Beaches There are a dozen beaches in the area, some of which are patrolled.

Coastguard Norah Head serves the ocean and Toukley serves the Lakes

Cycleways At Norah Head and Tuggerah there are dedicated cycleways where it is quite flat. In some of the hamlets locals ride bikes to the shops. The main circuit road is too busy, however, and the roads in the valleys are too narrow.

Bushwalking & National Parks The Great North Walk passes through the area, running all the way from Sydney to Newcastle. There are also two large reserves here, Wyrrabalong National Park and Munmorah State Recreation Area. Other walks include those along the shore and to Norah Head Lighthouse.

Dogs Three beaches and 11 reserves have off-leash exercise areas, otherwise dogs must be restrained.

SHOPPING

Shopping is extensive. A large Westfield Shopping Town is located at the Tuggerah Interchange with over 140 shops under one roof, including Coles, Woolworths, Target, Big W and David Jones. This centre is Westfield's fourth largest in Australia in terms of turnover and not yet 10 years old. Motorised mobility scooters are provided for those who need them. There are other substantial shopping malls at Toukley, Gorokan and the Entrance.

DINING

There's no fine dining but plenty of casual dining choices with an emphasis on seafood and steak.

SOCIAL ACTIVITY

The locals around here are very friendly, with time to talk, and shop staff are knowledgeable and helpful, noticeably more so than in the big smoke. There are many clubs, both sporting and social, and associations catering to older citizens, plus opportunities for further education. This is not an art and crafts region, and social interaction tends to be mostly outdoors. People do not dress up here so you won't have much opportunity to wear designer labels. There are cinema complexes at Westfield and the Entrance but don't expect to see art-house or foreign movies as they cater for mainstream audiences.

There are several golf courses; the one overlooking the ocean at Shelly Beach is a beauty and is open for new members.

• All community organisations • All religions • Boating
• Bushwalking • Cycling • Fishing • Horse riding • Prawning
• Surfing • Walking

REAL ESTATE

• Median house price: $337 000
• Median unit price: $248 000

The range is enormous. If you sold your three-bedroom bungalow in the city for $550 000, after subtracting the cost of sale and adding the stamp duty to the purchase price you could expect to buy a two-bedroom apartment at the Entrance with water views and still have $125 000 left in your pocket. To buy a larger, three-bedroom home and garden in a hamlet such as Gorokan or Long Jetty, without water views, you might end up with $100 000 left over. If money is not a limitation you could pick up a beach-side home, or one with acreage in one of the valleys, for between $700 000 to more than $1 million. New construction by quality developers such as Mirvac and Stockland provides opportunities to buy new properties, some of them off the plan.

WHY LIVE HERE?

Lots of great views of lake, ocean and natural bushland. The areas that have most appeal are the two valleys of Yarramalong and Dooralong. Of the two, Yarramolong is more intimate with trees overhanging the road and with its own general store; Dooralong is in the open countryside. The most appealing seaside area is Forresters Beach.

gosford
Retirement within easy reach of Sydney

Gosford is modern, clean and medium-rise, bordered by multi-level home units and the large, narrow-necked bay of Brisbane Water. The stretch of road from the expressway to Gosford and on to Wamberal is lined with retail outlets and light industry with a plethora of promotional signs, but once you pass Wamberal the advertising pollution disappears. Small rural holdings appear at Brook Hill, and then a chorus of bellbirds heralds you into the unique district of Matcham – one of the prettiest enclaves you could imagine. Tall gums mix picturesquely with deciduous trees, especially in the autumn; the effect is similar to Mount Wilson in the Blue Mountains outside Sydney or Victoria's Mount Macedon, but without the chilly temperatures.

Matcham is known for its horse studs although these are now being replaced by tastefully designed substantial homes on small acreages. Further on, the area around Terrigal and towards Avoca has smaller blocks but the residents are no less houseproud and there are plenty of plant nurseries around here. Terrigal is a holiday town located where the lagoon meets the ocean, with a larger number of high-rise apartments and middle-market holiday resorts. Avoca is appealing but crowded with pricey homes cheek to jowl. The stretch along the coast from Avoca towards Kilcare is very like Sydney's northern beaches, but with newer homes, and much of it is appealing to the eye.

Heading inland on the circuit is St Huberts Island, a well-established suburb connected to the mainland by road bridge. Many of the homes have waterfrontage to Brisbane Water and private boat jetties. Further along, Ettalong Beach and Woy Woy are cheaper suburbs made up of smaller, older cottages. There is bushland nearby and just before the national park there's the turn-off to Pearl Beach. Aptly named and protected from the ocean, it features exclusive holiday cottages and is a tranquil hideaway as the road ends here.

Gosford Shire is a mixed bag with plenty of options for would-be residents to explore. There are limited ocean views except from immediately adjacent to the coast as the bushland and topography hide the sea from the hinterland. Matcham and Pearl Beach are among the prettiest places you'll see. Other beach areas such as those near Terrigal and south of Avoca also have appeal and are cheaper. Unfortunately, many of the other villages are cluttered and rather characterless.

POPULATION

- 162 500 Est. June 2003
- 21.5% over sixty

This is a serious retirement magnet! Woy Woy, Ettalong, St Huberts Island, Umina and Pretty Beach attract the over-sixties more than Gosford, Terrigal and Avoca.

CLIMATE

Summer 17.1°C to 27.4°C
Winter 4.5° to 17.4°C
Sunshine 96 days
Rain 116 days

Rainfall 1321 mm

The temperature no doubt varies between the coast and hinterland.

LOCATION & GETTING AROUND

Sydney to Gosford is just a one-hour drive (75 kilometres). Avoid peak hours and Sunday afternoons as the freeway tends to gridlock.

Roads Roads are in reasonable condition but quite busy. A car is essential to enjoy this area.

Nearest airports Swansea, Belmont and Sydney

Nearest train Gosford and Woy Woy are both connected by City-Rail to Sydney and Newcastle with frequent services.

Buses Busways operates services around the area and to Gosford

Taxis ✓

INFRASTRUCTURE

Hospitals Gosford Hospital (with emergency services) and Woy Woy

Retirement villages Gosford, Terrigal, Erina, Daleys Point, Point Clare, Wyoming, Kincumber, Narara and Umina

Police stations Gosford, Terrigal, Woy Woy and Kincumber

Local newspaper *Central Coast Express* (Gosford edition)

RECREATION

Beaches There are many ocean and calm-water beaches, and some are patrolled.

Coastguard ✓

Cycleways Cycle lanes exist but there are few cyclists. The main roads are too busy and too narrow and are not recommended. Some areas where it is flat lend themselves to cycling, such as Matcham and around Woy Woy and Umina.

Bushwalking & National Parks Bouddi and Brisbane Water National Parks have walking tracks, secluded swimming beaches and great views of Broken Bay and the ocean.

Dogs Beaches have on-leash exercise areas as well as no-dog areas. No dogs are permitted in national parks.

SHOPPING

Gosford has a large variety of shops and Erina Fair is a huge refurbished shopping complex with all the major stores including Myer and Target. Woolworths has supermarkets at Erina, Gosford and Woy Woy. Coles supermarkets are at Erina, Gosford, West Gosford, Wyoming and Woy Woy.

DINING

There are limited fine dining and ethnic restaurants in the area but a wide range of casual dining.

SOCIAL ACTIVITY

There are many clubs, both sporting and social, and associations catering to over-fifties and senior citizens, plus opportunities for further education.

Golf courses are located at Gosford, Kincumber, Wamberal and Woy Woy. This is an outdoors place, and people don't dress up. The makeshift Avoca Beach Theatre shows 'movies with atmosphere', and occasionally they are the art-house variety, and there's a mainstream cinema at Erina Fair.

• All community organisations • All religions • Boating
• Bushwalking • Cinema • Fishing • Golf • Horse riding
• Prawning • Surfing

REAL ESTATE

• Median house price: $355 000
• Median unit price: $275 000

In Terrigal houses with views are mostly over the million-dollar mark. In Woy Woy villas start from around $280 000. At Avoca Beach or North Avoca you will be lucky to find a home for $400 000 without a view, and much more with views. In Matcham you might pick up five cleared acres for between $350 000 and $600 000 or a house with 1.5 acres for $750 000 but most will be more than $1 million.

WHY LIVE HERE?

There is a big population here with lots of lifestyle and housing choices, all fairly close to Sydney. 'I wouldn't move back to Sydney if you paid me. Who'd want to be in that madhouse?' So said Fred, the part-time fisherman.

sydney

upper north shore
The genteel life without going to Bowral

'All leaves and lawns' is the best way to describe Sydney's Upper North Shore. It's a bushy area and the houses are often large on oversized blocks with gum trees hiding whole suburbs from the air. Suburbs which are particularly popular with the over-sixties are in the Ku-ring-gai Shire, which extends from Roseville to Wahroonga.

Many homes have swimming pools, and although many of the tennis courts were sold off years ago to make way for battleaxe blocks they are still a feature of the area. These are Sydney's most elevated suburbs and it can get cold in winter, with occasional fogs; the area also receives Sydney's highest rainfall. Gardeners will enjoy living here as the gardens are beautiful, but certain areas are subject to bushfires as some of the houses literally have the bush for their backyard.

POPULATION

Ku-ring-gai
- 109 000 Est. June 2003
- 20.9% over sixty

CLIMATE

Temperate and humid. Local temperatures are not recorded by the Bureau of Meteorology; however, the maximums are similar to the rest of Sydney and the minimums probably a little cooler as it is at a higher altitude. The mean rainfall in Turramurra is 1400 mm, one of the highest in Sydney.

LOCATION & GETTING AROUND

CityRail has eight stations located along the axis. It should take 40 minutes to travel from Wahroonga to the city by train, but it invariably takes much longer as Sydney's rail service isn't as efficient as it used to be. By road it takes 30 minutes (off-peak) to travel the same

23 kilometres. Due to the expansion of the Chatswood shopping centre there is a frustrating bottleneck between the Upper North Shore and the city, which can make the trip take a lot longer.

Roads Main roads are heavily congested. The F1 freeway from the north spills out at Wahroonga.

Nearest airport Sydney Airport is 34 kilometres away, a 40-minute drive

Nearest train Roseville, Lindfield, Killara, Gordon, Pymble, Turramurra, Warrawee and Wahroonga. The railway runs up the middle of the suburbs, except St Ives. The nearest rail station to St Ives is Gordon.

Buses ✓

Taxis ✓

INFRASTRUCTURE

Hospitals The Sydney Adventist Hospital Turramurra, Hornsby Hospital (nearby) and Royal North Shore Hospital (nearby)

Retirement villages The Grange (Waitara), Killara, St Ives, Chatswood, Gordon, North Turramurra, Killara, Lindfield, West Pymble and Wahroonga

Police stations Gordon, and nearby at Chatswood and Hornsby

RECREATION

Cycleways Lane Cove National Park is not far from Lindfield, and there are plenty of back roads and quite a few hills

Bushwalking & National Parks Ku-ring-gai Chase National Park is enormous and includes pretty hamlets and boatsheds on Berowra Waters and many walking trails. The Great North Walk commences in Lane Cove National Park.

Dogs Dog regulations are fairly strict.

SHOPPING

Each suburb has its own shopping centres; Gordon, Lindfield and St Ives have the largest selection. Major stores are located just outside the area at Chatswood (huge) and Hornsby.

DINING

The choice within Ku-ring-gai Shire is limited but Chatswood has many restaurants, many of them specialising in Asian cuisines.

SOCIAL ACTIVITY

There are excellent golf and sports clubs, including croquet, tennis and bushwalking. Boating and picnicking at Bobbin Head in the national park on Pittwater are popular. The cinema complex at Roseville is good, and there are music clubs, two seniors centres, gardening clubs and nurseries, with more excellent nurseries close by at Terrey Hills.

• All community organisations • All religions • Boating
• Bushwalking • Cinema • Croquet • Golf • Libraries • Tennis

REAL ESTATE

• Median house price: $700 000
• Median unit price: $500 000

Prices vary quite a lot by suburb, and of course according to the size of the home, so it's worth spending some time getting familiar with real estate prices in each area.

WHY LIVE HERE?

The Upper North Shore is ideal if you like big gardens and the quiet life but want to stay near the family. You get more square metres for your bucks than harbourside, with rhododendrons thrown in for good measure, and you won't have the neighbours breathing down your neck – in fact, you may not even see your neighbours for days on end. Visits to the city to follow the arts can be managed without too much hassle once or twice a week.

northern beaches

Barefoot in the city

Sydney's northern beaches extend almost 30 kilometres from the Barrenjoey Lighthouse to tourist-thronged Manly, with twenty-two of the country's most stunning beaches along the way and picturesque Pittwater to the west. Pittwater is an expansive waterway bordered by national park bushland; it's a fabulous place to cruise or sail, without commercial traffic.

The northern beaches area has a remote, holiday feel about it – you could be a hundred miles away from the business action, and I'm sure some of the residents never go into the city at all. In the summer months many of them wear beach attire even when shopping.

POPULATION

Warringah and Pittwater Shires

- **194 500** Est. Jun 2003
- **18.8%** over sixty

This estimate includes several areas which are outside of what the locals refer to as 'the peninsula'. The area from Barrenjoey to Manly has a population of around 160 000, with approximately 30 000 residents aged over sixty.

CLIMATE

Summer 18.4°C to 26.6°C
Winter 7.9°C to 17.4°C
Sunshine 102 days
Rain 133 days
Rainfall 1220 mm

LOCATION & GETTING AROUND

The peninsula is a long, narrow strip of land with only a few single-lane access roads. There has been talk for decades about providing a light-rail service but it has never happened. There is also much debate about widening the Spit Bridge; this is a major bottleneck which opens for boats several times a day. The roads are clogged in summer as well as at peak times year-round; when they're moving freely, some of the roads take you on a pleasant journey through native bushland.

From Sydney to Mona Vale is 25 kilometres, which takes 37 minutes by car; Palm Beach is another 10 kilometres. The residents of Manly also have the choice of fast or slow ferries to the city and from Palm Beach there is the opportunity to catch a seaplane.

Roads Main roads are heavily congested, as you can't get around without a car.

Nearest airport Sydney Airport is 40 kilometres away, 50 minutes on average to drive

Nearest train ✗

Buses ✓

Ferries ✓

Taxis ✓

INFRASTRUCTURE

Hospitals Mona Vale Hospital and Manly Hospital. There has been talk of the Mona Vale Hospital closing and there has been strong resistance from locals.

Retirement villages Manly, Mona Vale, Dee Why, Narrabeen, Newport, Collaroy, Avalon Beach, Bayview and Warriewood

Police stations Manly, Dee Why, Mona Vale and Avalon

RECREATION

Beaches Of the many ocean beaches the best known is Manly, but little Shelly Beach may be the prettiest, Palm Beach and Whale Beach are the most social and the most private is certainly Bungan's ocean beach, with access only by foot. There are numerous calm-water beaches on Pittwater.

Cycleways There is not much opportunity to ride your bike off the busy roads; however, a lot of the area is flat if you are game.

Dogs Six beaches and reserves allow dogs off-leash, while others have a total ban on dogs.

SHOPPING

Warringah Mall is a large, undercover, multi-level shopping complex with department stores, supermarkets, cinemas, boutiques and cafés. Other major shopping areas are Mona Vale and Manly, which has interesting shops along the mall and in the side streets. Avalon is a relaxed beach with a village atmosphere and great little cafés.

DINING

The choice here is casual or casual – this is not a fine dining area. There are restaurants with atmosphere in Palm Beach, Avalon and Whale Beach and a sensational strip of restaurants with high-quality indoor and outdoor dining opposite the beach at Dee Why. Many of the beaches have cafés overlooking the surf. Manly offers the most variety as well as a number of hotels which provide good accommodation and food.

SOCIAL ACTIVITY

Marinas and boating clubs are located on Pittwater and at nearby Akuna Bay. If you don't want to buy a boat you can become a member of a leisure boating club, which works much the same as a golf club. There are several good golf courses and other sporting facilities for both participants and spectators. The walks around here are great, in particular North Head National Park to Barrenjoey Lighthouse and the very popular walk from Manly to Shelly Beach. There's excellent surfing and fishing on the ocean beaches. The region lacks the art galleries and libraries that are found closer to the CBD. All religions are represented here, including the Baha'i Faith.

- All community organisations • All religions • Boating
- Bushwalking • Fishing • Golf • Lawn bowls • Sailing
- Surfing • Tennis

REAL ESTATE

Northern Beaches
- Median house price: $850000

- Median unit price: $450 000

Manly

- Median house price: $1.25 million
- Median unit price: $635 000

Some Sydneysiders still maintain holiday homes on the northern beaches but with many beachfront properties selling in excess of $3 million it is hard to justify tying up so much money in a spare house.

WHY LIVE HERE?

If you don't want to hit the city too often but like to know it's there when you want it, then this is about as relaxed as Sydney living can be. For maximum enjoyment you need to be an outdoors person because this is definitely an outdoors place.

Pam from Newport: 'It's like being on holiday all year-round.'

Sue from Manly: 'I walk along the beach, breathe in the sea air or go for a swim before getting on with the day. Living here recharges your batteries.'

northern harbour suburbs
The best of harbourside living

The number of retirees living on the North Shore of Sydney Harbour, from Balmoral to Kirribilli, is well above the Australian average. This area has a lot going for it and is slightly cheaper and less busy than the Eastern Suburbs, with great harbour views and unique city views across the water. It also enjoys direct harbour access from many of the suburbs, one of the best harbour foreshore walks from Neutral Bay to Mosman, foreshore parks, good access to the city and North Sydney, and a good selection of restaurants and shopping centres. And not forgetting Balmoral Beach, without a doubt Sydney's best harbour beach (the only other harbour beach to rival it is Middleton in Albany, WA) – it's a paradise for swimmers and picnickers and for fine dining.

POPULATION

- 20000+
- 18% over sixty

CLIMATE

Summer 18.7°C to 25.8°C
Winter 8°C to 16.2°C
Sunshine 102 days
Rain 138 days
Rainfall 1217 mm

LOCATION & GETTING AROUND

Access to the city is excellent, via a frequent ferry service (usually every half-hour) and by train from Milsons Point or North Sydney rail stations. Access by car and bus is good outside of peak hours.

Roads The main road, Military Road, is always heavily congested. A sore point.

Nearest airport Sydney Airport is 18 kilometres away and averages only 20 minutes by car thanks to the Eastern Distributor.

Nearest train Milsons Point or North Sydney, by CityRail

Buses ✓

Ferries ✓

Taxis ✓

INFRASTRUCTURE

Hospitals Royal North Shore Hospital. The area is well supplied with medical facilities.

Retirement villages Neutral Bay, Mosman (several), North Sydney and Lavender Bay

Police stations North Sydney and Mosman

RECREATION

Beaches Balmoral Beach (partly netted), Chinamans Beach, Edwards Beach, Obelisk (nude), Clifton Gardens and Whiting

Beach plus the MacCallum Pool in Shellcove and the Olympic Pool at Milsons Point

Cycleways ✗

Dogs There are strict rules for dogs, which must be kept on a leash in most areas.

SHOPPING

Sydney's city centre is only a ferry ride away. For veggie and supermarket shopping, Neutral Bay and Mosman have large centres although they are a little tired. Woolworths has plans to upgrade in Neutral Bay. Warringah Mall and Chatswood are within driving range.

DINING

The choice is huge but not in the same league as the Eastern Suburbs, with Neutral Bay, Mosman and Balmoral providing a reasonably high standard. It takes only minutes by ferry to reach the city's wide range of excellent restaurants.

SOCIAL ACTIVITY

Marinas or boating clubs can be found at the Spit, Mosman, Cremorne, Careening Cove and Kirribilli.

• Everything

REAL ESTATE

• Median house price: $1.5 million
• Median unit price: $532 000

Interestingly, this area has always represented better value for money than its expensive neighbour on the eastern foreshore, despite its similar views.

WHY LIVE HERE?

If you can afford it, and you want to enjoy the best Sydney has to offer, this is a great retirement location.

eastern harbour suburbs
International buzz with a unique Australian view

The eastern foreshore of Sydney Harbour, from Watsons Bay to Darling Point, is one of the city's most sought-after retirement areas. Many people aspire to live in these suburbs but due to the expense of the real estate there is a greater skew towards older residents than in most other areas of Sydney. Included in this area are the suburbs of Watsons Bay, Vaucluse, Dover Heights, Bellevue Hill, Rose Bay, Point Piper, Double Bay, Edgecliff and Darling Point.

What makes this the most exclusive area in Sydney with the highest property prices is position, position, position! These suburbs have the best north-facing harbour views, excellent access to the city, a cosmopolitan population, boating facilities, netted harbour beaches, nearby ocean beaches, top competition golf courses, a choice of large shopping precincts and even bushwalks on the harbour foreshore.

If you can afford it, this is a great retirement location. However, there are down-sides: the area is oh so busy, the through streets are crowded with cars, parking is difficult and the cost of living is probably the highest in Australia. Having said that, for retirees with the ability to use any day of the week as their weekend, the beaches and facilities are remarkably quiet during the weekdays, the harbour is virtually unused except for afternoon sailing races and the pollution is minimal as it is swept away by harbour breezes. Many of the suburban streets off the main roads are quiet and leafy.

POPULATION

- 44 000
- 20.5% over sixty

CLIMATE

Summer 18.7°C to 25.8°C
Winter 8°C to 16.2°C
Sunshine 102 days
Rain 138 days
Rainfall 1217 mm

LOCATION & GETTING AROUND

These suburbs have arguably the best access to the city of any area in Sydney, thanks to the new cross-city tunnel, the Eastern Suburbs railway, Sydney Harbour ferries and government buses.

Roads Main roads are heavily congested.

Nearest airport Sydney Airport is 15 kilometres away, which averages a 20-minute drive.

Nearest train Edgecliff, CityRail

Buses ✓

Ferries ✓

Taxis ✓

INFRASTRUCTURE

Hospitals St Vincent's Hospital at Darlinghurst and Prince of Wales at Randwick. The area is well serviced by medical facilities.

Retirement villages Rose Bay, Elizabeth Bay, Watsons Bay, Woollahra and Waverley

Police stations Rose Bay

RECREATION

Beaches Seven Shillings Beach, Parsley Bay, Neilsen Park (Shark Beach), Lady Jane (nude), Camp Cove, Gibsons Beach, Kutti Beach and Lady Martins Beach

Cycleways Centennial Park is nearby with its popular four-kilometre loop for both walkers and cyclists. The harbour foreshore offers bushwalks with an amazing view.

Dogs There are strict rules for dogs, which must be kept on a leash in most areas.

SHOPPING

There's a choice from the largest shopping precincts in Australia. Within a few kilometres are the massive stores of the city of Sydney, the recently redeveloped Bondi Junction or the boutique fashion houses of Double Bay and Oxford Street, Paddington.

DINING

The choice within a 10-kilometre radius of these suburbs is infinite, as the cosmopolitan neighbourhood provides every type of ethnic cuisine imaginable. Sydneysiders have become very aware of what constitutes good food, so only consistently good restaurants survive. This doesn't mean that all restaurants are expensive, as Sydney residents feel equally comfortable eating on a laminated table top if the food is sensational.

SOCIAL ACTIVITY

This is the big smoke: whatever you want to do and whoever you want to play with, it's your choice.

Marinas or boating clubs are at Rushcutters Bay, Double Bay, Point Piper, Rose Bay and Watsons Bay. If you don't want to buy a boat you can become a member of a leisure boating club, which works much the same as a golf club.

- Everything

REAL ESTATE

- Median house price: $2.3 million
- Median unit price: $950 000

WHY LIVE HERE?

It is so convenient!

John and Trish: 'We moved from the North Shore, from a big home with an extensive garden; now we've downsized to an apartment in Double Bay that's a quarter the size of our former home and we love it. We can walk to everything and we can just shut the door and go away on holiday whenever we want to.'

kiama

Ireland by the sea

The Kiama Municipality on the New South Wales South Coast incorporates the townships of Kiama and the unhurried seaside villages of Gerroa and Gerringong. All three towns are crawling with retirees. Kiama is famous for its blowhole, and is the retail centre for the three towns, whilst Gerringong has a modest shopping centre and Gerroa has virtually no shopping facilities.

The coastline around Kiama is stunning, with rugged cliffs, pleasant beaches and rolling hills. The towns feature large Norfolk Island pines and are well suited to retirees who enjoy a seaside lifestyle. Retire here and you have the choice of visiting the beach, exploring rainforests, visiting quaint eateries, boutique shopping, walking in the national parks, fishing, going for country drives, searching for antiques, visiting local markets or just sitting back and enjoying the views.

Kiama will appeal to those who want to be close to facilities. The highway goes close enough to ensure that the town has passing traffic and is quite a busy place. In contrast, Gerringong and Gerroa are more remote and upmarket. Gerringong is elevated and has the most wondrous views of rolling green hills and the blue Pacific; the lack of trees gives the surrounding hills an Irish coastal appearance. Gerringong itself has many large Norfolk Island pines along its streets, an array of delightfully presented shops, well-renovated old buildings and nicely groomed houses. It is indeed a special area. Picturesque Gerroa overlooks Seven Mile Beach, at the southern end of which is Shoalhaven Heads. These are popular places for retirement, as is Avondale, 25 kilometres from Kiama.

POPULATION

- 20 000 Est. June 2003
- 20% over sixty

Kiama's population is both growing and ageing (it increased by 600 between censuses to exceed 12 000). Gerringong's population was estimated at 3500 (up by 600) at the last census and Gerroa's at 500 (down by 44).

CLIMATE

Summer 17.8°C to 25.1°C
Winter 8.4°C to 17.6°C
Sunshine 83 days
Rain 127 days
Rainfall 1261 mm
Temperatures are noticeably warmer here than in the nearby
Southern Highlands but often a little cooler than in Sydney, espe-
cially in winter.

LOCATION & GETTING AROUND

Kiama is 120 kilometres south of Sydney, a drive of one hour and
45 minutes. It's 30 minutes from the Southern Highlands and
just a 2.5-hour drive from Canberra. Gerroa to Sydney takes just
over two hours to cover the 135 kilometres.

Roads Highway One bypasses Kiama, which is a blessing as its
narrow main street winds through town and is lined with shops.
Gerringong and Gerroa are on the coast well off the main road.

Nearest train Trains run daily to and from Kiama and Gerringong. Services operate roughly every two hours. The trip to
Sydney's Central Station takes two hours.

Buses ✓
Taxis ✓

INFRASTRUCTURE

Hospitals Kiama has a hospital and community health service, plus four doctors' surgeries cover Kiama, Kiama Downs and
Gerringong.

Retirement villages Two in Kiama. Kiama Council operates the
Blue Haven Retirement Village, a 40-bed nursing home, a 30-
bed hostel and 115 independent living units.

Police stations Kiama and Gerringong

Local newspaper *Kiama Independent*

RECREATION

Beaches There are nine beaches, the best known being Seven Mile Beach. There are numerous locations to launch boats, and charter boats are also available.

Cycleways None to speak of, but many of the byroads are quiet.

Dogs Dogs are prohibited from running free in most places but there is an off-leash area at Bombo Head, which is close to Kiama.

SHOPPING

The Kiama Fair Shopping Centre is the main shopping centre; it has open-air parking and undercover shops, including a large Woolworths. There are many small shops on the main road through Kiama. Gerringong has an adequate supply of shops for its size, including an IGA supermarket, bank, day spa, newsagent and liquor store.

DINING

There are many restaurants, cafés and licensed clubs in Kiama, offering seafood with a view or specialising in cuisines including Italian, Chinese, Mexican, pizza and vegetarian. Gerringong has a range of excellent cafés including a vegetarian option and a formal restaurant with arguably the best ocean view in Australia.

SOCIAL ACTIVITY

The area has two golf clubs, lawn bowls clubs, bridge club, historical societies, neighbourhood centres, a garden club, woodcraft group, arts societies, game fishing club and arts and crafts associations.

• Arts & crafts • Boating • Fishing • Galleries • Golf
• Lawn bowls • Libraries • Most religions
• Some community organisations • Surfing

REAL ESTATE

• Median house price: $490 000
• Median unit price: $343 000

In Gerringong and Gerroa you should expect to pay more, with the median price for a house $549 000.

WHY LIVE HERE?

Gerringong has great appeal – in fact, it is sophistication by the sea and its views are postcard material. Both Gerringong and Gerroa are beautiful places with holiday cottages and permanent residences side by side. They are more appealing than Kiama, which is where suburbia meets the sea, although the town does have a good infrastructure.

shoalhaven
One of the most picturesque choices for retirement

Just a few hours south of Sydney in the picturesque Shoalhaven area, Nowra, Kangaroo Valley, Berry and Shoalhaven Heads are home to many retirees.

Nowra is on the meandering Shoalhaven River, with Bomaderry, its smaller sister town, just to the north. It's a well-planned township, with a naval base and naval airport. River cruises and fishing are popular pastimes, and there are several bushwalking trails, an attractive golf course and parkland all by the water's edge.

Kangaroo Valley is small and rural with the historic stone Hampden Bridge framing its western entrance. With its quaint shops, pub and cafés, it's the epitome of a small country village. The well-maintained eighteen-hole Kangaroo Valley Golf Course is nearby and, as the name suggests, often the only inhabitants are large grey kangaroos.

Berry is a pretty village filled with art and craft shops, galleries and cafés. Unfortunately, the Princes Highway thunders single file through the centre of town carrying scores of semi-trailers. Fortunately, a bypass is apparently on the cards and there is a bypass around Nowra. Shoalhaven Heads at the southern end of Seven Mile Beach is a popular fishing and surfing spot.

This area offers a choice of rural, beach or town living. Such is the lay of the land that even some of the rural retreats have a view of the Pacific Ocean. A very appealing and largely undiscovered rural area with panoramic views is Bellawongarah on the quiet mountain road between Berry and Kangaroo Valley; it's well worth considering if you are interested in acreage. Nowra provides the facilities and services but the smaller towns have the atmosphere, with winding roads and secluded nooks throughout. The escarpment from the Southern Highlands is an amazing backdrop and from it there are almost unlimited views. It is a beautiful drive down the escarpment from the Southern Highlands, the rainforest on either side parting to reveal lush fields and stunning views out to sea.

POPULATION

Nowra
- 25 000
- 20% over sixty

The population of Berry is around 1600, Shoalhaven Heads is 2750 and Kangaroo Valley has a population of only 340. All have substantial over-sixties populations.

CLIMATE

Summer 16.3°C to 25.8°C
Winter 6.2°C to 15.8°C
Sunshine 97 days
Rain 130 days
Rainfall 1135 mm

The temperature is noticeably higher here than in the nearby Southern Highlands, but it's cooler than Sydney, especially in winter.

LOCATION & GETTING AROUND

Nowra is about 160 kilometres from Sydney, which takes about 2.5 hours to drive; getting in and out of Sydney can be a bit of a nightmare. The main access road in the region is the very busy Princes Highway, which is narrow and mostly single lane each way, and is being upgraded. There is a two-lane expressway for part of the journey between Waterfall and Mount Ousley. Canberra to Nowra takes 2.5 hours to cover the 220 kilometres;

Bowral is a winding 60 kilometres away, which takes around 50 minutes.

Roads The main roads around Nowra are two-lane. The side roads are narrow but fairly quiet and picturesque.

Nearest train Trains run daily from Bomaderry (Nowra) and Berry stations. Access to Wollongong and Sydney areas involves changing to electrified trains at Kiama. Services operate roughly two hours apart from early in the morning to early evening. Extra commuter services run during the week.

Buses Daily interstate services operate through Nowra to Sydney and on to Cairns, as well as to Melbourne linking with a coach service to Canberra at Batemans Bay. Local services connect the villages to Nowra.

Taxis ✓

INFRASTRUCTURE

Hospitals The Shoalhaven District Hospital is located in Nowra, as are several health centres plus a large private hospital. Wollongong Hospital (80 kilometres from Nowra) is the major teaching and referral hospital for the region.

Retirement villages Three in Nowra and one in Berry

Police stations Nowra, Berry and Kangaroo Valley

Local newspapers *South Coast Register* and *Nowra News*

RECREATION

Beaches The Shoalhaven area is famous for its beaches – there are 109 of them along 160 kilometres of coastline. Shoalhaven Heads is at the end of Seven Mile Beach which is ringed with natural bushland. There are also many inland waterways and bays for protected boating and fishing with public boat ramps for ease of access.

Coastguard ✓

Cycleways Council has produced a guide containing 32 cycle routes throughout the Shoalhaven area.

Bushwalking & National Parks The Shoalhaven area is

renowned for its wonderful bushwalks. While the coastal walks are always very popular, those through the hinterland open up to some truly magnificent, rugged countryside.

Dogs Designated leash-free areas.

SHOPPING

Coles, Woolworths, Aldi and IGA supermarkets are all in Nowra, which also has a large choice of speciality shops. In Berry there are craft shops and cafés lining the streets but only a modest IGA supermarket. Shoalhaven Heads has an assortment of cottages, shops, cafés and a licensed club. This area has many galleries and craft centres selling ceramics, paintings, woodwork, knitted wear, handicrafts and Aboriginal art.

DINING

There are over fifty restaurants and cafés in and around Nowra, with a wide selection of cuisines and varying standards.

SOCIAL ACTIVITY

Nowra is a very active centre with festivals, markets, shows, a wide range of tourist attractions and more. The Shoalhaven City Arts Centre, which opened in Nowra in early 2004, is a vibrant and creative arts centre. There is a cinema complex in Nowra and a cinema in Bomaderry. Bundanon, on the banks of the Shoalhaven, is the rural property where Arthur Boyd painted and it's now a retreat for artists. There are lawn bowls clubs and golf courses in Nowra and Kangaroo Valley which welcome new members. The Berry Country Fair is held monthly. At Shoalhaven Heads there is a swimming pool open in warmer months and kite-flying is a ritual on the first Sunday of every month.

• All community organisations • All religions • Arts & crafts
• Bushwalking • Cinema • Galleries • Golf • Horse riding
• Lawn bowls • Surfing • Swimming

REAL ESTATE

Berry
- Median house price: $379 000
- Median unit price: $290 000

Land prices vary considerably throughout the Shoalhaven area, starting from a minimum of $160 000. Prices in Nowra are cheaper.

WHY LIVE HERE?

The landscape is more appealing than the coastal areas to the north of Sydney, the lifestyle is more relaxed and the towns are less crowded.

jervis bay
Where civilisation is lost in bush and ocean

Just south of Nowra, the spectacular waterway of Jervis Bay is ringed by small townships and communities, all of which are popular retirement spots. Callala Beach is on the northern shores of the bay and the larger townships of Huskisson and Vincentia are on the southern side. Hyams Beach, a small village to the south of Vincentia, has a perfect view of Point Perpendicular and the entrance to the bay. HMAS *Creswell*, a training college for the Australian Navy, is just a little further around on the southern peninsula, as are the villages of Erowal Bay and Jervis Bay. A little further around, St Georges Basin and Sanctuary Point also have small communities.

Jervis Bay Marine Park, Booderee National Park and Jervis Bay National Park protect the pristine waters and native bushland and give the bay the appearance of being virtually uninhabited. One local asked me not to reveal the area's secrets as she wanted it to remain relatively unpopulated – and who could blame her for that? One thing you won't find in the waters here are plastic bags, as they are banned. Good move.

This really is a pretty location. Huskisson is the gateway to Jervis Bay, but it is not large, and the main centre is Nowra. Some people may feel there's not enough social stimulation here, and the lack of a public hospital close by may not suit everyone, but both are only twenty minutes away.

POPULATION

- 14 000 people
- 29% over sixty

CLIMATE

Summer 18°C to 23.9°C
Winter 9.2°C to 15.1°C
Sunshine 97 days
Rain 136 days
Rainfall 1245 mm
Both the water and air temperatures are cooler than in Sydney.

LOCATION & GETTING AROUND

Sydney to Jervis Bay is 190 kilometres, taking about three hours to drive. The narrow and mostly single-lane Princes Highway is the main access road; it's busy and is being upgraded. There is a two-lane expressway for part of the journey between Waterfall and Mount Ousley. Canberra to Jervis Bay takes 2.5 hours to cover the 240 kilometres. An alternative route is via the Southern Highlands and Fitzroy Falls, a winding road with spectacular views.

Roads The local roads are narrow but fairly quiet, and so picturesque.

Nearest train The nearest option is Berry or Bomaderry. Jervis Bay is 30 kilometres from Bomaderry Station and 40 kilometres from Berry. Trains run daily from Berry and Bomaderry stations. Access to Wollongong and Sydney involves changing to electrified trains at Kiama. Services operate roughly two hours apart and extra commuter services run during the week.

Buses Various routes link the area with Nowra

Taxis Only on request from St Georges Basin

INFRASTRUCTURE

Hospitals The Shoalhaven District Hospital is located in Nowra (26 kilometres from Jervis Bay), as are several health centres plus a large private hospital. Wollongong Hospital (100 kilometres from Jervis Bay) is the major teaching and referral hospital for the region.

Retirement villages   One in the bay at Worrowing Heights, three in Nowra and one in Sussex Inlet

Police stations   Huskisson and Nowra

Local newspapers   *South Coast Register* and *Nowra News*

RECREATION

Beaches   Ten kilometres south of Huskisson is picturesque Hyams Beach, reputed to have the whitest sand in the world. Hyams is also a delightful small village with a general store/café and it's near Booderee National Park and the botanic gardens. Around the bay, Huskisson and Collingwood Beaches are popular, as are smaller more intimate beaches such as Greenfields and Blenheim, Murrays Beach and Greenpatch in Booderee National Park. The quieter waters of St Georges Basin are located to the south of Jervis Bay.

Coastguard ✓

Cycleways   The Bay and Basin cycle path, a 31-kilometre circuit, has great views over Jervis Bay and St Georges Basin. A leisurely circuit of 13 kilometres accesses the beaches and there are more strenuous rides requiring mountain bikes between Nowra and the Huskisson area. Shoalhaven City Council has produced a guide to 32 cycle routes throughout the Shoalhaven area.

Bushwalking & National Parks   There are many parks throughout the Shoalhaven area. Whilst the coastal walks and national parks are always very popular, the hinterland opens up to some truly rugged beauty.

Dogs   Rules are pretty relaxed and dogs run free.

SHOPPING

Vincentia has a Bi-Lo supermarket and Huskisson has a range of stores in a neatly laid out main street, including a small supermarket, some interesting boutiques and gift shops and post office;

outdoor markets are held every month. The nearest serious shopping is in Nowra with both Coles and Woolworths supermarkets and various department stores.

DINING

Dining is limited but offers value for money. Huskisson has several cafés with good fare and outside tables. Restaurants include Chinese, pizza and Thai, plus there are bistros at the Husky Pub and the RSL Club.

SOCIAL ACTIVITY

Jervis Bay is a water sports wonderland, wildlife haven and fisherman's paradise all in one place. Sightseeing for dolphins and whales is popular and other activities include bushwalking, birdwatching, sailing, sea kayaking and cycling. The Bay and Basin Leisure Centre offers wet and dry facilities throughout the year with heated pool, spa, gym and exercise classes. There is a choice of golf courses. The cinema (which they still call 'the pictures') in Huskisson shows recent releases as well as accommodating the Sydney Travelling Film Festival. The Lady Denman Museum Complex at Huskisson has one of the finest collections of marine surveying equipment in Australia.
• Birdwatching • Bushwalking • Cinema • Cycling • Diving
• Fishing • Golf • Horse riding • Leisure centre • Museum
• Sailing • Scuba diving • Waterskiing • Windsurfing

REAL ESTATE

• Median house price: $320 000
• Median unit price: $260 000
There are plenty of hidden villages to choose from.

WHY LIVE HERE?

The beaches are less crowded and the streets are unhurried. It is certainly one of the most natural environments to choose from and must be in your top ten list if this type of lifestyle appeals to you. As one of the locals said to me, 'It's a well-kept secret and that's the way we like it.'

ulladulla
Suburbia by the sea

The small town of Milton is 12 kilometres outside Ulladulla (driving from Sydney), perched on a ridge slightly inland. It has some interesting architecture, an assortment of shops and the local hospital, with emergency facilities. There is also a modern retirement village here and medical practices. A little further on is the turn-off to Mollymook, which has a protected beach and a well-developed community overlooking the ocean.

Ulladulla is a large coastal town with pleasant walks around the lighthouse and adjacent cliffs. Most of the streets in Mollymook and Ulladulla have fairly ordinary housing. The highway runs right through Ulladulla's main shopping centre and semis regularly plough through town, slowed down somewhat at the top of the hill by the roundabout. There is a substantial and protected boat harbour next to the highway.

Nearby Burrill Lake is a tiny village of just a few lakeside houses but as with the other towns/villages around here the highway splits the village in two. The highway bypasses Mollymook and Lake Conjola, both of which attract retirees no doubt because of the quieter neighbourhood. Lake Conjola is small, with a population of only around 600; it's a very pleasant lake for swimming, fishing and boating, and has a boardwalk suitable for wheelchairs which overlooks the lake entrance and Conjola Beach.

POPULATION

- 16 000
- 30% over sixty

Ulladulla (population 9600) grew by 1225 between censuses.

CLIMATE

Summer 18°C to 23.9°C
Winter 9.2°C to 15.1°C

Sunshine 97 days
Rain 136 days
Rainfall 1245 mm

LOCATION & GETTING AROUND

The 230-kilometre drive from Sydney to Ulladulla takes around 3.5 hours. The highway is narrow but with reasonable roads for a substantial part of the journey. From Canberra the trip takes around 2.5 hours to cover the 200 kilometres.

Roads Single lane each way with some overtaking lanes

Nearest airport Moruya (80 kilometres away)

Nearest train ✗

Buses Daily interstate services operate through Ulladulla to Sydney and on to Cairns, as well as to Melbourne, and link with a coach service to Canberra at Batemans Bay.

Taxis: ✓

INFRASTRUCTURE

Hospitals Milton/Ulladulla Hospital is in Milton, 10 minutes away from Ulladulla, and there are also medical and dental clinics in Ulladulla.

Retirement villages Milton and Sussex Inlet (45 kilometres away)

Police stations Ulladulla and Sussex Inlet

Local newspapers Ulladulla/Milton and Sussex Inlet *Times*

RECREATION

Beaches The area has some excellent beaches, especially at Cudmirrah, Narrawallee and Mollymook which are patrolled during summer.

Coastguard ✓

Cycleways Cycling is encouraged on the roads around Ulladulla harbour, with several trails mapped out

Bushwalking & National Parks The most challenging walk is to Pigeon House Mountain, and there are more leisurely walks such as the Coomee Nulunga Trail at Warden Head. 'The One

Track for All' at North Head is a disabled-access cultural trail that has been constructed in two loops with carved artworks along the way. Murramarang National Park, south of Ulladulla, has extensive walking trails.

Dogs Limited off-leash areas exist between the hours of 4 p.m. and 8 a.m.

SHOPPING

Ulladulla has ample shops on either side of the Princes Highway, including a large Coles supermarket. There are IGA supermarkets at both Milton and Mollymook. Open-air markets are held on Mollymook Beach.

DINING

There are plenty of cafés and restaurants in Milton and Ulladulla.

SOCIAL ACTIVITY

The Shoalhaven Shire is a big area and one council located in Nowra has to cover it all, which is a lot to ask; however, council has a branch office in Ulladulla as well as a community centre and library. There is a twin cinema in Ulladulla and another at Sussex Inlet. Art galleries are located at Milton, Sussex Inlet and Ulladulla. Mollymook has two golf courses, one beachside, and there is an 18-hole golf course at Sussex Inlet. Bowling greens are located at Ulladulla, Mollymook and Lake Conjola and an ex-servicemen's club in Ulladulla. The Wet and Dry Leisure Centre in Ulladulla is open year-round and has three heated indoor pools, an outdoor Olympic pool, gymnasium, spa and more.

There are village swimming pools at Milton and Sussex Inlet. The annual Blessing of the Fleet Festival at Ulladulla Harbour is the highlight of the Easter holiday period and in August the Ulladulla Food and Wine Festival by the Sea showcases the region's cuisine and local produce. The township of Milton is known for its arts and community festivals, such as Tabula Rasa and the Milton Settlers Fair.

- Cinema • Diving • Fishing • Galleries • Golf • Lawn bowls
- Leisure centre • Library • Most community organisations
- Most religions • Swimming

REAL ESTATE

- Median house price: $362 000
- Median unit price: $335 000

A four-bedroom, two-bathroom house with ocean views in Ulladulla sells from $650 000. In Mollymook and Lake Conjola prices for houses with views are likely to be higher. Sussex Inlet prices start at around $320 000 and climb over $800 000.

WHY LIVE HERE?

Ulladulla offers suburban living conditions in a more pleasant environment than might be experienced in a capital city. Mollymook has developed substantially and is starting to resemble some of the built-up coastal areas north of Sydney. This location is quite a long way from Sydney, but with the benefit of slightly cheaper real estate, and Canberra isn't too far away.

One couple who were happily ensconced in Mollymook said they didn't feel guilty about being away from the kids as one daughter lived in Brisbane and the other in Melbourne, so 'Whatever we do one is going to miss out, this way we are between them both.'

sussex inlet
Island hideaway

Sussex Inlet is between Nowra and Ulladulla, and only a thirty-minute drive away from both, but it deserves its own heading as it is quite separate. It is referred to as the 'island township', and indeed you cannot help but be impressed by this very quaint little village. It consists of older-style small houses and has a number of shops as well as a bank, RSL Club, community health clinic, police station and an old fibro cinema. The population is around 4000, growing by almost 400 between censuses.

The inlet is popular for fishing and boating in still waters (ideal for kayaking) as well as cycling and bushwalking. It also has a well-frequented caravan park with many permanent caravans, some used as holiday homes by folk from Wollongong.

WHY LIVE HERE?

It's surrounded by water, and very secluded – a great 'get away from it all' spot.

batemans bay
Self-contained, with no reason to leave

This is a very popular retirement area indeed, encompassing Batehaven, Denhams Beach, Lilli Pilli, Malua Bay, Broulee and Mossy Point. Nearby are Dalmeny, Moruya, Narooma and Tuross Heads. Most of these towns rate well within the top 100 in Australia in terms of the proportion of over-sixties in their populations.

Batemans Bay is a well-presented, modern town at the mouth of the Clyde River and the junction of the Princes Highway and the Kings Highway to Canberra. Moruya is a historic rural town, slightly inland on the Moruya River and less than twenty minutes' drive south of Batemans Bay. It's surrounded by dairy and beef cattle farms, and nearby Bodalla is a picturesque inland village that's home to Bodalla cheese. Moruya is designated as the location for the shire's light-industrial expansion, and it's where you'll find the Eurobodalla Shire Council and the airport.

Narooma is on the Wagonga Inlet, about a fifty-minute drive south of Batemans Bay. This beautiful coastal town is known for its deep-sea fishing; it also has magnificent beaches and Montague Island National Park is just off-shore. Dalmeny is a small town on a headland whose older-style cottages with spacious gardens overlook the beaches and ocean. You can hear the bellbirds calling as you leave the highway and drive along the few kilometres to the village.

POPULATION

Greater Batemans Bay	Moruya	
• 15 600	• 2550	
• 30% over sixty	• 26% over sixty	

Dalmeny	Narooma	Bodalla
• 1785	• 3400	• 1060
• 40% over sixty	• 33% over sixty	• 21% over sixty

In Dalmeny one in every 2.5 residents is aged over sixty, making it one of the oldest communities in Australia.

CLIMATE

Summer 16.3°C to 24.1°C
Winter 5.9°C to 16.1°C
Sunshine 137 days
Rain 109 days
Rainfall 963 mm

LOCATION & GETTING AROUND

Batemans Bay is located at the junction of the Princes Highway leading to Sydney and the Kings Highway to Canberra. The normal driving time from Sydney is about four hours (282 kilo-metres) and to Canberra it's just two hours (150 kilometres).

Roads The Albion Park to Kiama by-pass currently under con-struction will substantially reduce the trip to and from Sydney.

Nearest airport Moruya Airport is 20 minutes' drive south of Batemans Bay and five minutes east of Moruya. Rex Airlines operates daily flights out of Moruya to Sydney; it's a spectacularly scenic flight along the coast, taking 55 minutes. Also daily flights to Melbourne.

Nearest train The NSW State Rail network terminates north of the Eurobodalla Shire at Nowra, about midway between Sydney and Batemans Bay. Daily coach services directly link with train services at Nowra.

Buses Local, intrastate and interstate buses

Taxis ✓

INFRASTRUCTURE

Hospitals Batemans Bay has a modern 22-bed hospital with full emergency care facilities. Moruya has 45 beds, with theatres, general and maternity wards. Community Health Centres are located in Batemans Bay, Moruya and Narooma, and each of the three towns has an ambulance service. The region is serviced by 24-hour emergency retrieval helicopter services.

Retirement villages Several quality aged-care and retirement facilities are located at Batemans Bay, Malua Bay, Moruya, Broulee and Batehaven, and there's a large modern village in Dalmeny. More nursing home and retirement village developments are planned.

Police stations Batemans Bay, Bodalla, Moruya and Narooma

Local newspapers *Batemans Bay Post*, *Moruya Examiner* and *Narooma News*

RECREATION

Beaches There are more than 60 beaches lining the Eurobodalla Coast – from pounding surf to tranquil bays – and they are among the cleanest in Australia. During the holiday season, the main beaches are patrolled at Batemans Bay, Malua Bay, Broulee, South Head (Moruya), Tuross, Dalmeny and Narooma.

Coastguard ✓

Bushwalking & National Parks There are plenty of opportunities for bushwalking in the many parks, including Murramarang, Budawang, Eurobodalla, Wadbiliga, Montague Island, Monga and Clyde River.

Dogs Dogs are permitted to run free on some beaches, while others have limitations or total bans on dogs, as do national parks.

SHOPPING

Woolworths has supermarkets in Batemans Bay, Moruya and Narooma. Moruya's shops are quite extensive and tucked off the main street. Bermagui has a small shopping strip overlooking a park and the bay, and Dalmeny has a very compact shopping square. Tilba Tilba has craft and gift stores as well as a winery.

DINING

There's a range of restaurants to choose from in Batemans Bay, Moruya and Narooma, from fine dining to cafés. Bodalla has an excellent restaurant.

SOCIAL ACTIVITY

There are three great golf courses: Batemans Bay has a championship 27-hole golf course; the Narooma Golf Club has arguably the most stunning views from any course in Australia, perched on the cliff top overlooking Montague Island; and there's a course at Moruya. There are tennis courts and a lawn bowls club at Dalmeny and Bermagui. Fishing is very popular in the region, with a choice of deep-sea fishing via charter boat or estuary fishing. There are many bushwalking opportunities including a club at Batemans Bay. A regional TAFE campus is located at Moruya.

The region has a full calendar of events, including the Festival of the Sea, Great Southern Blues and Rock Music Festival, Moruya Jazz Festival, Tollgate Island Fishing Classic, Eurobodalla District Show and Batemans Bay Blues Music Club.
• All community organisations • All religions • Bushwalking
• Fishing • Golf • Lawn bowls • Surfing • Swimming • Tennis

REAL ESTATE

• Median house price: $338 000
• Median unit price: $270 000

In areas away from Batemans Bay the median house price is a little lower at $280 000, with units at $230 000.

WHY LIVE HERE?

The area is ideal for retirees, especially from Canberra, who want an affordable coastal change with all the trimmings.

sapphire coast
Affordable sea change but a little too remote

The Sapphire Coast in south-eastern New South Wales extends from Bermagui in the north, through the Bega Valley to Eden on the Victorian border. A lot of Melbourne folk are attracted here and a local told me it is their equivalent of the Gold Coast. This is a long stretch of coastline and some parts are fairly isolated.

The commercial centre is the typical country town of Bega, surrounded by rolling hills; this is where the Bega Valley Shire is located. Bega is well known for its dairy products, especially Bega cheese. Bega itself is not a magnet for retirees, however; they prefer to live in the coastal resorts of Bermagui, Tathra and Merimbula. If you're looking for something more rural, the village of Cobargo might be perfect, and if you want beach as well as farm there's Pambula.

Although small, Bermagui has a high proportion of over-sixties. It sits right on the bay and has a protected marina, fisherman's co-op, shops and a spacious park between the main street and the beach, with an appealing restaurant built over the water. Tathra is breathtaking, partly perched high on the hill with 270-degree views of the ocean from the pub with the best view in the country, as well as from many of the homes. Merimbula is a large town with quite a buzz; it's where things happen and it attracts many retirees. Pambula has interesting shops and galleries slightly inland as well as beachside residences. Eden is more remote with rugged beauty and overlooking historic Twofold Bay. The sport followed here is AFL not League as the border is only a few miles away. Eden is a working town, with a large fishing and logging industry, and it has fewer retirees. It used to be a depot for fuel shipments but that has closed, as has its cannery; the locals say they are a forgotten community. As in most coastal retreats, tourism is important in Eden and there is an unusual Killer Whale Museum which tells the truly amazing story of the town's whaling past.

POPULATION

Bega Valley LGA
- 31 500 Est. June 2003
- 23.8% over sixty

Tathra
- 1650
- 25% over sixty

Eden
- 3157
- 19.5% over sixty

Bega
- 4383
- 22.3% over sixty

Pambula
- 1840
- 25% over sixty

Merimbula
- 5000
- 39% over sixty

Bermagui
- 1320
- 35.3% over sixty

CLIMATE

Summer 14.5°C to 27°C
Winter 1.4°C to 16.7°C
Sunshine 86 days
Rain 90 days
Rainfall 870 mm

It gets cold down here when the wind blows in from the Snowy. According to one local, they have three-sock days.

LOCATION & GETTING AROUND

From Sydney to Bega is 430 kilometres, which takes almost six hours to drive. From Melbourne to Bega is 640 kilometres, a drive of just over eight hours.

Roads The Princes Highway is the main access road. It is single lane each way except for overtaking sections and fairly busy, but by New South Wales standards the road is in reasonable condition. The coastal alternative route from Tilba to Eden is fairly fast and picturesque.

Nearest airport Merimbula, with daily services to Sydney and Melbourne

Nearest train Not very satisfactory. If you're travelling from Sydney you need to take the XPT train to Canberra then a coach to Bega or Merimbula – it's a long, roundabout journey that takes over nine hours.

Buses Coach from Canberra to Bega takes just over three hours.

Taxis There's no taxi service but a volunteer transport service provides some assistance to the elderly.

INFRASTRUCTURE

Hospitals Bega has a district hospital open 24 hours providing accident and emergency, maternity, medical, surgical and diagnostic services including pathology, X-ray and microbiology. Pambula has a district hospital just seven kilometres from Merimbula. There are various other health services in Bega.

Retirement villages Merimbula

Police stations Bega, Tathra, Merimbula, Bermagui and Eden

Local newspapers *Bega District News*, *South East Town & Country Magazine*, *Eden Imlay Magnet* and *Merimbula News Weekly*

RECREATION

Beaches Lifeguards patrol seven beaches between Bermagui and Eden, from Boxing Day to Australia Day. Horse Shoe Bay at Merimbula is considered one of the safest beaches in the area. Aslings Beach in Eden is a good place to escape the crowds and Short Beach at Merimbula is a good vantage point for whale watching.

Coastguard ✓

Cycleways Tathra leads the way, with a well-patronised concrete trail running into town.

Bushwalking & National Parks There are nine national parks in the vicinity, abundant with animal and bird life, rainforest and old-growth forests.

Dogs Dogs are permitted to run free on some of the beaches.

SHOPPING

There are Woolworths supermarkets in Bega, Moruya and Merimbula, and a Coles supermarket in Bega. IGA also has supermarkets throughout the district. Pambula holds markets every month.

DINING

Merimbula has a range of good restaurants as well as casual dining, and Eden has an oyster bar and surprisingly good pub fare. As the waiter said to me, 'You will never eat fresher oysters because I just shucked them.'

SOCIAL ACTIVITY

This area is renowned for its fishing – game, deep-sea, reef, rock and beach – and diving is also very popular. Golfers can play a round in Bega, Pambula-Merimbula (27-hole course), Tathra, Tura Beach and Eden, and there are swimming pools at Bega, Cobargo, Merimbula and Eden. Plenty of social clubs meet in the area, and some of the more unusual pastimes covered are spinning and weaving, woodcraft and heritage motoring. Other clubs and associations include amateur theatre, cameras, potting, dance and music. Merimbula has a bowling alley and Bega has its own band and a small art gallery. A number of artists live in the hinterland and there are numerous art galleries and craft shops, especially in Cobargo.

• All community organisations • All religions • Arts & crafts
• Dancing • Diving • Fishing • Galleries • Golf • Horse riding
• Libraries • Museums • Swimming • Theatre

REAL ESTATE

Bega
• Median house price: $229 000
• Median unit price: $174 500
Merimbula
• Median house price: $390 000
• Median unit price: $243 000

Eden
- Houses: $283 000
- Units: $210 000

WHY LIVE HERE?

Tathra and Merimbula are my picks for retirement. If it is solitude and beautiful scenery that you are after, then Tathra could
be perfect; after all, Bega is only twenty minutes away for that
big weekly shop. Merimbula has all the facilities you need in one
place and much more to offer in terms of social life. If you want
to pursue craft and maybe run a small farm, Cobargo or Pambula
would be worth looking into.

tamworth
Guitars and stetson hats

Approximately four hours from the coast, the Peel River city of Tamworth is
on the New England Highway, with road links to the Gold Coast, Melbourne,
Port Macquarie, Adelaide and Sydney. Tamworth is widely recognised as the
'Country Music Capital of Australia' so it won't be a surprise to hear that it
has a Regional Conservatorium of Music. The city has beautifully landscaped
parks and gardens, and numerous outdoor cafés and paved walkways shaded
by palm trees. This is a country centre with major appeal, and it's also at the
heart of a popular gemstone-fossicking region.

POPULATION

Tamworth LGA
- 37 000 Est. June 2003
- 17.6% over sixty

CLIMATE

Summer 17.1°C to 31.9°C
Winter 2.9°C to 15.5°C
Sunshine 134 days

Rain 82 days
Rainfall 673 mm

LOCATION & GETTING AROUND

Tamworth is 415 kilometres from Sydney, a driving time of 5.5 hours; it's 570 kilometres from Brisbane, which takes just under seven hours.
Roads Tamworth is at the intersection of the New England and Oxley Highways. Local traffic is light
Nearest airport Tamworth, with regular flights to Sydney and Brisbane
Nearest train Tamworth; the Armidale XPT from Sydney takes just over six hours
Buses ✓
Taxis ✓

INFRASTRUCTURE

Hospitals Tamworth Base Hospital and Tamara Private Hospital. Tamworth is the major health centre for the New England region.
Retirement villages Five in the area
Police stations Tamworth
Local newspapers *Northern Daily Leader* and *Tamworth Times*

RECREATION

Cycleways There's a network of cycleways through the urban area and along the Peel River foreshore
Bushwalking & National Parks The Kamilaroi Walking Trail is close to Tamworth, starting at the Oxley Scenic Lookout. The Warrabah National Park is 80 kilometres from Tamworth on the upper Namoi River for bushwalking, canoeing, fishing and swimming. The Ponderosa Park and Nundle State Forest Drive have established walking trails, barbeques and camping. The Sheba Dams Reserve has similar facilities and is also popular for swimming and fishing.

SHOPPING

There is a good range of shopping in Tamworth, with all the major national retailers represented. Supermarkets include Bi-Lo, Coles, IGA and Woolworths. Monthly craft and produce markets are held and there are many antique and craft shops in the area.

DINING

Tamworth has a large range of cafés and some award-winning restaurants; Peel Street in particular has many outdoor cafés. Cuisines include Modern Australian, international and vegetarian.

SOCIAL ACTIVITY

In addition to the Regional Conservatorium of Music and Regional Craft Centre, there's also a musical society, dramatic society and eisteddfod, new art gallery and library. There is also a cinema complex and entertainment centre – this is where the Country Music Festival is held. There is trout fishing at Nundle and Hanging Rock, and waterskiing at Chaffey Dam, Split Rock and Keepit Dam.

- All community organisations • All religions • Arts & crafts
- Cinema • Fishing • Gallery • Golf • Horse racing
- Lawn bowls • Library • Waterskiing

REAL ESTATE

- Median house price: $218 000
- Median unit price: $170 000

WHY LIVE HERE?

For high-quality health-care services, friendly locals and a large range of hobbies and interests – and not forgetting the great entertainment, although it helps if you like country music.

mudgee
Sea change without the sea

Mudgee is a backwater below the Great Dividing Range, on the road to nowhere but itself. Its remoteness is the attraction: there's no passing parade of people and perhaps for this reason it is a happy town, without pretence. The streets of Mudgee are spacious and much of the architecture is appealing, notably the beautiful churches, train station and clock tower. The stately mansions in the vicinity now tend to be used as B&Bs. Local arts and crafts and produce are evident everywhere you look; ceramics are particularly popular as a number of professional potters live here and the now-defunct train station has been converted into a gallery presenting local wares. Trains occasionally visit on specially chartered trips.

The town is surrounded by undulating volcanic hills, lush vineyards and forests. Henry Lawson spent a significant part of his life here. The agriculture is diverse, including lavender farms, alpacas, sheep, beef cattle, vineyards and honey. Mudgee means 'nest in the hills', although Mudgee itself is flat. The historical impetus for its growth was the discovery of gold, and to this day people still enjoy fossicking in the area.

POPULATION

Mudgee Shire
- 18 500 Est. June 2003
- 18.9% over sixty

The township of Mudgee added 424 between censuses to bring its population to 8620.

CLIMATE

Summer 15.5°C to 31°C
Winter 1.3°C to 14.4°C
Sunshine 113 days
Rain 81 days
Rainfall 675.4 mm

LOCATION & GETTING AROUND

Mudgee is 270 kilometres north-west of Sydney, which is approximately four hours by car.

Roads Mudgee's roads are wide and typical of a proud country town. The surrounding roads are single lane but in good repair and relatively quiet.

Nearest airport Mudgee; flights to Sydney are just under an hour and run every weekday.

Nearest train CityRail from Sydney to Lithgow then coach to Mudgee takes approximately 5.5 hours.

Buses National coach services only

Taxis ✓

INFRASTRUCTURE

Hospitals Mudgee District Hospital; there's also a Community Health Centre.

Retirement villages Mudgee

Police stations Mudgee and Gulgong

Local newspaper *Mudgee Guardian*

RECREATION

Cycling There are plenty of opportunities to cycle as the roads are flat and relatively quiet.

SHOPPING

Mudgee's attractive veranda-shaded streets are lined with shops and cafés. Supermarkets include Bi-Lo, Southside Mini Market, Woolworths, Go-Lo, Target Country and general stores. Monthly community markets feature local produce, arts and crafts and second-hand goods.

DINING

Food is an important part of life in Mudgee, although dining opportunities are not gourmet, and of course Mudgee wines are featured. Some vineyards have their own restaurants, but vineyard dining hasn't been exploited to the extent that it has in other wine-producing areas.

SOCIAL ACTIVITY

Mudgee has many craft groups and a number of clubs. There are libraries in Mudgee and Gulgong, plus a mobile service. Over twenty-five wineries have cellar doors, and other activities include bushwalking, gold fossicking, horse riding and punting at the race track. Windemere Dam, only 24 kilometres from Mudgee, is popular for fishing, sailing, swimming and canoeing. The area is also known for its arts and crafts, and there are a number of antique shops and galleries selling pottery, woodwork and paintings. Festivals include the Wine Celebration, Henry Lawson Festival, Music Festival, Mudgee Cup Race Meeting, Gulgong Folk Festival and Farm Field Days.

- Arts & crafts • Bushwalking • Fishing • Galleries • Golf
- Horse racing • Horse riding • Lawn bowls • Libraries
- Most community organisations • Most religions • Sailing
- Swimming

REAL ESTATE

- Median house price: $250 000
- Median unit price: $265 000

Homes on a small acreage sell from $300 000.

WHY LIVE HERE?

Mudgee is a relaxed, sociable place where it would be easy to drop out of the rat race. If you are the sort of person who could happily take up a hobby (from raising alpacas to knitting jumpers from alpaca wool), then this could be for you. It would be a distinct advantage if you enjoy open fires, as it does get quite cold in winter.

blue mountains
Mountain valleys and beautiful gardens

The Blue Mountains take you back in time, with plenty of opportunities to sit in front of a log fire and enjoy the spectacular scenery. It seems there are breath-taking views everywhere you look: cliffs dropping vertically into deep valleys, tumbling waterfalls and spectacular rock formations. Much of the architecture in the area is from yesteryear, and it's a gardener's paradise, especially if you like rhododendrons, azaleas and other cold-climate plants. Nearby Mount Wilson has its own unique flora.

The proportion of over-sixties in the Blue Mountains is highest in Blackheath, Wentworth Falls, Leura and, to a lesser extent, Katoomba, which is the largest town in the mountains. The main street of Leura is like a film set from the 1930s, and is very popular with tourists who frequent the town's antique shops and cosy cafés. Mount Victoria, a charming village with a number of historic buildings, is the most westerly township in the Blue Mountains.

For many people, the main attraction of the Blue Mountains is bushwalk-ing, from easy half-day walks to serious hiking and overnight camping and mountaineering.

POPULATION

Blue Mountains LGA
- 77 500 Est. June 2003
- 16.9% over sixty

In Wentworth Falls almost one in every four residents is aged over sixty, and in Blackheath the percentage is only slightly lower. The total population of the region from Katoomba to Wentworth Falls is 18 400, up by 700 between censuses.

CLIMATE

Summer 12.6°C to 23.1°C
Winter 2.5°C to 9.2°C
Sunshine 69 days
Rain 131 days

Rainfall 1402 mm

You should expect some snowfalls in winter.

LOCATION & GETTING AROUND

Sydney to Blackheath is 115 kilometres, approximately a two-hour drive.

Roads The local roads are well surfaced but narrow and winding, typical of mountain access routes. If travelling from Sydney, there are motorway conditions to Glenbrook at the foot of the mountains.

Nearest airport Sydney Airport is 120 kilometres away, a travelling time of just over two hours.

Nearest train Regular Sydney CityRail services connect all the towns in the Blue Mountains. Travel time from Blackheath to Sydney is approximately two hours and 15 minutes.

Buses ✓

Taxis ✓

INFRASTRUCTURE

Hospitals Blue Mountains District ANZAC Memorial Hospital at Katoomba and Boddington Red Cross and Queen Victoria Memorial hospitals at Wentworth Falls. A health centre is also located in Katoomba.

Retirement villages One in Katoomba and two in Leura. There are several retirement villages closer to Sydney in Springwood and Glenbrook.

Police stations Blackheath, Katoomba and Mount Victoria

Local newspaper *Blue Mountains Gazette*

RECREATION

Cycleways It's a wee bit hilly and dangerous on the highway. Cycling needs to be localised, for instance in the Megalong Valley or the backstreets of Blackheath.

Bushwalking & National Parks The Blue Mountains National Park has finally become a listed World Heritage area, and the

Grose and Megalong Valleys in particular are spectacular. The Blue Gum Forest is the largest stand of blue gums in the world. It's on the 'must see and hug before you die' list.

Dogs Off-leash areas are not easy to find. Katoomba, Leura and Blackheath all have one but they tend to be somewhat obscure; for example, the old airstrip in Blackheath.

SHOPPING

Katoomba's shopping centre is the bread basket of the mountains with a large Coles supermarket and other shops; surprisingly, given the climate, there are no undercover shopping malls. Blackheath and Leura retain a village atmosphere.

DINING

There are a number of fine restaurants in Blackheath, Leura, Katoomba and Mount Victoria. Some of the area's upmarket hotels and guesthouses also offer fine dining, typically traditional French cuisine, enjoyed in a cosy atmosphere warmed by log fires. Tea houses serving Devonshire teas are also common.

SOCIAL ACTIVITY

One of the main activities in this part of the world is bushwalking, with paths leading to spectacular waterfalls, magnificent views and an opportunity to see a large array of bird life. The Fairfax Heritage Track has wheelchair access and is also suitable for people with poor vision. For the fit and adventurous there are strenuous treks into places such as the Blue Gum Forest, the Grose Valley and the Giant Staircase. There are golf courses with spectacular views and Katoomba has an aquatic centre with heated indoor and outdoor pools.

For less strenuous activities there are six branches of the Blue Mountains Library, the Blackheath Art Society holds exhibitions and workshops, and there are a number of museums to visit. The Railway Station Museum at Mount Victoria details the area's history and the gallery at Blackheath exhibits fine art and drawings.

The Blue Mountains is well known for its antiques and public and private gardens, which are open for inspection at various times of the year. Spring and autumn are special times in the mountains, and the annual Rhododendron Festival in spring is a major drawcard.

The University of the Third Age runs over sixty courses for retired people, including, art, ceramics, law, computers and music.

• All community organisations • All religions • Aquatic centre
• Bushwalking • Galleries • Golf • Lawn bowls • Libraries
• Museums • University of the Third Age

REAL ESTATE

Katoomba, Leura and Medlow Bath
• Median house price: $333 000
• Median unit price: $270 000
Blackheath
• Median house price: $321 000
Mount Victoria
• Median house price: $301 000
This is still a relatively affordable area even though it is close to Sydney.

WHY LIVE HERE?

Because you like gardening, sitting in front of log fires and dressing up in coats and scarves. Add to that, you like to read, write or paint and go for long walks in the forest. There could be a little corner of the Blue Mountains waiting just for you. I always think of the mountains as somewhere you go to recuperate, and the Blue Mountains are the perfect place to recover from forty years in the rat race.

southern highlands
An English climate within easy reach of Sydney

The attraction here, for some at least, is the cold weather. The brisk climate has encouraged residents to create English cottage gardens, replicate English housing estates and hold annual flower festivals. However, the presence of the Australian bush proves we're in the southern hemisphere, and the huge gum trees and deciduous imports happily coexist.

The Southern Highlands is a very popular area for retirement, as well as for holiday homes and hobby farms. On weekends Sydneysiders visit the art galleries and various festivals in the area, which is more elevated than Sydney (parts of it to around 600 metres), and so gets very cold and is sometimes covered in snow. Fogs are common, often nightly at certain times of year, and driving can be hazardous.

There are many towns in the shire, some with large shopping strips such as Mittagong, Bowral and Moss Vale. Others are more intimate with small shopping strips such as Berrima, Bundanoon and Robertson; towns such as Burrawang and Exeter have little more than a general store. Minor roads criss-cross the shire so nowhere is too far away.

POPULATION

Southern Highlands
- **44 000** Est. June 2003

Bowral
- **10 400**
- 27.5% over sixty

Bundanoon has almost 28 per cent over-sixties (over 500 in number). In total, Berrima, Moss Vale and Kangaroo Valley have a similar number of over-sixties to Bowral.

CLIMATE

Summer 12.2°C to 26.6°C
Winter 1°C to 11.9°C
Sunshine 90 days
Rain 115 days

Rainfall 945.8 mm

For much of the year it is very cold here, and in winter the temperature often falls to freezing. It snows occasionally and frosts are common.

LOCATION & GETTING AROUND

It's a 1.5-hour drive from Sydney to Bowral (120 kilometres). The dual-carriage tollway is excellent as it offers a run free of any traffic lights from Sydney to Mittagong. No other freeway from Sydney offers such a slick egress.

Roads Roads are in reasonable to good condition, although some are fairly narrow. However, traffic off the freeway is relatively light and it's generally easy to travel around the area.

Nearest airports Sydney and Wollongong

Nearest train Mittagong, Bowral, Exeter, Moss Vale, Burradoo and Bundanoon are connected by CityRail to Sydney, with a one- to two-hour schedule depending on the time of day. There is also a twice-daily CityRail bus service to and from Wollongong.

Buses Berrima Buslines runs a limited service within Bowral, Mittagong and Moss Vale.

Taxis ✓

INFRASTRUCTURE

Hospitals Bowral Hospital and Southern Highlands Private Hospital, plus numerous health-care groups for older citizens.

Retirement villages There are a number in Bowral and one in Bundanoon.

Police stations Bowral, Mittagong, Moss Vale, Bundanoon, Robertson and Kangaroo Valley

Local newspaper *Southern Highland News*

RECREATION

Cycleways There are hills, but a lot of the area is flat and cyclists have plenty of opportunities to enjoy interesting trips. The Bowral Bike Path is an extensive trail for cyclists and walkers.

Bushwalking & National Parks There's bushwalking at Mount Gibraltar and nearby Fitzroy Falls.

Dogs Dogs are required to be microchipped and on leads.

SHOPPING

Given the cold climate, you would expect that there would be at least one large undercover shopping mall in these parts, but there's only a medium-sized one in Bowral. That doesn't mean that there's a shortage of shops: the major supermarkets are represented and the main streets of Mittagong, Bowral and Moss Vale are lined with retail outlets, including those selling farming equipment and hardware. The old general store in Exeter is a fascinating place to visit, and they also claim to make the best cappuccino in the Southern Highlands – and, who knows, perhaps they do!

DINING

One of the advantages of this cold climate is the choice of restaurants with fine dining and good wine lists. If you don't wish to spend up, a range of bistros offer good food at reasonable prices, and local wines are included on the menus. There aren't a lot of ethnic dining choices beyond Italian and Asian.

SOCIAL ACTIVITY

The Southern Highlands is a cultural centre attracting well-known performers, artists and jazz musicians. It seems there is always something arts-related happening, and if forced indoors by the weather one can always while away the hours in the art galleries or at the Berkelouw Book Barn. Libraries are located in Bowral, Mittagong and Moss Vale. There are loads of associations, including bridge clubs, dancing clubs, music societies and garden clubs, as well as several excellent golf courses.

This area is home to a relatively high number of professional people, often referred to as 'Pitt Street Farmers', who have established hobby farms here. The four definite seasons provide plenty of opportunities for locals to dress up in their fashionable R. M. Williams gear.

• All community organisations • All religions • Dancing
• Galleries • Golf • Horse riding • Lawn bowls • Libraries

REAL ESTATE

Bowral

• Median house price: $540 000
• Median unit price: $445 000

These figures are well above the average for country New South Wales but the range of real estate is extensive. There are cheaper areas such as New Berrima and parts of Mittagong and Moss Vale where small homes start at $250 000. Modest homes in Bowral are usually over $400 000, but homes with street appeal and established gardens will cost a lot more. Outlying areas such as Bundanoon, Exeter and Robertson are worth exploring and all three have local shopping facilities. Acreage is the other alternative and property sizes range from one to 100 hectares with prices up to several million dollars.

Here is a tip: I have spoken to many people who have bought in the Southern Highlands and their advice is to rent in the area while looking because it will take weeks to familiarise yourself with the localities and to compare values. I was surprised at the number of properties for sale and the variation in prices, even within the same area. Understanding the real estate market here will take time and you will certainly need to do your homework more carefully than in other areas. Fortunately, there are virtually no auctions so at least you know what the vendors are wanting.

WHY LIVE HERE?

Picture an open fire, a glass of red wine, the sound of classical music and the smell of roast lamb from the oven. Outside your window there are fields of spring daffodils or autumn colours and in the nearby bushland grey kangaroos are grazing and birds chattering. Cosy pubs and restaurants are just around the corner. This is the

Southern Highlands. Does it get any better than this? According to a local part-time librarian it doesn't: 'I can't stand the heat and I don't like the beach. I like reading. Here is perfect.'

I like the idea of being a part-time cocky, and it's only an hour and a half from Sydney. Five hectares would do, and I would grow the flowers, fruits and veggies I can't grow in Sydney – but then I might find I have a full-time job again!

new south wales' top 10

1. **BEST RETIREMENT HOTSPOT: Byron Bay**
   Excellent climate, beaches, nature reserves, shopping and dining, plus the many small surrounding villages offer rural, coastal or village lifestyles.

2. **BEST RETIREMENT LIFESTYLE: Sydney – Northern Beaches**
   Good food, shopping, beaches, facilities and nature reserves, and close to Sydney's art and culture.

3. **BEST SMALL LOCATION: Jervis Bay**
   Peaceful and affordable, with a pristine natural environment on a wonderful bay.

4. **BEST LARGE LOCATION: Coffs Harbour**
   Good infrastructure, lots of fresh air, beaches and easy access to Sydney.

5. **BEST SHOPPING: Sydney**

6. **BEST DINING: Sydney**

7. **BEST PLACE TO CURL UP WITH A GOOD BOOK: Southern Highlands**

8. **BEST BEACHES: Manly, Byron Bay**

9. **BEST OUTDOOR ACTIVITIES: Blue Mountains**
   For bushwalking, climbing, abseiling, golf and gardening.

10. **BEST-VALUE REAL ESTATE: Grafton**

victoria

Mallacoota 199

Lakes Entrance 201

Inverloch 205

Phillip Island 208

Mornington Peninsula 210

Melbourne 216

  By the Bay 216

  Toorak 219

Bellarine Peninsula/Queenscliff 221

Apollo Bay/Lorne 225

Colac & District 228

Hepburn Springs/Daylesford 230

Wangaratta to Yarrawonga 234

Horsham 237

Mildura 239

Victoria's Top 10 243

Opposite: The ever-popular Boathouse Café on Lake Daylesford

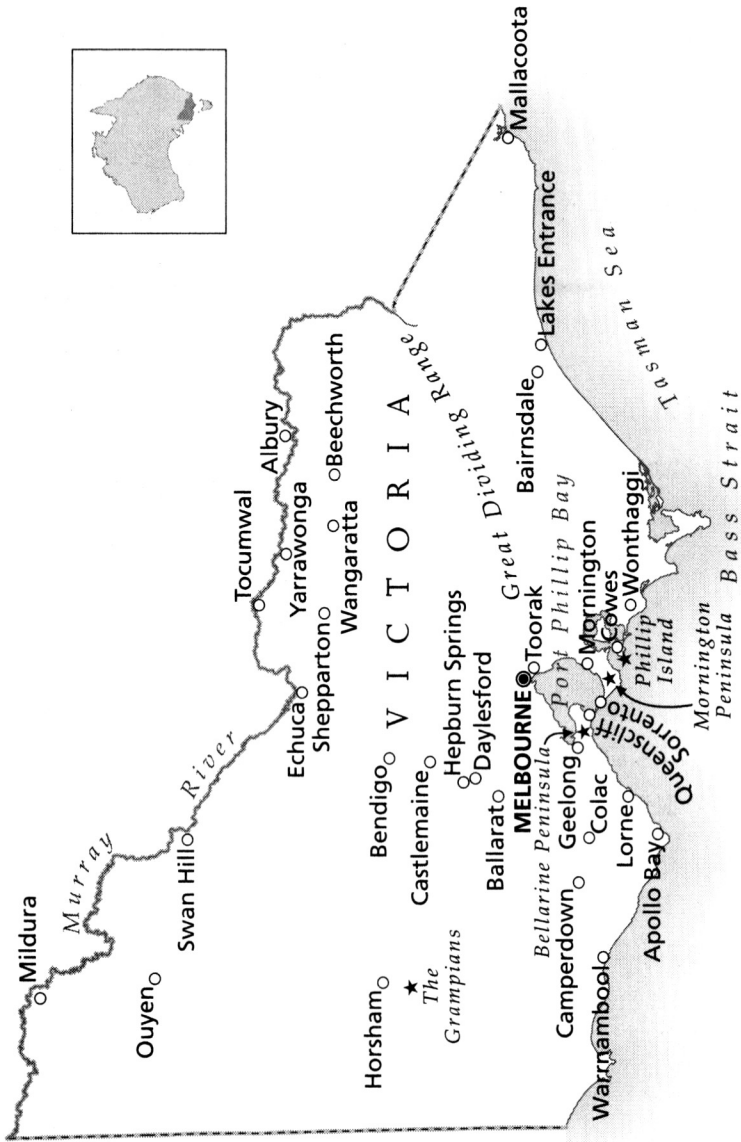

mallacoota

Get lost!

Mallacoota is a cosy community 200 kilometres north-east of Lakes Entrance and 85 kilometres south of Eden. This is as about as remote as it gets, for Mallacoota has no near neighbours. The town is on an inlet, separated from the Tasman Sea by sand dunes and small grassy islands that are home to numerous waterbirds.

The town has an older population and is growing in numbers, although the total population only broke through the thousand mark at the last census. Whoever designed the road system around here had a sense of humour: I have never seen such a confusing set of intersections in such a tiny area. The small shopping centre is well laid out though, with a car park in the middle of a tree-lined one-way street. A caravan park overlooks the inlet, as do some of the town's modest houses. Dirt roads branch off to log cabins and other secluded areas, and Mallacoota is surrounded by bush and water.

POPULATION

- 1150
- 26% over sixty

CLIMATE

Summer 16.2°C to 21.5°C
Winter 8.2°C to 14°C
Sunshine 59 days
Rain 145 days
Rainfall 949 mm
The cold wind blows off the Snowy and even summer maximums are a little cool for sunbaking.

LOCATION & GETTING AROUND

From Melbourne to Mallacoota is 510 kilometres, a drive of 6.5 hours. This is as far east from Melbourne as you can go and still be in the same state. From Canberra it is 360 kilometres, which takes 4.5 hours to drive.

Roads The 20-kilometre road into Mallacoota off the Princes Highway is narrow and winding.

Nearest airport The small local airport has air ambulance facilities

Nearest train ✗

Buses ✗

Taxis ✗

INFRASTRUCTURE

Hospitals There is an ambulance, medical clinic and doctor.

Retirement villages ✗

Police station Mallacoota

Television stations Satellite only

Radio Satellite only

Local newspaper ✗

Communications No Internet access or mobile phone reception

RECREATION

Beaches Surfing is good at Bastion Point Beach, which is patrolled in season. Another nearby beach is Betka Beach where the river enters the ocean.

Coastguard ✓

Cycleways There are plenty of opportunities to cycle as the roads are quiet and flat and there are also some bush trails for mountain biking.

Bushwalking & National Parks Mallacoota is surrounded by the Croajingolong National Park

Dogs No restraints.

SHOPPING

There's a Food Works supermarket plus several small stores.

DINING

The hotel has a bistro, as does the golf club, and there are several restaurants and cafés in town.

SOCIAL ACTIVITY

• Boating • Bushwalking • Cycling • Fishing • Golf
• Lawn bowls • Surfing

REAL ESTATE

• Median house price: $278 000

Prices have been rising rapidly; however, you may still be able to pick up an unassuming three-bedroom house without views for as low as $175 000. There's nothing much to buy, though, so you may have to build, and that could cost a lot of money this far from the nearest big town.

WHY LIVE HERE?

This is an unspoilt part of Australia which would appeal to nature lovers, though many people might find it just a bit too remote.

lakes entrance
Waterway wonder

The resorts of Lakes Entrance and Paynesville are outposts, away from every-thing. To the north there's nothing until Eden on the New South Wales border; coming from the south-west you pass through Bairnsdale, which is the gate-way and provides the infrastructure for the district. As you descend the last stretch, driving from Melbourne, there are spectacular views of lakes and of Ninety Mile Beach. The lakes make up the largest inland waterway system in Australia.

The townships of Lakes Entrance, Paynesville and Metung all have sig-nificant older populations. In fact, Paynesville was listed in the last census as having the thirteenth-highest proportion of over-65s in Australia. Lakes Entrance is geared to tourism, with plenty of shops and even a McDonald's. Not surprisingly, it's on the lake and fishing is one of the area's all-consuming passions and also part of the local industry. The town is low rise and well laid out, with wide streets. Paynesville is on Lake King to the north and Lake Vic-toria to the south. It's a yachting and power-boating enthusiast's Mecca with an extensive system of marinas and boat ramps. A series of canals have been constructed to provide sheltered moorings and lakeside housing for retirees and holiday-makers.

POPULATION

Lakes Entrance	Paynesville	Metung
• 5500	• 2850	• 500
• 35% over sixty	• 40% over sixty	• 36% over sixty

The population of Lakes Entrance swells to over 30 000 in the summer holidays. The lakes district populations as a whole are growing steadily.

CLIMATE

Summer 14.9°C to 23.9°C
Winter 5.9°C to 14.6°C
Sunshine 64 days
Rain 136 days
Rainfall 716 mm

LOCATION & GETTING AROUND

Melbourne to Lakes Entrance is 320 kilometres and a drive of just under four hours. Melbourne to Paynesville is 300 kilometres, a driving time of 3.5 hours.

Roads The roads in Lakes Entrance are wide and the Princes Highway is well maintained in this part of the world.

Nearest airport Bairnsdale, 40 kilometres or a 30-minute drive away

Nearest train V/Line buses have replaced the rail but they continue to use the old train station

Buses Daily V/Line buses from Melbourne. Buses also connect with trains at Sale, which is just over an hour away from Paynesville and one hour and 20 minutes from Lakes Entrance.

Taxis ✓

INFRASTRUCTURE

Hospitals Bairnsdale Regional Hospital has 100 beds, 500 staff and includes an emergency department. Lakes Entrance and Paynesville both have medical clinics.

Retirement villages Bairnsdale has a private nursing home which accommodates 60 residents. Lakes Entrance has an aged-care facility for 46 residents.

Police stations Lakes Entrance and Bairnsdale, and water police at Paynesville

Local newspapers *Bairnsdale Advertiser*, *Lakes Post* and *East Gippsland News*

RECREATION

Beaches Eastern Surf Beach is just a small distance away from Lakes Entrance.

Coastguard ✓

Cycleways There are plenty of cycleways in the area, a large part of which is flat, and also a number around Paynesville

Bushwalking & National Parks There are good walks throughout the area. Close to Lakes Entrance there is a very good walk along Eastern Beach, which is separated from the town by an arm of water. Seven parks are nearby including the Snowy River National Park.

Dogs No strict policy.

SHOPPING

Lakes Entrance has fairly comprehensive shopping with several supermarkets including Woolworths and a large Mitre 10 hardware store. Paynesville has two modest general stores as well as two hotels. Bairnsdale has more comprehensive shopping including supermarkets, clothing shops and hardware stores.

DINING

There are many restaurants, mostly middle-of-the-road, a few specialising in Italian cuisine and of course local seafood. There are only a few coffee shops to choose from but the café fare is pretty ordinary and the cappuccinos did not pass muster! There's no outdoor dining in Lakes Entrance – perhaps because you can feel those winds blowing down from the Snowy.

SOCIAL ACTIVITY

All water-based activities are available here. The excellent golf course which runs alongside the ocean at Lakes Entrance is rated in the top 100 in Australia. There's also a nine-hole course above the town and the Bairnsdale Golf Course is between Bairnsdale and Paynesville. Lakes Entrance has an Aquadome with heated pool, spa, sauna and gym. You'll find cinemas in Lakes Entrance and Bairnsdale (triple screen). This is not an arts and culture area although galleries are scattered here and there. Local associations include music and drama, poetry and painting. Angling, motor boating and yachting clubs are located in Paynesville.

• Aquatic centre • Boating • Cinema • Cricket • Fishing
• Galleries • Golf • Lawn bowls • Most religions • Sailing
• Some community organisations • Squash • Tennis

REAL ESTATE

Lakes Entrance
• Median house price: $224 000
• Median unit price: $260 000
Paynesville
• Median house price: $242 000
The cheaper housing option of relocatable homes can be found in Lakes Entrance. The homes are built in nearby Bairnsdale and then transported to sites where other relocatable homes form small retirement-style villages. They are very neat and cost significantly less than a normal home. However, the owners of these homes do not own the land on which they are located and so they have to pay a small rent for the space.

WHY LIVE HERE?

This is a charming area of waterways and bushwalks, which will suit many retirees who love fishing or boating and prefer a cooler climate with virtually no humidity. I prefer Paynesville as a retirement destination to Lakes Entrance. Both attract many tourists during the summer months, but Paynesville is more secluded and the prettier of the two. One word of warning: mosquitoes can be a problem in this neck of the woods.

inverloch
Windswept rural villages for keen fishing types

The Bass Coast is exposed to the Southern Ocean and it's not always inviting, although the juxtaposition of rolling fields, sea-ravaged coast and windswept foreshore is dramatic. The infrastructure and shopping facilities for the surrounding district are provided by Wonthaggi, a hardy town set slightly inland, which continues to reflect its mining origins. Ten minutes away is the more picturesque village of Inverloch, which is protected from the sea by an inlet providing a safe mooring for the growing number of boats. This is a village in transition as newer homes are appearing with the influx of retirees, who are attracted by the affordable land, the water-based activities and the coastal walks. In fact, it is one of Victoria's fastest-growing areas, as many people have moved here to take advantage of the cheaper real estate.

POPULATION

Bass Coast

- 24 000
- 27% over sixty

Within Wonthaggi and Inverloch more than one in three residents are aged over sixty. Wonthaggi grew slowly between censuses to reach a population of just over 6000; meanwhile, Inverloch grew a massive 50 per cent to 3740 in the same period.

Fifty per cent of the region's housing is not permanently occupied, and when the shire's holiday accommodation is occupied the population almost triples. The Bass Coast population is projected to increase to over 26 000 by 2011 and to around 30 000 by 2021.

CLIMATE

Summer 13.2°C to 24.6°C
Winter 6°C to 13.4°C
Sunshine 39 days
Rain 147 days
Rainfall 938 mm

LOCATION & GETTING AROUND

Inverloch is 150 kilometres from Melbourne, which takes around two hours to drive.

Roads The roads are good, and mostly dual carriageway
Nearest airport Tullamarine (155 kilometres away), taking a little under two hours to drive
Nearest train ✗
Buses Daily V/Line buses travel from Melbourne, taking under three hours
Taxis ✓

INFRASTRUCTURE

Hospitals Wonthaggi and District Hospital
Retirement villages Inverloch
Police stations Wonthaggi and Inverloch
Local newspaper *South Gippsland Sentinel Times*

RECREATION

Beaches There are several beaches close to Wonthaggi, including beautiful Harmer's Haven. Inverloch has clean beaches suitable for swimming and surfing. Cape Paterson is a tranquil beachfront town known for its surf beaches and good fishing.
Coastguard ✓
Cycleways The area has beautiful cycling tracks, including Victoria's only coastal rail trail.

Bushwalking & National Parks There are numerous walks such as the seven-kilometre George Bass Cliff Walk along the coast from San Remo. The 16-kilometre Bass Coast Rail Trail starts at the old Wonthaggi train station and runs to the Anderson train station site at the turn-off to Phillip Island. From Wonthaggi, the first five kilometres of the trail are fully constructed and suitable for cycling, walking and horse riding; the remainder of the trail is fine but cyclists will need to mountain bike. At Inverloch the Screw Creek Nature Walk meanders through bushland for 1.5 kilometres.

Dogs Some areas are restricted but there's generally a positive attitude towards pet owners.

SHOPPING

Wonthaggi has the largest shopping centre in the district, with an extensive range of shops, two large supermarkets and three hotels.

DINING

Dining is pretty casual around here.

SOCIAL ACTIVITY

Boat ramps and facilities are located at Grantville, Corinella and Inverloch.
- Boating • Bushwalking • Croquet • Fishing
- Golf • Horse riding • Lawn bowls • Most religions
- Some community organisations • Surfing • Swimming

REAL ESTATE

- Median house price: $308 000
- Median unit price: $318 000

WHY LIVE HERE?

For those seeking a remote location by the sea which represents value for money and is still within reach of Melbourne.

phillip island
Understated and relatively undiscovered

Connected by bridge to the mainland, and measuring 26 kilometres in length and nine kilometres wide, Phillip Island is a piece of paradise removed from the rest of the world. The island is large enough for locals to go about their business undisturbed by the motor racing and the tourists who flock to see the penguin parade. Most of the island is rural with grazing cattle and hidden villages.

The cost of living is cheaper here, and the pace of life slower. The drive into Cowes takes you through an old arbour of cypress trees to reach a harbour foreshore with inviting picnic areas and shops. Many of the homes are modest, but they enjoy privileged views onto the bay. The sheltered villages of Cowes, Rhyll and Ventnor have lovely beaches but the island also has a wild side with barren headlands pounded by the sea and bracing winds. Other villages on the island which suit retirees are Cape Woolamai, Smith's Beach, Surf Beach and Newhaven.

POPULATION

Cowes	Cape Woolamai	Ventnor	Rhyll	Newhaven
• 3570	• 1000	• 550	• 450	• 400

• 37% over sixty

The over-sixties on Phillip Island totalled some 1700 at the last census.

CLIMATE

Summer 14.1°C to 24.4°C
Winter 7°C to 13.2°C
Sunshine 39 days
Rain 153 days
Rainfall 765 mm
Some parts of the island are affected by strong winds and occasional fogs.

LOCATION & GETTING AROUND

Phillip Island is 135 kilometres from Melbourne, a little under a two-hour drive.

Roads The roads are good, and mostly dual carriageway

Nearest airport Tullamarine, 160 kilometres away, taking a little more than two hours to drive.

Nearest train Stony Point on the mainland, which is reached via passenger ferry from Phillip Island

Buses The daily V/Line bus service from Melbourne to Cowes takes around three hours.

Ferries Stony Point–French Island–Phillip Island

Taxis ✓

INFRASTRUCTURE

Hospitals Wonthaggi and District Hospital. Warley Hospital in Cowes is a 24-bed hospital and 30-bed nursing home. There are medical clinics at Cowes, Newhaven and San Remo.

Retirement villages ✗

Police stations Cowes

Local newspapers Phillip Island and San Remo *Advertiser*

RECREATION

Beaches There are 26 beaches, some protected and some surf. The Esplanade in the centre of Cowes has safe beaches for family swimming.

Coastguard ✓

Cycleways A combination of shared paths and roads allows you to cycle around the island.

Bushwalking & National Parks There are many walks, taking from 15 minutes to two hours. The Rhyll boardwalk winds through mangrove swamp which abounds in bird life and takes approximately one hour.

Dogs Some restricted areas but there's generally a positive attitude towards pet owners.

SHOPPING

Cowes is the retail hub of Phillip Island and has a supermarket, a range of smaller shops, restaurants and cafés. The nearest large shopping centre is Wonthaggi, some 40 kilometres away.

DINING

The restaurants and cafés on the island are mostly casual, and certainly not to the high standard of Melbourne.

SOCIAL ACTIVITY

There are various clubs, including amateur theatre, gardening and art. Cowes has a leisure centre with gym, squash and spa facilities and a picturesque 18-hole golf course.
• Boating • Cinema • Croquet • Fishing • Golf
• Lawn bowls • Leisure centre • Most religions
• Some community organisations • Surfing • Theatre

REAL ESTATE

• Median house price: $259 000
• Median unit price: $227 000

WHY LIVE HERE?

For many retirees, Phillip Island is every bit as appealing as the more popular Mornington Peninsula, but without the expensive price tag.

mornington peninsula
Retirees' playground

The Mornington Peninsula is a special place. Many residents live here part time, coming down from Melbourne and even Sydney to play golf or holiday by the water. There are hills here, which are generally lacking in Melbourne and elsewhere around Port Phillip Bay, and they afford extensive views over the bay and all the way to the Melbourne CBD.

Flanked by water, with Port Phillip Bay on one side, ocean beaches to the south and the more sheltered waters of Western Port to the east, the Mornington Peninsula is often described as Melbourne's playground for well-off retirees. Apple orchards have made way for wineries (there are reputedly over 170 vineyards and fifty cellar doors in the area), golf links, stylish accommodation and sensational gardens.

The Peninsula includes exclusive towns such as Portsea and Sorrento, as well as parts of Mornington and Mount Eliza. There is more modest housing in Dromana, Rosebud, Tootgarook, Rye, Hastings, Tyabb and Balnarring. There are coastal hideaways such as Flinders, a peaceful seaside village with walks and a cliff-top golf course, and inland gems like the hinterland village of Red Hill, which offers sensational views in a rural environment. The calm bay beaches sport colourful bathing boxes and the wild back beaches are popular with surfers. In all, there is an amazing variety of attractive locations comfortably arranged within a relatively small area, with plenty of forested and open areas. Importantly, council has committed to maintain 70 per cent of the Peninsula as rural.

POPULATION

- 137 500 Est. June 2003
- 22.5% over sixty

This is a popular retirement magnet, and it is estimated that the Peninsula's population will continue to age. In Rosebud, Sorrento and Portsea more than one in every three people are aged over sixty.

CLIMATE

Summer 13.9°C to 25°C
Winter 6.5°C to 12.8°C
Sunshine 46 days
Rain 137 days
Rainfall 737 mm
Inland, the temperatures can fall below freezing from June to September.

LOCATION & GETTING AROUND

Mornington is an hour's drive south of Melbourne. Sorrento, towards the tip of the Peninsula, is 110 kilometres from the CBD, taking 1.5 hours to drive along the Nepean Highway or the Mornington Peninsula Freeway. Alternative access is by ferry from Queenscliff.

Roads The Mornington Peninsula Freeway runs almost the entire length of the Peninsula and is a multi-lane dual carriage-way. There are many good secondary roads within the Peninsula, which there needs to be, as the traffic can get heavy.

Nearest airport 125 kilometres to Tullamarine, which takes just under two hours to drive.

Nearest train The Stony Point service is a single-track route via Hastings to Frankston, from where regular suburban services travel to Melbourne.

Buses Buses meet the trains at Frankston and provide regular services along the Peninsula to Portsea.

Ferries Portsea and Sorrento to Queenscliff

Taxis ✓

INFRASTRUCTURE

Hospitals Mornington Peninsula Hospital has its main base at Frankston with 336 beds and another 75 beds at Rosebud. Medical clinics, dental surgeries and five private hospitals are also in the area.

Retirement villages Mornington, Mount Eliza, Mount Martha, Rosebud and Frankston

Police stations Rosebud, Dromana, Frankston, Mornington, Hastings, Rye and Sorrento

Local newspapers *Mornington Peninsula Leader* and *Southern Peninsula Mail*

RECREATION

Beaches There are many beaches to choose from, including sheltered bays at Portsea, Sorrento, McCrae, Safety Beach, Balnarring and Shoreham, and wild surf at Sorrento back beach, St Andrews and Gunnamatta.

Coastguard ✓

Cycleways Cyclists are well served with numerous shared pathways along the bay.

Bushwalking & National Parks The entire back beach from Portsea to Cape Schanck is protected by the Mornington Peninsula National Park. Briars Park in Mount Martha is a wildlife reserve with bushland trails. There are also a number of foreshore boardwalks, including those at Mount Martha, Coolart and Cape Schanck. The Point Nepean walk takes in the old fortifications at Fort Nepean which guards the opening to Port Phillip Bay.

Dogs There are more than 30 leash-free exercise areas for dogs on the Peninsula.

SHOPPING

Mornington has a huge retail neighbourhood, including warehouses such as one of the larger Bunnings hardware stores as well as boutique-style shops. Frankston, Hastings and Rosebud have large but not particularly attractive centres. Sorrento has the most appealing shopping strip, shaded by trees with wide footpaths and many small shops and cafés. Markets are held in a range of locations on the Peninsula every weekend.

DINING

Tourists, food and wine all go together and so there are lots of choices on the Peninsula, from informal cafés to fine dining and award-winning vineyard restaurants.

SOCIAL ACTIVITY

There is plenty to keep you busy on the Peninsula, from wine and food, culture and heritage to gardens and wildlife. It is truly a golfer's paradise, with a dozen outstanding courses, including world championship courses, and links courses overlooking the water. Sailing is popular and there are large yacht clubs at

Mornington, Blairgowrie, Sorrento and Hastings. The gardens are magnificent, particularly Heronswood at Dromana, Seawinds at Arthurs Seat and the Ashcombe and Arthurs Seat mazes. Sorrento and Rosebud have cinemas and Dromana even has a drive-in cinema – there's not too many of those left. There is a race course at Mornington. A Life Activities Club has been formed on the Peninsula for active over-fifty-year-olds, to keep them fit and socially stimulated, and the University of the Third Age is located in Mornington and Dromana. Adult education opportunities are available through TAFE and other local programmes.

- All community organisations • All religions • Arts & crafts
- Boating • Bushwalking • Cinema • Golf • Horse racing
- Horse riding • Lawn bowls • Libraries • Sailing • Surfing
- University of the Third Age • Yachting

REAL ESTATE

Portsea and Sorrento
- Median house price: $1 million

Flinders and Mornington
- Median house price: $543 000

Dromana
- Median house price: $315 000
- Median unit price: $329 000

Rosebud
- Median house price: $250 000
- Median unit price: $241 000

Hastings
- Median house price: $218 000
- Median unit price: $200 000

Prices vary considerably across the Peninsula.

WHY LIVE HERE?

To be so close to the Melbourne CBD and yet so removed is very appealing. There is the opportunity to lead a rural, beach or village lifestyle, and an hour after you pull off your wellies you can be sipping coffee in Melbourne. This is one of my favourite places for retirement near a capital city. Few places come near it, as it has everything you'd need.

Two retired advertising executives I spoke to claimed: 'Our lives revolve around golf and eating, as there are great choices for both here. We have a good view of Melbourne from our property but that's as close as we want to get.'

melbourne

by the bay
Village living within sight of the city

The attraction of living here is the proximity to the bay and the great village atmosphere of suburbs like Brighton, Hampton, Sandringham, Black Rock and Mentone. The homes have character and their gardens are established and leafy. Each of the above suburbs has its own village centre with good opportunities for dining at numerous cafés. Yachties and motor boat enthusiasts are well catered for with marinas and clubs. Walkers and cyclists have an excellent pathway around the shoreline – one advantage of the flat landscape is that it's easier for older folk to get around and there are plenty of them here enjoying the open air and quiet surrounds.

POPULATION

The suburbs by the bay where the over-sixties have a greater than average representation include Brighton, Sandringham, Black Rock and Mentone. The total number of over-sixties living in the Bayside and Kingston LGAs was in excess of 45 000 at June 2003. In neighbouring Glen Eira there were another 25 000 over-sixties. In total, 20 per cent of this population is aged over sixty (one in every five people).

CLIMATE

Summer 14°C to 26°C
Winter 6°C to 13.2°C
Sunshine 34 days
Rain 142 days
Rainfall 705 mm

LOCATION & GETTING AROUND

Sandringham to the Melbourne CBD is 17 kilometres, a drive of around 25 minutes. The Nepean Highway is the major arterial road linking the bay suburbs to the centre of Melbourne. Beach Road from St Kilda is the more scenic route and it has two lanes each way. The railway terminates at Sandringham, connecting with regular bus services to the southern bay suburbs. There are no trams here.

Roads Typical suburban roads

Nearest airport Tullamarine, 38 kilometres and 35 minutes to drive.

Nearest train Brighton, Hampton and Sandringham

Buses ✓

Taxis ✓

INFRASTRUCTURE

Hospitals Sandringham and District Memorial Hospital has 86 beds. There are also several private hospitals and a hospice, as well as rehabilitation centres.

Retirement villages There are a number of retirement villages and aged-care accommodation in Sandringham, Brighton, Hampton and Cheltenham.

Police stations Throughout the area

Local newspaper *Bayside Leader*

RECREATION

Beaches Safe sandy beaches are dotted along the 30 kilometres of coastline

Coastguard ✓

Cycleways No hills! A bike trail runs around the bay

Bushwalking & National Parks There are plenty of parks throughout the Bayside district as well as walks along the coast, including the popular Arts Trail.

Dogs This is a dog-friendly area, with many off-leash areas.

SHOPPING

Hampton Street has trendy shops, galleries, antique shops and eateries as well as Safeway. Sandringham has quite a large shopping area and Middle Brighton has both Coles and Safeway in popular

Church Street, as well as designer-label boutiques and a two-screen cinema. Bay Street in North Brighton has a mix of retail and fashion outlets, cafés and an art-house cinema.

DINING

Church Street in Brighton has a good choice of eateries but the food is good everywhere, with choices from seafood to sushi and international cuisines. Curiously, there are few opportunities to dine overlooking the bay.

SOCIAL ACTIVITY

Bayside offers culture and history plus plenty of outdoor activities with its beaches, boating facilities and sailing clubs. The area is ideal for walking, cycling and beach picnics as there are forty parks and reserves in the area. There are also a number of tennis clubs, including an over-55's club. Famous artists such as Streeton, Condor and Roberts painted on this coast so it is not surprising that Bayside is committed to the arts; the Bayside Arts and Cultural Centre, set in large gardens, is a good example of this commitment and the Bayside Coastal Arts Trail is a 17-kilometre walk celebrating the notable artists who painted the Bayside coast. There are half a dozen excellent golf courses, including Royal Melbourne. Six libraries operate in the area and there are various social groups, including dance, music and arts and crafts.

• All community organisations • All religions • Cycling
• Galleries • Golf • Libraries • Sailing • Swimming • Tennis
• Walking • Yachting

REAL ESTATE

Sandringham
• Median house price: $645 000
• Median unit price: $440 000
Brighton
• Median house price: $950 000
• Median unit price: $477 000

Many of Sandringham's homes have interesting architecture, established gardens and, often, tennis courts. Brighton homes are more expensive and tend to be hidden behind high walls. Black Rock's housing is cheaper at $635 000 and homes in Hampton are also less grand but many of them are appealing Federation-era weatherboards.

Many over-sixties also live nearby in the neighbouring LGA of Glen Eira where properties are cheaper; for instance, the median price for a house in Caulfield is $535 000 and a unit is $335 000.

WHY LIVE HERE?

Village life is highly appealing especially when in view of the CBD yet far enough away to feel a sense of beauty, in both the homes and the environment. There's space and social stimulation here to satisfy most retirees.

toorak

The ritziest village in the country

Toorak is Melbourne's most expensive suburb, yet it doesn't overlook the bay or much of the river. It doesn't have great views of anything, other than of itself, but it does have a great position off busy Toorak Road. Homes are individually designed on large blocks with colourful gardens and the suburb's picturesque parks include historic Victoria Gardens and the unique ecosystem of the Urban Forest. Kooyong Lawn Tennis Club as well as the exclusive Royal South Yarra Tennis Club are close by.

POPULATION

- 12 765
- 23.5% over sixty

Toorak's over-sixties number around 3000, almost one in four of the population.

CLIMATE

Summer 14°C to 26°C
Winter 6°C to 13.2°C
Sunshine 34 days
Rain 142 days
Rainfall 705 mm

LOCATION & GETTING AROUND

It's just a seven-kilometre hop, step and jump into the heart of Melbourne by tram, bus or car.

Roads Toorak Road is busy, with trams and cars competing for space. Off the main roads, the streets are quiet.

Nearest airport Tullamarine is 30 kilometres away, a 40-minute drive outside peak hour.

Nearest train Toorak Station is only four stops from Flinders Street.

Buses Met buses crisscross the area as well as private bus companies.

Trams Toorak Road, running to and from the city.

Taxis ✓

INFRASTRUCTURE

Hospitals The Alfred Hospital is not far away in Prahran and the Cabrini Hospital is in Malvern.

Retirement villages None in Toorak, some in nearby Malvern

Police stations ✗

RECREATION

Cycleways The backstreets are quiet enough for a leisurely cycle

Dogs This is a dog-friendly area with many off-leash areas.

SHOPPING

Toorak village has designer boutiques, delis and cafés. Behind the main road is an off-street parking area accessing a large Safeway supermarket.

DINING

There are many excellent places to dine, both in Toorak Road and in surrounding streets such as Malvern Road and High Street.

SOCIAL ACTIVITY

• Everything

REAL ESTATE

Prices for houses in Toorak range from $900 000 to $10 million. The median price is somewhere around $1.5 million.

WHY LIVE HERE?

Because you can afford to.

bellarine peninsula / queenscliff
More affordable than Portsea

The Bellarine Peninsula is dotted with farms and vineyards, beautiful old cypress trees, quiet country lanes and coastal villages. In many places the water views tend to be a little obscured by dunes and tea-trees. The villages are unpretentious but there are signs of transition as older shacks make way for stylish beach houses.

There are many villages to choose from, each with a relatively small population which only becomes meaningful when you add the whole Bellarine Peninsula and Queenscliff together. They include Barwon Heads (where the TV series *SeaChange* was filmed), Breamlea, Clifton Springs, Connewarre, Curlewis, Drysdale, Indented Head, Leopold, Mannerim, Marcus Hill, Ocean Grove, Wallington, Point Lonsdale and Queenscliff.

St Leonards, Queenscliff and Portarlington are all in the top forty in terms of having the highest proportions of over-65s in urban centres in Australia. In fact, St Leonards has the highest proportion of over-65s of any urban area in Victoria and the fourth highest in Australia.

The largest towns are Queenscliff/Point Lonsdale and Ocean Grove; the latter is growing and modern residential estates are being developed. Queenscliff is made up of old cottages and historic town buildings dating back to the 1860s. Its main street is wide and leads to the car ferry which plies back and forth from the Mornington Peninsula. Bellarine is slightly elevated and has some good views of Port Phillip Bay, although overall the country and views here are not as appealing as from the Mornington Peninsula. Clifton Springs, on the north coast of the peninsula, is home to a large number of retired people and Mannerim is a farming community with a number of homesteads on large acreages. Portarlington is an appealing village with established shops and open parkland running down to the bay and its extensive boating facilities. St Leonards has views over Swan Island towards Port Phillip Heads, as well as across the bay as far as Melbourne.

POPULATION

Over 5000 over-sixties live on the Bellarine Peninsula. In Queenscliff and St Leonards one third of the population is over sixty years of age. The remainder of the Bellarine Peninsula is only slightly younger, with one in four aged over sixty.

CLIMATE

Summer 14.7°C to 22.4°C
Winter 6.7°C to 12.8°C
Sunshine 59 days
Rain 138 days
Rainfall 605 mm
Geelong, 30 kilometres up the road, is several degrees warmer!

LOCATION & GETTING AROUND

Queenscliff is 100 kilometres from Melbourne, a drive of 1.5 hours past the city of Geelong and onwards via the Bellarine Highway. Ferries run to the Mornington Peninsula every day on the hour from 7 a.m. to 6 p.m.

Roads Roads are in reasonable condition on the Bellarine Peninsula

Nearest airports Avalon Airfield is a 45-minute drive (60 kilometres) and it's just under a two-hour drive to Tullamarine Airport (110 kilometres).

Nearest train Tourist service only on the historic Bellarine Railway.

Buses Private coaches run regularly every day, taking 40 minutes from Geelong to Point Lonsdale and Queenscliff.

Ferries Queenscliff to Portsea and Sorrento

Taxis ✓

INFRASTRUCTURE

Hospitals Geelong District Hospital and Mayne Health Private Hospital

Retirement villages None on the Bellarine Peninsula but there are some in Geelong.

Police stations Queenscliff and Portarlington

Local newspaper *Geelong Independent*

RECREATION

Beaches The major surf beaches are patrolled in summer.

Coastguard ✓

Cycleways The Bellarine Rail Trail is a shared trail for cyclists and walkers that stretches 33 kilometres, linking Geelong to Queenscliff. Many of the roads are also safe for cyclists.

Bushwalking & National Parks The Bellarine Rail Trail is suitable for walking, jogging and cycling.

Dogs Dogs are restricted on many beaches in the district for certain months of the year, whether on leash or off leash.

SHOPPING

Geelong is close by for the large shops. Ocean Grove, Portarlington and Queenscliff all have reasonable shopping centres.

DINING

There aren't many dining choices outside of Queenscliff, where there are a number of fine eateries and a sizable café culture. There is a restaurant on the beach at Barwon Heads.

SOCIAL ACTIVITY

The Barwon River offers opportunities for water sports, walking, cycling and fishing. There are several protected boating marinas and golf courses at Point Lonsdale, Portarlington and Curlewis (the latter is arguably the best). There are senior citizens clubs throughout the district, and antique collecting is a popular pastime.

- Boating • Cycling • Fishing • Golf
- Most religions • Some community organisations
- Surfing • Swimming • Walking

REAL ESTATE

Barwon Heads
- Median house price: $368 000

Ocean Grove
- Median house price: $309 000
- Median unit price: $269 000

Queenscliff and Point Lonsdale
- Median house price: $445 000
- Median unit price: $360 000

Indented Head, Portarlington and St Leonards
- Median house price: $268 000
- Median unit price: $195 000

The construction of an 18-hole golf course and residential development of up to 1000 dwellings has been proposed at Point Lonsdale.

WHY LIVE HERE?

The Bellarine Peninsula offers good value for retirees who prefer anonymity to the show of wealth from their neighbours on the Mornington Peninsula (although, of course, it may not remain such a bargain for ever). It suits those who enjoy the natural environment of country, bay or beach without the crowds and are prepared to forgo some facilities.

apollo bay / lorne
The long and winding road

The Great Ocean Road towns of Apollo Bay and Lorne are as picturesque as it gets, and there are high concentrations of over-sixties in both centres. Apollo Bay is protected by a breakwater which shelters an active shipping fleet. Many homes have great water views, and in Lorne the views are even better as the town is elevated and backed by the forests of the Otway Ranges. On the weekends and in summer the area is inundated with tourists. In terms of domestic visitors, the Great Ocean Road is the fifth most popular region in Australia and quite possibly the busiest tourist attraction in Victoria. If you choose to live here, you should expect a lot of company! The area's popularity is good for the local economy but perhaps not so good for those over-sixties who are seeking a quiet lifestyle.

POPULATION

Although in the 2001 census Apollo Bay and Lorne each had a population of under 1500 people, one in every four residents was over sixty.

CLIMATE

Summer 14.6°C to 21.9°C
Winter 7.3°C to 13.1°C
Sunshine 37 days
Rain 167 days
Rainfall 1053 mm
There are often strong winds blowing off the ocean which can make weather conditions quite unpleasant.

LOCATION & GETTING AROUND

Apollo Bay is 190 kilometres from Melbourne, a drive of 2.5 hours; it's a 1.5-hour drive to Geelong. Lorne is 40 kilometres east of Apollo Bay and a little closer to things: two hours from Melbourne and one hour from Geelong.

Roads Good overall, but the Great Ocean Road is narrow and winding and very crowded on weekends and holiday periods.

Nearest airport Colac, one hour's drive from Apollo Bay and 50 minutes from Lorne

Nearest train There are three passenger services daily between Melbourne and Colac.

Buses ✓

Taxis ✓

INFRASTRUCTURE

Hospitals Apollo Bay has a small hospital with nine acute beds and offering hospice care and nursing home care facilities. Lorne has a community hospital. Colac (just under an hour away by car from Lorne) has a hospital with 56 acute beds.

Retirement villages Lorne has a nursing home

Police stations Apollo Bay and Lorne

Local newspaper *Apollo Bay News*

RECREATION

Beaches Main Beach at Apollo Bay is a safe swimming beach which is patrolled during summer. Lorne's golden beach is directly opposite the main street.

Coastguard ✗

Cycleways There are four well-established paths in Lorne taking from 30 minutes to three hours.

Bushwalking & National Parks Bushwalking is very popular with many kilometres of well-marked walking tracks along the beach and in the bush behind Lorne that include waterfalls, rainforest and rivers.

Dogs Beaches have either permanent dog-free areas or time restrictions in place.

SHOPPING

The locals do their major shopping in Colac or Geelong. Apollo Bay has two medium-sized supermarkets and a range of other retail outlets, banking facilities and commercial services. The fishermen's co-op sells lobsters, local fish, oysters and prawns.

Lorne has a range of interesting shops and boutiques, plus an independent supermarket.

DINING

There are many restaurants in Apollo Bay and Lorne, from fine dining to fish and chips, catering for the regular influx of tourists.

SOCIAL ACTIVITY

There are numerous arts and crafts groups in Apollo Bay and Lorne, in particular ceramics and painting. The Apollo Bay Music Festival is held in March with performances held in multiple venues. There's no cinema in Apollo Bay but the local hall improvises during the holiday period. Apollo Bay and Lorne have very picturesque coastal golf courses and lawn bowls clubs. Other than the above, there's not a lot of opportunity for social stimulation – no library and not many community groups. Nearby Colac offers more variety, including regular horse racing.

• Arts & crafts • Golf • Lawn bowls • Most religions

REAL ESTATE

Apollo Bay
• Median house price: $348 000
• Median unit price: $365 000

Lorne
• Median house price: $652 000
• Median unit price: $600 000

It is possible to buy a one-bedroom apartment with good ocean views in Apollo Bay for $320 000 and a two- or three-bedroom apartment without views for $350 000. Even a waterfront property with acreage is under $1 million. The architecture is often new and appealing although there are not a lot of properties available. Lorne is more expensive.

WHY LIVE HERE?

For the spectacular scenery, nearby bushland and fresh sea air.

colac & district

Lush countryside for a lush retirement

Ah, peace and quiet at last. This is an area of picturesque rural hamlets surrounded by lush countryside, and there are a number of lakes in the area for fishing and water sports.

Winchelsea is an attractive rural town on the banks of the beautiful Barwon River, just a thirty-minute drive from Geelong. Camperdown has an avenue of elms, Terang an avenue of English oaks, while Cobden has lush dairy pastures. Colac is bigger, with shopping and other facilities, but it's still unpretentious and appealing. There are high concentrations of over-sixties in all of these towns.

POPULATION

Colac	Camperdown	Terang	Cobden	Winchelsea
• 10 000	• 3000	• 1800	• 1400	• 1100

One in every four residents is aged over sixty in Colac, Camperdown and Winchelsea, and the percentage is even higher in Cobden and Terang.

CLIMATE

Summer 11.4°C to 23.9°C
Winter 4.9°C to 11.4°C
Sunshine 40 days
Rain 204 days
Rainfall 1018 mm

LOCATION & GETTING AROUND

Colac is 150 kilometres south-west of Melbourne, a drive of just under two hours along the Princes Highway. It's 75 kilometres from Geelong, a drive of one hour. Cobden and Terang are 40 minutes or so from Colac and Camperdown is a little closer. The closest town to Melbourne is Winchelsea, 110 kilometres and a drive of 80 minutes.

Roads Roads are good overall. The Princes Highway is well maintained, if not always two lanes each way.

Nearest airports Colac, and Avalon is 100 kilometres away
Nearest train There are three passenger services daily between Melbourne and Colac, Camperdown, Terang and Winchelsea.
Buses ✓
Taxis ✓

INFRASTRUCTURE

Hospitals Colac Hospital has 56 acute beds. Cobden District Health Service has a largish hospital with a 24-hour emergency department.
Retirement villages Two aged-care facilities, Eventide Mercy and Barongarook Gardens
Police stations Colac, Camperdown, Terang, Cobden and Winchelsea
Local newspapers *Cobden Times, Camperdown Chronicle, Colac Herald, Echo, Colac Corangamite Extra* and *Terang Express*

RECREATION

Cycleways There are plenty of opportunities to cycle around here
Bushwalking & National Parks Bushwalking is very popular and there are many choices from the volcanic crater lakes near Camperdown, Lake Terang, Mount Leura and Mount Sugarloaf.
Dogs The area is dog friendly.

SHOPPING

The locals do their major shopping in Colac or Geelong (population 200 000). Murray Street in Colac is the main thoroughfare with hotels, cafés, restaurants, supermarkets (including Safeway) and a major department store as well as Sunday markets.

DINING

There are plenty of casual dining choices.

SOCIAL ACTIVITY

In Colac there are a number of groups associated with the arts as well as community facilities such as the Colac Otway Performing Arts and Cultural Centre (COPACC). From Terang to Colac, there are ample opportunities to play golf. Fishing is not limited to the coast and there is good trout and redfin fishing in Lake Elingamite near Cobden. Horse racing is held regularly in Colac.

• Fishing • Golf • Horse racing • Lawn bowls
• Most community organisations • Most religions • Theatre

REAL ESTATE

Colac
• Median house price: $185 000
• Median unit price: $145 000

WHY LIVE HERE?

These rural areas are peaceful and pretty and not too far from Geelong and Melbourne. One of the best reasons to move here is the proximity to many beautiful attractions such as the Otways and the Great Ocean Road. If you like the country life with reasonable facilities, you could do a lot worse than Colac or one of its satellite towns. I asked one lady why she chose to move here, and she replied: 'It is a very friendly, safe community. We don't lock our doors here.'

hepburn springs / daylesford
Spa country hideaway

This area is like a more intimate version of the Southern Highlands in New South Wales, but with a twist: the natural spa waters. It wasn't always this way. Most of the towns in the region were gold towns, in particular Clunes and Creswick, and they remain steeped in the history of the gold rush. Clunes in particular is frozen in time: small miners' cottages dot the countryside and the shops are original, not even renovated, many of them empty and decaying. It has the appearance of a Wild West ghost town, but it is slowly growing, with more than 1000 residents.

Nowadays, Hepburn Springs and Daylesford are known for their mineral waters and spa facilities. Many tourists go there to 'take the waters' and enjoy spa treatments in the numerous resorts. Creswick, just 30 kilometres west of Daylesford, is a small commercial centre with wide streets and a high proportion of over-sixties. Castlemaine, to the north, is a much larger, historic and culturally active town. All the villages have wonderful old buildings and leafy streets, and a sense of thriving communities. The landscape is attractive, with European trees mingling with wonderful wattles and other Australian natives. For me, the pick of this area is Daylesford: it's a picturesque, hilly town with a main street lined with wonderful old shops and cafés, and attractive homes in the surrounding streets.

POPULATION

Hepburn LGA
- **14 500** Est. June 2003
- **20.6%** over sixty

Castlemaine, 40 kilometres from Daylesford and out of the Hepburn LGA, has an even higher percentage of over-sixties. Its population grew 150 between censuses to 6830.

CLIMATE

Summer 11.9°C to 26.3°C
Winter 2.4°C to 10.3°C
Sunshine 60 days
Rain 149 days
Rainfall 743 mm

In a word, cold! On average there are twenty-seven days a year when the temperature falls below freezing, and sometimes it even snows in spring. Just how do they get out of bed?

LOCATION & GETTING AROUND

Daylesford is 110 kilometres from Melbourne via excellent freeways (four lanes each way near Melbourne). Driving time 1.5 hours. Ballarat is just 45 kilometres further on, taking an extra 30 minutes.

Roads Local roads are mostly in good condition, though they are single lane each way and some of them are a little narrow. Secondary roads are of packed earth, but these see little traffic.
Nearest airport Ballarat, with daily flights to Melbourne
Nearest train Ballan, 30 minutes from Daylesford.
Buses ✗
Taxis ✓

INFRASTRUCTURE

Hospitals There are hospitals in Creswick and Daylesford, and health services in Clunes.
Retirement villages Two in Ballarat
Police stations Clunes, Creswick, Daylesford and Trentham
Local newspaper *Daylesford Advocate*

RECREATION

Cycleways It can be hilly but the roads are suitable for cycling.
Bushwalking & National Parks The area is a bushwalker's paradise. Long walks of up to 30 kilometres pass natural springs, and for the casual walker there are easy walks around picturesque Daylesford Lake. The Tipperary Track is also popular.
Dogs Dog friendly, and there are plenty of trails to walk the dogs, which is a popular pastime for the locals.

SHOPPING

For major shopping Ballarat is only a short drive away. Daylesford has a substantial strip including a large Coles and Liquorland. Creswick and Castlemaine are also well served. Sunday markets are held in Trentham.

DINING

There are some particularly fine restaurants in the area, some with award-winning chefs. I can recommend the upmarket Mercato, Lake House and the evergreen Boathouse Café, all in Daylesford.

SOCIAL ACTIVITY

This area is home to many artists and craftspeople, and Castlemaine has a particularly good art gallery. Castlemaine also has a quirky old cinema and there's a multiplex in Ballarat. There are three golf courses: Hepburn Springs (with big grey kangaroos as spectators), Trentham and Creswick. Outdoor swimming pools can be found in Daylesford, Trentham and Clunes, but they're only open from December to March. Spas and massages are a speciality of Hepburn Springs and Daylesford. For a lot of the year the locals seem to pass much of the time reading or watching telly by the fire, with a brief walk with the dogs to stretch the legs.

• Arts & crafts • Bushwalking • Cinema • Galleries • Golf
• Some community organisations • Some religions

REAL ESTATE

Hepburn Springs
• Median house price: $206 000
Daylesford
• Median house price: $240 000
Trentham
• Median house price: $222 000

A miner's cottage in Clunes could be a lot cheaper still. There are a lot of properties for sale and some places stay on the market for quite a long time before being sold. Homes on acreage are available for $200 000.

WHY LIVE HERE?

For the intimacy of village life, the cold climate, low cost of living, alternative lifestyles, long bushwalks and attractive scenery.

wangaratta to yarrawonga
Rowing down the river of content

The sprinkling of towns on the border of central Victoria and New South Wales are home to high proportions of over-sixties, and unlike much of rural Australia these towns are growing. They include Wangaratta, Yarrawonga, Tocumwal, Barham, Numurkah, Corowa, Rochester, Tongala, Cobram, Euroa and Benalla.

This region has spectacular scenery and is well known for its wine and gourmet food. It is also a gateway to Victoria's ski fields and numerous national parks. The area's largest urban centre is Wangaratta. Elsewhere, the Murray, Ovens and King Rivers wind through townships that dot the valleys and plains, and there are also large lakes in the area, such as Lake Mokoan.

Yarrawonga and twin town Mulwala are on pretty Lake Mulwala on the border of New South Wales, with pelicans and paddle-steamers as added attractions. Cobram is a likeable town on the Murray River, with unexpectedly sandy beaches. The architecture is reminiscent of Drysdale's paintings, with posted verandas jutting over the town's footpaths. Tiny Tocumwal is on the New South Wales side of the Murray River.

POPULATION

Wangaratta
- 18 000
- 22% over sixty

Yarrawonga and Mulwala
- 5500
- 34% over sixty

Cobram
- 5000
- 25% over sixty

Over-sixties represent 20 to 35 per cent of the various towns' populations, and all the towns grew between censuses. Other towns in the area such as Shepparton, Echuca and Albury have a younger profile.

CLIMATE

Summer 16.9°C to 31°C
Winter 3.9°C to 13.4°C
Sunshine 115 days
Rain 82 days
Rainfall 516 mm

LOCATION & GETTING AROUND

Wangaratta is 235 kilometres north-east of Melbourne, a drive of 2.5 hours; it's 650 kilometres south of Sydney. Yarrawonga is another 30 kilometres further from Melbourne.

Roads Roads are in good condition and unhurried

Nearest airports Yarrawonga, Albury, Corowa, Shepparton and Tocumwal

Nearest train A regular service runs between Wangaratta and Melbourne's Spencer Street Station, taking 2.5 hours.

Buses Coaches connect Wangaratta to Beechworth and Mount Beauty. Wangaratta has a local bus service.

Taxis ✓

INFRASTRUCTURE

Hospitals Wangaratta Base Hospital has 190 beds and a 70-bed nursing home, plus a private hospital with 40 beds. Yarrawonga and District Health Services, Cobram and District Hospital and Numurkah District Health Service all have 30 beds plus aged-care facilities. Nathalia District Hospital has 10 beds.

Retirement villages Wangaratta, Yarrawonga, Cobram, Nathalia and Numurkah

Police stations Throughout the district, even in the smaller towns

Local newspapers *Wangaratta Chronicle*, *Yarrawonga Chronicle*, *Numurkah Leader* and *Cobram Courier*

RECREATION

Cycleways The Murray to the Mountains Rail Trail is a 94-kilometre sealed trail for cyclists which links Wangaratta with Beechworth, Myrtleford and Bright.

Bushwalking & National Parks Cobrawonga State Forest has attractive river redgums, King Valley has spectacular waterfalls and there are bushwalks through the Warby Ranges around Mount Glenrowan and along the Sunrise Walking Trail.

Dogs Dog friendly.

SHOPPING

Yarrawonga, Wangaratta and Cobram have a Safeway and IGA. Wangaratta has two department stores and a Coles, and there's a Target in Yarrawonga.

DINING

Yarrawonga, Wangaratta, Tocumwal and Cobram are your best bets when dining out.

SOCIAL ACTIVITY

Horse-riding trails run throughout the area and are especially scenic along the Murray. Many of the towns have swimming pools, open during the summer months. There are plenty of golf courses, including a 45-hole golf course in Yarrawonga/Mulwala. Education courses for adults are offered in Cobram. Wangaratta has an indoor sports and aquatic centre, and both Cobram and Nathalia have sports centres. Clubs and interests include theatre, art, crafts and various sports. There are libraries in Wangaratta, Cobram, Nathalia, Numurkah and Yarrawonga.

• Aquatic centre • Arts & crafts • Boating • Bushwalking
• Fishing • Golf • Horse riding • Libraries
• Most community organisations • Most religions
• Sports centre • Swimming • Waterskiing

REAL ESTATE

Yarrawonga
- Median house price: $242 000
- Median unit price: $155 000

Wangaratta
- Median house price: $190 000
- Median unit price: $150 000

Your money goes further out in the sticks.

WHY LIVE HERE?

It's simply country living at its best.

horsham
A safe haven

Horsham Council's slogan is 'Stay connected – start living'. Staying connected relates to the distance from Melbourne and Adelaide, while the second part of the equation is about enjoying life again instead of treading the mill in the big smoke. It's certainly quiet around here – there's not even whale watching on offer because Horsham is a 2.5-hour drive from the coast. What it does offer is a range of rural and semi-urban housing options and many social activities.

Horsham is well laid out, with wide streets and parks, and there are walk-ways along the Wimmera River and wetlands which are home to many species of birds. The villages and towns outside Horsham have very high proportions of over-sixties, including Nhill, Warracknabeal and Dimboola (remember the play?).

POPULATION

- 18 700 Est. June 2003
- 21% over sixty

CLIMATE

Summer 13.4°C to 29.8°C
Winter 3.7°C to 13.3°C
Sunshine 86 days

Rain 106 days
Rainfall 449 mm
The temperature range is quite large, dropping to as low as −6°C and soaring to around 45°C.

LOCATION & GETTING AROUND

Melbourne to Horsham is 300 kilometres and a drive of 3.5 hours. From Adelaide to Horsham it's 430 kilometres, which takes five hours to drive.
Roads Typical country roads
Nearest airport ✗
Nearest train Regular train services connect Horsham with Ballarat and Melbourne, taking 4.5 hours.
Taxis ✓

INFRASTRUCTURE

Hospitals Wimmera Base Hospital is in Horsham and there are many associated health-care organisations in town, including at least six medical clinics.
Retirement villages Sunnyside Lutheran Village
Police stations Horsham and Natimuk
Local newspapers *Horsham Weekly Advertiser* and *Horsham Wimmera Mail-Times*

RECREATION

Cycleways The Horsham to Mount Arapiles Rail Trail via Natimuk is a 48-kilometre round trip taking you though reasonably flat terrain.
Bushwalking & National Parks There are walking tracks along the banks of the Wimmera River. Grampians National Park, a short drive away, is a hugely popular destination for climbers and walkers.

SHOPPING

Horsham is home to both Safeway and Coles supermarkets.

DINING

Horsham has a range of eateries, including a couple of Chinese restaurants.

SOCIAL ACTIVITY

Horsham has a Regional Art Gallery specialising in photography, a Performing Arts Centre and Art-Craft Workshop. Associations include a Performing Arts Society, botanical groups, a brass band, choirs, dance and music. Horsham also has a library, a three-cinema complex and an Art Deco art gallery. There's a very good 18-hole golf course and the nearby Grampians provide unlimited opportunities to mix with nature, with good fishing in the many lakes for golden perch, Murray cod, redfin and rainbow trout. If you are game there is world-class rock climbing at Mount Arapiles.

• Bushwalking • Cinema • Fishing • Gallery • Golf
• Lawn bowls • Library • Most community organisations
• Most religions • Theatre • University of the Third Age

REAL ESTATE

• Median house price: $163 000
• Median unit price: $173 000

WHY LIVE HERE?

For the quiet country life and the opportunity to commune with nature.

mildura

Paddling down the Murray

Picture a paddle-steamer on the Murray and you sum up the ambience of this part of Victoria. Not all the towns in the bush are getting smaller, and this is one of a number of outback areas that are growing significantly. Mildura Council includes the towns of Mildura, Red Cliffs, Ouyen, Merbein and Irymple – you'll probably need a local to help you pronounce the last three placenames!

Mildura, Red Cliffs and the hamlet of Ouyen have the highest concentrations of over-sixties in this district. It was the Mediterranean climate and fertile countryside that first brought people from a range of cultures to live on the banks of the Murray, resulting in today's richly multicultural society. There's a colourful year-round calendar of festivals and celebrations – not to mention twenty-something wineries.

POPULATION

Mildura Municipal Council

- 50 000 Est. June 2003
- 20% over sixty

In Ouyen and Red Cliffs one in four residents is aged over sixty.

CLIMATE

Summer 16.3°C to 32.8°C
Winter 4.4°C to 15.4°C
Sunshine 150 days
Rain 58 days
Rainfall 268 mm

The weather in these parts is a roller-coaster ride of extremes, although locals claim that winters are mild here compared to other parts of the state. The highest maximums recorded were 50.7°C in January and the high forties in February, March, November and December. Air-conditioning is recommended.

LOCATION & GETTING AROUND

Mildura is 550 kilometres from Melbourne by road, taking 6.5 hours; from Adelaide it's 400 kilometres, taking just under five hours to drive.

Roads Roads are a mix of sealed and unsealed surfaces.

Nearest airport Mildura Airport is one of the largest regional airports in Australia. Qantas and Rex Airlines fly frequent services to Melbourne (75 minutes flight time) and there are also services to Sydney.

Nearest train A V/Line bus service goes to Swan Hill, where you can pick up a train to Melbourne.

Buses Regular services to Red Cliffs, Irymple and Merbein as well as local services around Mildura. A bus also runs direct to Bendigo.

Taxis ✓

INFRASTRUCTURE

Hospitals Mildura Base Hospital

Retirement villages Mildura and Irymple

Police stations Mildura, Red Cliffs, Ouyen and Merbein

Local newspapers *Sunraysia Daily*, *Independent Star* and *Mildura Midweek*

RECREATION

Cycleways They are into cycling around here; the Port to Port two-day cycle tour travels from Mildura via Swan Hill to Echuca.

Bushwalking & National Parks Mungo National Park in the Willandra Lakes World Heritage area is an ancient lake system showcasing the history, both geological and cultural, of Australia's outback region. Ancient fossils of people and giant marsupials have been found here. Kings Billabong is an important wetland and dryland reserve and is home to many bird species and native animals. Seventy kilometres south of Mildura is the Hattah/ Kulkyne National Park comprised of mallee, floodplain and dune country. The Murray/Sunset National Park is the second largest in the state and the wild flowers in spring here are outstanding.

Dogs This is dog-friendly territory – they even have a lost dog register.

SHOPPING

There are two Woolworths and one Coles supermarket in Mildura.

DINING

Mildura has a cosmopolitan flavour with excellent wines and fresh produce, and in Mildura alone there are over 50 restaurants and around 40 casual cafés. Venues range from paddle-steamers on the Murray to wineries. In town there's outdoor dining at numerous cosmopolitan restaurants on Langtree Avenue.

SOCIAL ACTIVITY

The Mildura region boasts some famous names in wines and most wineries have cellar door sales. There are eight swimming pools, open from November to the end of March, and the city's swimming centre has a heated indoor pool as well as an outdoor pool. The Mildura Country Music Festival is held every September. Golf clubs include Mildura Golf and Country Club, Merbein Golf Club, Riverside Golf Club and Wentworth Services Golf Club. Racing and harness racing is held in Mildura and the city's cinema has four screens.

• Aquatic centre • Cinema • Golf • Horse racing • Lawn bowls
• Most community organisations • Most religions
• Swimming • Tennis

REAL ESTATE

• Median house price: $185 000
• Median unit price: $132 500

Cheaper housing is available in neighbouring towns such as Ouyen and Red Cliffs, where the median price for a house is $145 500.

WHY LIVE HERE?

A totally self-sufficient, if somewhat isolated, metropolis with a highly valued sense of community.

victoria's top 10

1. **BEST RETIREMENT HOTSPOT: Bellarine Peninsula/Queenscliff**
   Loads of potential, with open spaces and beaches, close to the city of Geelong.

2. **BEST RETIREMENT LIFESTYLE: Mornington Peninsula**
   A variety of rural and beach alternatives, excellent facilities, shopping and dining, and good access to Melbourne.

3. **BEST SMALL LOCATION: Hepburn/Daylesford**
   Picturesque villages with café culture and log fires.

4. **BEST LARGE LOCATION: Melbourne – By the Bay**
   Good food, shopping, beaches and sporting facilities only twenty or so minutes from Melbourne's CBD.

5. **BEST SHOPPING: Melbourne**

6. **BEST DINING: Melbourne**

7. **BEST PLACE TO CURL UP WITH A GOOD BOOK: Mallacoota**

8. **BEST BEACHES: Apollo Bay/Lorne**

9. **BEST OUTDOOR ACTIVITIES: Wangaratta to Yarrawonga**
   For golf, horse riding, boating and fishing.

10. **BEST-VALUE REAL ESTATE: Horsham**

tasmania

Wynyard 248

Port Sorell 251

Bridport 254

St Helens 258

Launceston 261

Hobart 264

Tasmania's Top 10 269

Opposite: The small, rather quaint
fishing fleet at Wynyard

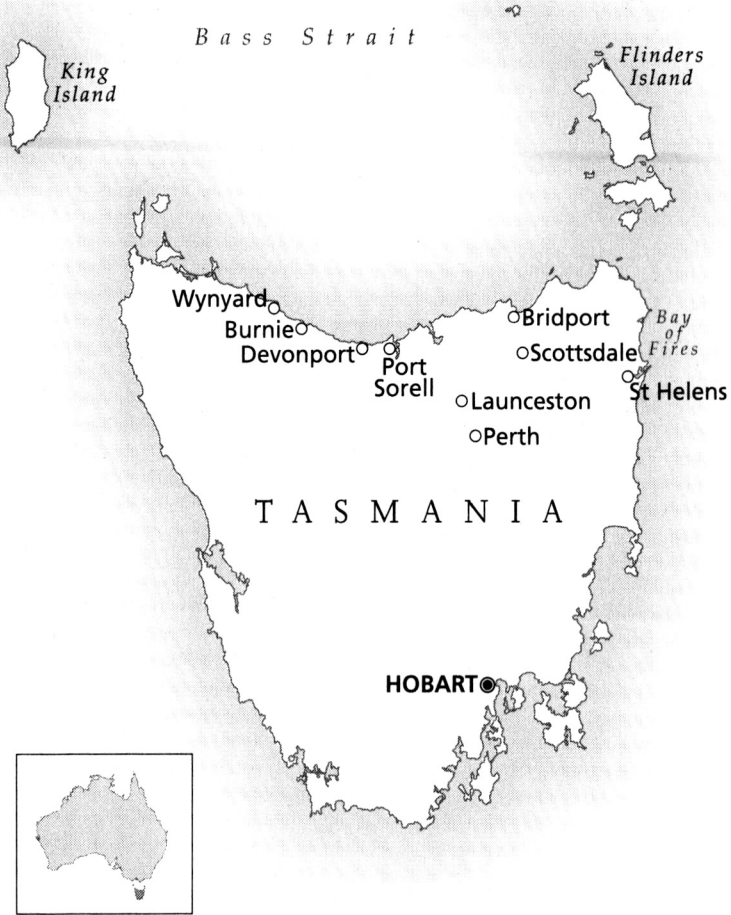

Bass Strait

King
Island

Flinders
Island

Wynyard
Burnie
Devonport
Port
Sorell

Bridport
Scottsdale

Bay
of
Fires

St Helens

Launceston
Perth

TASMANIA

HOBART

Taswegians refer to 'the mainland', where the rest of Australia's population lives, as though it's another country – there's the mainland, and then there's Tassie. They are also keen to dispel some of the myths which they believe mainlanders hold; for example, the idea that Tasmania is cold and remote. They are of the opinion that many parts of Tassie have a milder climate than Melbourne, and that as the island is easily accessed by air and the *Spirit of Tasmania*, it's not at all isolated. Even so, you get the feeling that they're quite happy to have that large expanse of Bass Strait between them and the rest of us.

Over the years, quite a number of mainlanders have ventured to Tasmania for a holiday and never returned home. It was a recurring comment from the retirees I spoke to, who tended to come from Melbourne, Sydney and Adelaide. One clear benefit is the cost of living: meat, veggies and real estate are all reputed to be cheaper in Tasmania. The seafood produce is first-rate and the beef and dairy products from King Island are excellent. They brew some good beers in Tassie – Boags in the north, Cascade in the south – and they also produce superb wines.

There are three groups of Tasmanians: the pro-loggers, the pro-green and, perhaps the largest group, those who believe that logging and conservation can coexist. The logging issue is the number one festering sore in Tasmania's future. I noticed many bearded men on my travels in Tasmania (not the neatly trimmed type, either) but I don't know whether they were loggers or greens!

In terms of climate and appearance, Tasmania is very reminiscent of the English countryside. Unlike the rest of Australia, you don't see canal-side housing developments, golf-course estates or high-rise apartment blocks. Instead, old weatherboard cottages and gracious 150-year-old mansions sit side by side with the occasional architect-designed contemporary home. Tasmania has loads of history and character, the streets are clean and the air is pure. Even the houses seem to be better maintained than on the mainland. As for parking meters, they are virtually nonexistent except for Launceston and Hobart, and even in those cities twenty cents will buy you some time! One drawback to Tasmania's delightfully old-fashioned ways is its lack of complete mobile phone coverage. This can be a problem, especially if you are with the 'wrong' provider.

The trip to Tasmania aboard the *Spirit of Tasmania* puts you in contact with an interesting potpourri of people, ranging from semi-trailer drivers to holiday-makers to business commuters. I met a number of people who are spending their retirement travelling around the country and who now call their campervans or caravans home. One chap, who had 'been on the wallaby for three years', as he put it, had only a post box number in Sydney; he lives in his caravan and goes wherever he feels the urge. Having spent three months in Tasmania he was heading north to Sydney, although he only planned to stay there as long as it took to get out. He had met many others like him on his travels. He told me that one couple he met had been 'on the wallaby' for thirty-three years. Some wallaby!

wynyard
An English country garden within reach of the world

Wynyard is my pick of Tasmania's coastal townships. Located on the north coast, it's in the centre of a patchwork-patterned agricultural district at the mouth of the Inglis River. It is a beautiful stretch of coastline, where rolling hills and grassy headlands meet beaches and bays. One of the area's dominant features is Table Cape, which has a lighthouse surrounded by magnificent tulip fields and spectacular views of Bass Strait. Table Cape was originally volcanic and the area is very fertile.

Several factors make Wynyard appealing as a retirement destination: it has an airport with regular commercial flights to Melbourne; it is only 16 kilometres from the large township of Burnie; the road connections to Burnie and Devonport are excellent and largely 110 km/h dual-carriage freeway; and, lastly, it has a mild climate. A retiree working in the tourist information centre told me: 'I sold up in Melbourne and bought in Wynyard and ended up with a sizable nest egg left over.'

POPULATION

Wynyard	Burnie and Somerset
• 4600	• 18 000
• 22% over sixty	• 19% over sixty

Wynyard's population is growing slowly; in Burnie and Somerset (Tassie's fourth-largest urban centre) and in many rural locations, the population is decreasing.

CLIMATE

Summer 12.2°C to 21.7°C
Winter 3.9°C to 12.9°C
Sunshine 49 days
Rain 189 days
Rainfall 1042 mm

An old lady who has lived in Wynyard all her life told me she has only experienced snow here twice.

LOCATION & GETTING AROUND

Wynyard is 160 kilometres from Launceston, a driving time of about 1.5 hours. Devonport, and the *Spirit of Tasmania*, is only 50 minutes by car. The neighbouring town of Somerset is eight kilometres east of Wynyard.

Roads An excellent freeway connects Wynyard to Devonport. The road on to Launceston is mostly single lane each way but the traffic moves well.

Nearest airport Wynyard Airport has daily services to Melbourne with Rex and Qantas. A regional service also provides several daily flights to King Island and Hobart.

Nearest train ✗ (there are no passenger trains in Tasmania)

Buses Local weekday services to Burnie and Somerset

Taxis ✓

Ferries Devonport to Melbourne and Sydney

INFRASTRUCTURE

Hospitals Northwest Regional Hospital, Burnie
Retirement villages There are a few clusters of units for elderly people but no retirement villages.
Police stations Wynyard and Burnie
Local newspaper *Advocate*

RECREATION

Beaches There is no surf on the north coast due to Bass Strait. There are safe beaches along the Wynyard foreshore with grassed reserves, walking tracks and three boat ramps. Only the beach at Burnie is patrolled on summer weekends. Sisters Beach, in Rocky Cape National Park, is also good for swimming and connected to Boat Harbour by a walking track. Somerset has safe swimming and is near the mouth of the Cam River.

Coastguard ✓

Cycleways There are some cycle lanes in Wynyard, and the roads are fairly quiet around town. Sections of the Inglis River walking trails are also suitable for cycling.

Bushwalking & National Parks A 14-kilometre walking circuit along the Inglis River leads to a bird rookery and Fossil Bluff. Rocky Cape National Park, further west along the coastline, has an easy walking track with coastal views, Aboriginal caves, wild flowers and bird life. Inland, the Hellyer Gorge State Reserve offers wilderness to explore, trout fishing, gold panning and mine tours.

Dogs Parts of the beaches at Somerset, Wynyard and Sisters are designated exercise areas for dogs.

SHOPPING

Wynyard has a reasonably good shopping strip by Tasmanian country village standards, including two supermarkets. It also has one of the biggest antique and craft markets on the coast at the Old Theatre Market, which is held monthly. The Car Boot Sale is also held monthly and the Farmers' Market twice a month. Burnie has a substantial shopping centre.

DINING

There are three hotels, a number of restaurants, a pizzeria and two Chinese restaurants. There are more choices in Burnie, Somerset and Boat Harbour Beach.

SOCIAL ACTIVITY

Fishing is a popular pastime in these parts, particularly trout fishing in the Inglis and Flowerdale Rivers. The Cam River and Cape Bridge Reserves are also good for fishing and boating, and there are a number of sailing clubs. Wynyard has a nine-hole golf course and Seabrook has an 18-hole course. Wynyard has a number of social clubs, including birdwatching, Scrabble, gardening, singing, lacemaking, leadlight and pottery.

- Arts & crafts • Boating • Croquet • Fishing
- Golf • Indoor bowls • Library • Sailing
- Some community organisations • Some religions • Tennis

REAL ESTATE

- Median house price: $200 000

WHY LIVE HERE?

Smaller towns such as Wynyard are cohesive neighbourhoods, rich in community activities like the Bloomin' Tulips Festival and monthly markets. Retirees are attracted by the proximity of everything, including access to the mainland. The flat townscape makes walking or cycling easy and the fishing is great.

port sorell
Lost on the Rubicon

Port Sorell attracts boating and fishing enthusiasts, and claims to be the fastest-developing area in Tasmania. The low-lying town is on the Rubicon River, only 20 kilometres from Devonport. There's not too much to it – just a jetty, a small number of shops, holiday houses, caravan parks and B&Bs – although it's the oldest township on the north-west coast.

The adjoining hamlet of Shearwater has been more recently developed and is the area's shopping centre for basic requirements. It is a little hillier than Port Sorell and has some good views over the river. Hawley Beach, five minutes away at the mouth of the river, is booming and described by enthusiastic locals as a mini Noosa.

Shearwater is the more appealing of the two towns, but overall the area feels as if it has grown in a rather higgledy-piggledy fashion, without sufficient planning and infrastructure.

POPULATION

Port Sorell and Shearwater

- 2000
- 27% over sixty

This area has grown significantly since the last census.

CLIMATE

Summer 16.3°C to 21.3°C
Winter 6.7°C to 12.2°C
Sunshine 68 days
Rain 150 days
Rainfall 899 mm

LOCATION & GETTING AROUND

Port Sorell is 100 kilometres north-west of Launceston, a driving time of 75 minutes via the Bass Highway. It's 20 kilometres from Devonport, which takes around 20 minutes to drive. It takes only 15 minutes or so to drive to the *Spirit of Tasmania* car ferry, which sails regularly to Melbourne (10 hours) and Sydney (20 hours).

Roads The road linking Port Sorell to Devonport is quite narrow.
Nearest airport Devonport Airport, 15 minutes' drive.
Nearest train ✗
Buses ✗
Ferries Devonport to Melbourne and Sydney
Taxis ✗

INFRASTRUCTURE

Hospitals Latrobe (near Devonport), Burnie and Launceston
Retirement villages There are up to nine in Shearwater, Port Sorell and nearby, but most of them have long waiting lists
Police stations Shearwater and Devonport
Local newspapers *Advocate* and *Launceston Examiner*

RECREATION

Beaches This area is known for its long stretches of beach and sand dunes. Swimming and boating are popular at Port Sorell Beach, Hawley Beach and Freers Beach near Shearwater, which has a Surf Life Saving Club; Bakers Beach, to the south, is also popular. There are some deserted beaches to be found in Narawntapu National Park.

Coastguard ✘

Cycleways Port Sorell has shared walking/bike tracks and Devonport has more than 20 kilometres of cycle/walkways.

Bushwalking & National Parks Narawntapu National Park has walking trails to isolated beaches through sand dunes and heathlands covered in wild flowers. It is also a breeding colony for fairy penguins and has a diverse variety of fauna. As well as well-marked walking trails, there is an elevated boardwalk over wetlands that is particularly popular with birdwatchers. The Port Sorell Conservation Area protects 70 hectares of foreshore and woodland.

Dogs Exercise areas are located at Squeaking Point and portions of Freers and Hawley Beaches, as well as on the Port Sorell foreshore.

SHOPPING

Port Sorell has limited shopping, as Shearwater's modest modern centre is the area's commercial centre. Devonport has a large shopping centre for more substantial purchases.

DINING

Port Sorell's dining is limited to a Mediterranean-style licensed café and little else, while Shearwater has a Country Club restaurant. Devonport has numerous cafés and a small range of restaurants, and good wines are available from the local vineyards in the Tamar Valley.

SOCIAL ACTIVITY

Port Sorell's water-based activities include fishing and boating. You would need to go to Devonport for more entertainment, hobby groups and cinema. The closest churches are also in Devonport.

• Boating • Bushwalking • Fishing • Golf • Lawn bowls
• Surfing • Swimming • Tennis

REAL ESTATE

Port Sorell
• Median house price: $270 000

A two-bed unit in the Shearwater Retirement Village costs under $220 000. Acreage is also available at reasonably low prices, but beach blocks at Hawley Beach are selling at prices up to $500 000.

WHY LIVE HERE?

For the opportunity to own a small acreage or a house in the village, to fish, go for walks in the national parks or visit Launceston. You won't be able to walk to a range of restaurants, cafés or shops, but you could feasibly leave the farm or beach here and be in Melbourne in around three hours.

bridport
Alone on Bass Strait

The isolated little town of Bridport is 20 kilometres from substantial supermarkets and infrastructure such as police and medical facilities; you'll find those at Scottsdale, 20 kilometres inland en route to Launceston. The Tasmanian landscape is known for its lushness and Bridport's is no exception, with beautiful rivers, ocean and bays, natural bush and bucolic green fields. The small fishing village is on the island's north-east coast on the southern end of Anderson Bay. For much of the year it's the centre of scallop, trout and lobster industries, but in the summer months the town creaks and groans under the pressure of up to 10 000 tourists (thankfully, they don't tend to arrive all at once) who descend on the Bridport Caravan Park, in prime position on the water's edge, providing much-needed revenue.

Although this is a beautiful part of the world to live, some locals claim there are issues to be addressed: out-of-date infrastructure, inadequate funding, grossly overused roads and generally insufficient services for an ageing population.

Neighbouring Scottsdale is a charming, picturesque town with a number of heritage buildings, set on a hill with views of the surrounding valleys. If your retirement plan involves buying a small rural holding, Scottsdale could be the ideal choice. The local economy is driven by logging, so if you are thinking of moving here it might help if you have no issues with that industry.

POPULATION

Bridport
• 1351
• 27% over sixty

Bridport grew by 10 per cent between censuses. Scottsdale's population of 2000 is stagnating.

CLIMATE

Summer 13.3°C to 20.9°C
Winter 5.9°C to 11.9°C
Sunshine 66 days
Rain 141 days
Rainfall 677 mm

LOCATION & GETTING AROUND

Bridport is on Tasmania's north-east coast, all by itself. Launceston is 85 kilometres away, a driving time of 1.5 hours (outside of the summer tourist season).

Roads The roads to Bridport are narrow but relatively quiet out of season.

Nearest airport Launceston; Bridport has a small non commercial airport

Nearest train ✗

Buses Both Bridport and Scottsdale have local scheduled services.

Taxis ✗

INFRASTRUCTURE

Hospitals The North-Eastern Soldiers Memorial Hospital at Scottsdale. Two medical practices in Scottsdale also have surgeries in Bridport which they visit on selected days. There is a chemist in Bridport.

Retirement villages One group of cluster homes in Bridport and there are retirement villages in Scottsdale

Police stations Bridport, manned only in summer

Local newspapers *Advocate* and *Launceston Examiner*

RECREATION

Beaches Bridport's beaches range from wide stretches of golden sand to secluded, rocky coves, but there's no surf. There's safe swimming and rock diving at Mermaids Pool. The secluded foreshore beaches run all the way to Granite Point and Adams Beach, with access via an unsealed road.

Cycleways Dual-use cycle/running paths run along the foreshore.

Bushwalking & National Parks There are many trails to be found in this north-eastern area. At Bridport the walking trail follows the foreshore, passing through a wild-flower reserve and sand dunes. Scottsdale's Northeast Park has walking trails.

Dogs Approved dog exercise areas include two beach areas in Bridport – Adams Beach and Tread Water.

SHOPPING

Bridport is a small village with a supermarket, some general stores, a shopping complex and a range of shops on Main Street but no bank. Scottsdale, being the larger town, has good shopping facilities including the Channel Court Shopping Centre. The small country towns throughout the area have arts and crafts centres and antique shops.

DINING

As dining in Bridport is very restricted, the best place for a meal is the Bridport Resort Restaurant. Otherwise there's only a bakery, a couple of coffee shops and the occasional takeaway food outlet. Scottsdale has far more eating options.

SOCIAL ACTIVITY

Beach and ocean fishing are popular pastimes, as is sailing. Scottsdale has a heated swimming pool, but it is only open from November to March as it is not undercover. There are golf clubs at both Bridport and Scottsdale, including the newish Barnbougle Golf Links at Bridport. The well-known Pipers Brook vineyard is nearby, as well as a lavender farm.
• Arts & crafts • Bushwalking • Fishing • Golf • Lawn bowls
• Library • Sailing • Swimming • Tennis

REAL ESTATE

• Median house price: $270 000
Housing in Bridport includes some very substantial and attractive older-style buildings. Locals bemoan the rising prices, which have partly been pushed up because of mainlanders buying into the area. Prices are still comparatively cheap although new developments are more expensive, especially those with sea views. In outlying hamlets acreage is available at relatively low prices.

WHY LIVE HERE?

Bridport has a mild climate and is so quiet that many of the locals still don't lock their doors. One local I spoke to was originally from Manly. She's been in Bridport for twenty years, and her husband worked on a fishing boat before retiring. 'It's the sort of place that once you are here you forget everywhere else,' she told me. Another 29-year resident, originally from Melbourne, said, 'I just couldn't stand winter in Melbourne. It's much milder here. But I still like to go back twice a year to shop.'

st helens

Cottages by the bay

Not a lot of people live on Tassie's north-east coast. At the last census St Helens had a total of only 1800 people, but that was enough to make it the largest community in the vicinity. It sits on a beautiful stretch of beach on Georges Bay, and predominantly relies on tourism, timber, fishing and farming, including grapes, potatoes, dairy cattle and sheep. This is another seaside location that claims to have a unique microclimate which is warmer than Melbourne during the winter. Large stretches of natural bushland border Georges Bay and the east coast, covering more than 50 kilometres of shore line. One of the best ways to explore the coast is by foot, as the beaches extend well beyond the access roads.

The council has the unusual name of Break O'Day, and also administers the neighbouring townships of Ansons Bay, Binalong Bay, Beaumaris, Scamander, Stieglitz, St Marys and Fingal. This is an area of beautiful scenery, with natural wonders such as St Columba Falls and the Bay of Fires. Condé Nast's *Traveller* magazine recently named the Bay of Fires as the second-best beach in the world. A big statement!

So how do people find living in this remote paradise? One couple from Adelaide said, 'We came here for a holiday twenty years ago and only went back to sell up.' One issue which would-be residents might want to investigate further before moving into this area are claims of water contamination from chemicals used in agriculture and forestry. There are different versions of the story and council regularly samples the water. However, most locals drink bottled water.

POPULATION

- 1800
- 31% over sixty

CLIMATE

Summer 12.0°C to 23.0°C
Winter 2.5°C to 13.8°C
Sunshine 87 days

<u>Rain</u> 142 days

<u>Rainfall</u> 779 mm

This is Tassie's Sunshine Coast, the warmest place in the Apple Isle.

LOCATION & GETTING AROUND

Access is only by road. St Helens is 150 kilometres from Launceston, via Conara, which is about two hours' travelling time. Hobart is 250 kilometres, a drive of around three hours. The roads are winding and dangerous in these parts. The coastal Tasman Highway to Hobart is one of the most picturesque routes in the whole of Australia, but it's made unnecessarily dangerous by the big timber rigs which tend to be in a hurry (even aggressive) when they are not laden, as the road is not policed.

<u>Roads</u> The local roads are barely adequate and become very congested in holiday seasons.

<u>Nearest airports</u> Launceston Airport. There is a small airport at St Helens with charter flights.

<u>Nearest train</u> ✘

<u>Buses</u> Coaches run almost daily to Launceston

<u>Taxis</u> ✓

INFRASTRUCTURE

<u>Hospitals</u> St Helens District Hospital and St Mary's Community Health Clinic, both fairly small. Air ambulance is available.

<u>Retirement villages</u> Sun Haven Villas and Medea Residential Care

<u>Police stations</u> St Helens

<u>Local newspapers</u> *Advocate* and *Launceston Examiner*

RECREATION

<u>Beaches</u> On the southern side of the bay from St Helens through Stieglitz to St Helens Point the beautiful stretches of white-sand beaches are ideal for swimming, surfing and fishing. Beaches include St Helens, Burns Beach, Maurouard Beach and Peron Dunes, looking onto St Helens Island. To the north, Binalong Bay and Dora Point are also good swimming beaches.

Coastguard ✓

Cycleways Many of the local streets are quiet enough to ride on the flat.

Bushwalking & National Parks Georges Bay walking track is a good flat walk or ride around the bay. Humbug Point Reserve has long walks around the coast from Binalong Bay to Moulting Bay. The Bay of Fires Coastal Reserve to the north of St Helens has spectacular coastal scenery enhanced by red rocks, blue water and white beaches. It is also popular for its fishing lagoons. Blue Tier is an old tin-mining mountain plateau with six walking tracks, one with wheelchair access. Mount William National Park to the north has an abundance of native flora and fauna; however, roads into the area are unsealed.

Dogs Fairly relaxed regulations, but there have been some concerns about dogs attacking sheep and other farm animals.

SHOPPING

St Helens has a large newish supermarket development and retail complex.

DINING

Scallops, abalone, crayfish and oysters are in abundance, and there are at least fifteen informal restaurants to choose from.

SOCIAL ACTIVITY

St Helens hosts the Suncoast Jazz Festival annually. Clubs include a film society, Jazz club, dancing and art and craft. St Helens' cinema is the only one on the east coast. Scamander, to the south, has golf, tennis and lawn bowls. Marlin and tuna fishing are very popular, with numerous fishing charters available, and of course there is plenty of beach, bay and river fishing. The Scamander River has some of the best bream and trout fishing in Tassie.

• Arts & crafts • Bushwalking • Cinema • Fishing • Golf
• Horse riding • Lawn bowls • Surfing • Swimming • Tennis

REAL ESTATE

- Median house price: $270 000
- Median unit price: $200 000

These prices would get you something near the beach but perhaps not with water views.

WHY LIVE HERE?

To live on a beautiful coastline, surrounded by beautiful parkland, away from the bustle: no traffic lights, no parking meters, no traffic jams and no high-rise buildings. Now that does sound appealing! One keen advocate told me, 'This is a healthy place to live – even the kids grow quicker here.'

launceston
Gateway to the north

The Tamar River winds through the beautifully landscaped garden city of Launceston, Tasmania's second-largest commercial hub. The city has a distinctive low-rise charm because of its Georgian and Victorian architecture, wide streets and views of the surrounding hills and countryside. The rugged Cataract Gorge Reserve on Launceston's western edge is a hugely popular attraction, with walking tracks along the gorge.

East Launceston, on the hill overlooking the city, is the best retirement option as it has a mixture of comfortable and often grand old homes, a number of which have been turned into B&Bs.

POPULATION

- 68 000
- 18.5% over sixty

Launceston is growing slowly, at only 1 per cent between censuses.

CLIMATE

<u>Summer</u> 12.0°C to 24.4°C
<u>Winter</u> 2.1°C to 12.5°C

Sunshine 50 days
Rain 126 days
Rainfall 683 mm

LOCATION & GETTING AROUND

Launceston is 200 kilometres from Hobart, approximately 2.5 hours' drive; it is 100 kilometres south-east of Devonport.

Roads The Tasman, Bass and Midland highways all meet in Launceston. The West and East Tamar highways run along either side of the river, heading north to the sea.

Nearest airport Launceston's very good provincial airport is 20 minutes south of the city near Evandale, with frequent services to Sydney, Melbourne and Adelaide.

Nearest train ✗

Buses ✓

Taxis ✓

INFRASTRUCTURE

Hospitals Launceston General Hospital, St Vincent's Private and Calvary Health Care (private)

Retirement villages There are five aged-care facilities including retirement villages and nursing homes within Launceston.

Police stations Launceston

Local newspaper *Launceston Examiner*

RECREATION

Cycleways There are cycleways in the parklands of the Inveresk Railyards as well as many other opportunities around the city.

Bushwalking & National Parks Cataract Gorge Reserve, a 10-minute walk west of the city centre, has walking and hiking trails, a chairlift, lookouts and rock pools, plus a restaurant, kiosk and gardens. The Trevallyn State Recreational Reserve is in the hills west of Launceston by the South Esk River and is a popular spot for bushwalking, archery and aquatic activities.

Dogs There are assigned areas in the parks and reserves.

SHOPPING

Launceston's major retail outlets can be found in the Brisbane Street Mall. Yorktown Square has a mix of speciality shops and eateries plus a market on Sunday. Craft and fresh produce markets are held weekly at Esk, Evandale and Perth. Both Launceston and Longford have interesting craft shops, and the former also has an excellent wine gallery selling wines from all over Tasmania.

DINING

Restaurateurs claim that Tasmania's best dining opportunities are found in the north of the island rather than Hobart, and Launceston's award-winning Synergy restaurant is a fine example. The late Premier Jim Bacon compared the Tamar Valley to the food and wine regions of France.

SOCIAL ACTIVITY

Outdoor activities include golf, fly-fishing, sailing, river cruises and historic walks around the town. The Water Park has three heated swimming pools and the city also has a spa centre in the style of an ancient Roman bathhouse. Grindelwald Village, a replica of a Swiss village, has a nine-hole golf course. There is also a casino, theatre and Queen Victoria Museum and Art Gallery (with exhibitions and a planetarium); outside the city, the vineyards are not too far away.

• All community organisations • All religions • Bushwalking
• Fishing • Galleries • Golf • Libraries • Museums • Sailing
• Swimming • Theatre • Walking

REAL ESTATE

• Median house price: $265 000

Launceston's houses are solid and appealing, and your dollar goes a long way. At the top of the market are fabulous, three-storey Federation-style homes for under a million (just bursting to be turned into yet more B&Bs).

Launceston's retirees can enjoy the pleasures of city life while feeling that they live in the country. I met a retiree from Sydney's North Shore who'd retired to a cattle station just north of Launceston, preferring the cooler climate and the rainfall. When the cattle got too much for him he moved down the road to Launceston. 'Although I was a Sydney boy, I prefer the climate here,' he told me. 'I only go back to Sydney to visit my daughter.'

hobart
The jewel in the bay

Australia's southernmost capital city nestles comfortably below Mount Wellington, surrounded by bushland on the Derwent River. It is a beautiful, compact city and the second-oldest site of European settlement in Australia. With its well-maintained Georgian sandstone buildings, Hobart is surely Australia's most charming city. Hotels and restaurants line its wharves but it remains a working port, bustling with fishing boats, cruise boats, ferries, visiting yachts and naval vessels.

The pick of the retirement suburbs is Battery Point, with its café society and lovely architecture; you can walk to everything from here. Sandy Bay, a short distance from the CBD, is also a good option, with solid old homes and great views. A little further along the shore are Taroona (childhood home to Mary Donaldson, now better known as Denmark's Princess Mary) and Kingston, just outside of which is good acreage for growing grapes.

Hobart is also a city of classic parks, featuring English trees, rhododendrons and roses. Queens Domain, to the north of the CBD, is a large green expanse on the Derwent that's ideal for walking, cycling and other outdoor activities, as well as being home to the botanic gardens.

POPULATION

- **125 000** Est. June 2003
- **19.9%** over sixty

A slightly higher percentage of over-sixties live in the hamlets of Midway Point and Sorell, just 20 minutes out of Hobart.

CLIMATE

Summer 12.0°C to 21.6°C
Winter 4.5°C to 11.6°C
Sunshine 101 days
Rain 122 days
Rainfall 619 mm

LOCATION & GETTING AROUND

Hobart is in the south of the island, flanked by Mount Wellington and the Derwent River.

Roads The streets are well laid out and exits from the city are easily accessed. The peak-hour traffic is not heavy. What joy!

Nearest airport Hobart Airport is 18 kilometres from the city centre. Direct flights to Melbourne take 70 minutes and to Sydney it's just under two hours.

Nearest train ✗

Buses ✓

Taxis ✓

INFRASTRUCTURE

Hospitals The city's public hospitals are Royal Hobart Hospital, May Shaw Health Centre, Midlands Multi Purpose, Ouse District Hospital and WP Holman Clinic. Private hospitals include the Hobart Private, Calvary Health Care and St Helens Private.

Retirement villages There are at least 20 retirement villages, including Abbeyfield House, Derwent Waters, Independent Life Cottages, Maranatha Retirement Homes, Queen Victoria House and Vaucluse Gardens.

Police stations ✓

Local newspaper *Hobart Mercury*

RECREATION

Beaches There are a number of sandy river beaches around Hobart, including Sandy Bay, Long Beach (popular for picnics, barbeques, boating, sailing and sailboards), Nutgrove Beach, Lords Beach, Red Chapel Beach, Short Beach and Kingston Beach.

Coastguard ✓

Cycleways Around 20 kilometres of mostly flat cycleway run from the city centre past Queens Domain, along the water's edge at Cornelian Bay to vineyards further north.

Bushwalking & National Parks There is plenty of bushland around Hobart, starting with Wellington Park which sweeps up from the south-western suburban fringe to the pinnacle of Mount Wellington, with scenic bushwalks year-round and snow in winter. Also close by is the bushland that spreads across the slopes of Knocklofty. The Hobart Rivulet Linear Park has walking tracks which run from the heart of the city to the foothills, following the banks of the Hobart Rivulet through extensive gardens. On the foreshore there are 21 parks to enjoy.

Dogs This is a dog-friendly area with 34 off-leash exercise areas, including reserves and riverfront areas. Dogs are prohibited on cycleways.

SHOPPING

The CBD includes major department stores and a shopping mall with various fashion outlets. Battery Point specialises in arts and crafts, bookshops and antique stores, and there are art galleries and fashion boutiques in north Hobart. Salamanca Place is the showcase of Tasmanian arts and crafts, displayed in beautiful heritage-listed former warehouse buildings near the waterfront. The popular weekend markets here sell produce as well as arts and crafts.

DINING

Hobart has many good restaurants and cafés, serving a wide variety of cuisines. The waterfront restaurants offer fine dining with atmosphere and nearby Salamanca Place is home to restaurants, specialist food shops and bars. Battery Point is known for its dining and north Hobart has a restaurant strip with pubs, restaurants and cafés.

SOCIAL ACTIVITY

Hobart's attractions include its Heritage Museum, botanic gardens, Wrest Point Casino and Carnegie Gallery, with an annual programme of art exhibitions. The city is a gardener's paradise, with four distinct seasons. The 50 and Better Centre (for over-fifties) offers indoor bowls, table tennis, activities, seminars, Internet access, snacks and meals. Hobart hosts a number of festivals, including the Summer Festival which coincides with the finish of the Sydney to Hobart Yacht Race. All major religions are represented, plus a few not so well-known ones such as Huon Christian Church, World Wide Church of God, Faith Baptist, First Church of Christ and the Presentation Sisters.

- All community organisations • All religions • Bushwalking
- Cinemas • Croquet • Fishing • Galleries • Golf
- Lawn bowls • Library • Museums • Sailing • Swimming
- Tennis • Theatre

REAL ESTATE

- Median house price: $375 000
- Median unit price: $300 000

Prices vary, of course, and values in Battery Point have crept up; a comfortable terrace-style home without views in Battery Point would cost around $700 000.

WHY LIVE HERE?

A recently retired gentleman who works part time in a CBD library put it in a nutshell: 'I can be fly-fishing fifteen minutes after I finish work. How good is that?' Another said to me: 'Where else can you live in the country, in the city?' And a retired couple told me: 'We lived a very, very hectic life and Hobart was about as far away from that as we could get.' Add to this the cosmopolitan atmosphere and facilities that come with city life and you can see why the residents of Hobart feel they have got it made.

tasmania's top 10

1. **BEST RETIREMENT HOTSPOT: Wynyard**
Rural or village lifestyle on the Bass Coast, close to Devonport.

2. **BEST RETIREMENT LIFESTYLE: Hobart**
A variety of rural and city alternatives, excellent facilities, arts and culture, and good food and wine.

3. **BEST SMALL LOCATION: St Helens**
Picturesque seaside village with great beaches, fishing and nature reserves.

4. **BEST LARGE LOCATION: Hobart**
The choice of nearby rural options or a relaxed take on cosmopolitan city life.

5. **BEST SHOPPING: Hobart**

6. **BEST DINING: Launceston**

7. **BEST PLACE TO CURL UP WITH A GOOD BOOK: Bridport**

8. **BEST BEACHES: St Helens**

9. **BEST OUTDOOR ACTIVITIES: Hobart**
For golf, walking, cycling, sailing and fly-fishing.

10. **BEST-VALUE REAL ESTATE: Wynyard**

south australia

Robe/Kingston 273

Murray Bridge 276

Adelaide 279

　Eastern Suburbs 279

　Beach Suburbs 281

McLaren Vale 285

Strathalbyn 287

Victor Harbor 289

Barossa Valley 293

Copper Coast 296

South Australia's Top 10 299

Opposite: Boys with their toys, Glenelg

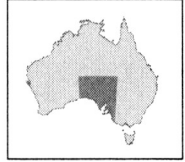

Coober Pedy

SOUTH AUSTRALIA

Great Australian Bight

Port Augusta

See Enlargement

ADELAIDE

Kingston SE
Robe
Mount Gambier

Wallaroo
Moonta Kadina
Yorke
Peninsula
Barossa
Valley Nuriootpa
Lake
Alexandrina
ADELAIDE
Glenelg Murray Bridge
McLaren Vale Strathalbyn
Victor Harbor
Kangaroo
Island
Encounter
Bay
Fleurieu
Peninsula

robe/kingston
Laid-back-as-it-gets lifestyle

Robe is a very attractive historic port on Guichen Bay, on the state's south-east Limestone Coast. It's a popular tourist destination in the summer months and has some charming heritage buildings, such as the Customs House; it's also used as a safe harbour for fishing and lobster fleets. There is a choice of housing in Robe, both old and new, including some modern townhouses over-looking the bay.

Kingston (also known as Kingston SE – South-East – to distinguish it from Kingston-on-Murray to the north) is also a fishing and lobster port and tourist destination. It's slightly larger than Robe and also has a number of historical buildings. It has an extremely long jetty, still in use and over 100 years old, from where you can spot sea lions, seals and dolphins.

POPULATION

Robe
- 1000
- 25% over sixty

Kingston
- 1500
- 25% over sixty

CLIMATE

Summer 13.7°C to 22.5°C
Winter 8.1°C to 13.6°C
Sunshine 56 days
Rain 153 days
Rainfall 634 mm

There are definite seasons here and it gets a little cool in winter but not as cold as places inland.

LOCATION & GETTING AROUND

Robe is 335 kilometres south-east of Adelaide, a drive of over four hours. It is 580 kilometres north-west of Melbourne, taking over seven hours. Kingston is 44 kilometres north of Robe.

Roads Robe is on the Alt Highway which connects to Kingston via the Princes Highway.

Nearest airports There is a small airfield at Robe but no regular commercial flights. The main airport is at Mount Gambier, 130 kilometres to the south.

Nearest train ✗

Buses Daily buses run from Adelaide to Mount Gambier via Kingston and Robe.

Taxis In Kingston and during the summer months in Robe

INFRASTRUCTURE

Hospitals Kingston Soldiers Memorial Hospital and Robe Community Health Centre

Retirement villages Kingston has a retirement village and an aged-care hostel (Lighthouse Lodge) within walking distance of the Kingston Soldiers Memorial Hospital.

Police stations Robe and Kingston

Local newspapers *South Eastern Times* and *Coastal Leader*

RECREATION

Beaches Robe's beaches are excellent, with safe swimming, snorkelling and surfing. Town Beach is good for swimming but the water here is cold. West Beach to the south is very exposed and unsuitable for swimming but popular for its cliff walking tracks and plant and bird life. Kingston's Wyomi Beach is popular, and to the north there's the 100-kilometre Long Beach, considered one of the best surf fishing beaches in Australia.

Coastguard ✓

Cycleways Both Kingston and Robe have shared bike paths and walkways.

Bushwalking & National Parks There are good views of the coast, lakes and township from Robe's Beacon Hill Walk. A cliff track runs from Robe along the beaches and estuary to Long Beach. The Obelisk track starts at the Old Gaol and follows the cliff along to the quieter waters of Guichen Bay. Little Dip Conservation Park is interesting due to its diversity, including beaches, windblown sand dunes, sheltered coves and saltwater lakes, which are good for bushwalkers and birdwatchers. Butcher's Gap Conservation Park, six kilometres south of Kingston, has interesting walking trails through wetlands with lots of bird life. Mount Scott Conservation Park is 20 kilometres to the east of Kingston and has bushwalking trails through dunes and forest.

Dogs Robe has a restriction of two dogs per household. There are some off-leash beaches, and others where dogs are prohibited.

SHOPPING

The shopping in Robe is quite good and includes tourist shops and boutiques as well as a large local supermarket and antique stores. Kingston, being rural, carries supplies for the local farmers and has a large shopping centre with two supermarkets, several hotels and some antique and craft shops.

DINING

There are a few restaurants and smart cafés offering outdoor dining. Christine Manfield started her foodie career here. The specialities are seafood (including fresh crayfish), local produce and wines.

SOCIAL ACTIVITY

Outdoor activities include reef snorkelling, scuba diving, sailing and windsurfing. Robe has a twin cinema complex and an art gallery showcasing the work of local artists. The Robe Village Fair is held on the last weekend of November and features art, wines and gourmet food. There are numerous local wineries in Mount Benson between Robe and Kingston. Kingston has a museum and holds the Cape Jaffa Wine Festival every January.

• Birdwatching • Bushwalking • Cinema • Fishing • Gallery
• Golf • Lawn bowls • Library • Museum • Sailing • Surfing
• Swimming • Tennis

REAL ESTATE

Robe
• Median house price: $243 500

- Median cottage price: $175 000
- Land: from $80 000

Kingston

- Median house price: $168 000
- Land: from $50 000

WHY LIVE HERE?

Perfect for those who like being away from the city and who enjoy the seasons and coastal life.

murray bridge
A bridge too far, or just right?

Unlike many inland towns, the population of Murray Bridge is on the rise. This is largely due to Woolworths, which has a distribution centre here the size of two football fields, and the local abattoirs and agricultural industries also provide much-needed employment. Without these industries Murray Bridge would not make an entry in this book – it's only just hanging in there! But there are a lot of over-sixties, more than one in five of the population, many of whom have retired here from surrounding villages.

As the name suggests, the town is on the Murray River. There is plenty to do here, including watching the houseboats and riverboats plying the waters on the way to Victoria or south to Lake Alexandrina.

POPULATION

- 13 000
- 20.6% over sixty

CLIMATE

Summer 14.6°C to 29.2 °C
Winter 5.4°C to 16.2°C
Sunshine 77 days
Rain 97 days
Rainfall 346 mm

LOCATION & GETTING AROUND

Murray Bridge is 75 kilometres from Adelaide, a one-hour trip by car.

Roads There's good road access to Adelaide, with two lanes each way.

Nearest airport Pallamana is a small private airfield which offers private charter flights

Nearest train The train runs through here from Melbourne to Adelaide, but there's a hitch: passengers can alight coming from Melbourne and they can board going to Melbourne but there is no service between Murray Bridge and Adelaide, even though the train goes there – quite odd!

Buses Coaches pass through travelling to and from Melbourne to Adelaide.

Taxis ✓

INFRASTRUCTURE

Hospitals Murray Bridge Soldiers Memorial Hospital, 56 beds.

Retirement villages Lerwin Aged Care, a 50-bed high-level care facility; Murray Bridge Lutheran Homes, 73 units; Southern Cross Village, independent units; Murray Lands Village, 73 units; Resthaven, 73 low- and high-care units; and Waterford Estate.

Police stations ✓

Local newspaper *Murray Valley Standard*

RECREATION

Cycleways ✗

Bushwalking & National Parks The challenging, 58-kilometre Federation Walking Trail heads off from Murray Bridge and passes through forests, wetlands and rugged gorge territory.

Dogs Dog friendly, with few rules.

SHOPPING

Murray Bridge has a major shopping centre including, of course, a large Woolworths.

DINING

Dining is casual around here, with clubs and pubs the best options.

SOCIAL ACTIVITY

Murray Bridge has a heated pool and spa centre. Most sports are catered for and the river offers fishing, boating, skiing and swimming.

- Boating • Fishing • Golf • Horse racing • Lawn bowls
- Library • Most religions • Some community organisations
- Swimming

REAL ESTATE

- Median house price: $180 000
- Median unit price: $161 000

WHY LIVE HERE?

For the Mighty Murray and the huge water playground of Lake Alexandrina, an enjoyable boat ride away.

adelaide

eastern suburbs

Convenient, leafy and value for money

Adelaide is a terrific city for those who want the comforts and convenience of a city without the chaos and stress – it's just the right size. The CBD is open and welcoming, surrounded by parkland. It's also flat, making it ideal for 'gophers', the local vernacular for the motorised mobility scooters used by older folk to buzz around the shops and run over slow pedestrians.

The suburbs a few minutes east of the CBD are popular with over-sixties. Many of these areas are on the Torrens River, which is bordered by substantial reserves of bushland. It's an ideal playground for locals to picnic, walk and ride bikes on shared pathways. Popular suburbs include the middle-income belt of Payneham, Felixstow, Royston Park, Marden, Joslin, Firle, Trinity Gardens and Glynde; Burnside and Kensington Gardens are more upmarket and even shadier suburbs. All these suburbs are crisscrossed by very busy through streets, in total contrast to the empty and fairly narrow side streets. If you're looking to purchase in this area, check the traffic flow around your chosen spot.

POPULATION

Burnside
• 40 000
• 24% over sixty

In the suburbs of Felixstow, Marden, Royston Park, Joslin, Firle, Trinity Gardens and Glynde, 27 per cent of the 15 000 residents are aged over sixty.

CLIMATE

Summer 17.2°C to 29.4°C
Winter 7.4°C to 15.3°C
Sunshine 87 days
Rain 121 days
Rainfall 558 mm

LOCATION & GETTING AROUND

Adelaide's eastern suburbs are only seven kilometres from the city centre, a 10-minute trip by car.

Roads The roads are busy but they flow well and are mostly two lanes. Adelaide has some creative ways to move traffic; for example, by altering the direction of flow and traffic light rules at certain times of the day.

Nearest airport Adelaide Airport is 13 kilometres away, a travelling time of 20 minutes.

Nearest train No trains run to the east of Adelaide.

Buses ✓

Taxis ✓

INFRASTRUCTURE

Hospitals Burnside War Memorial Hospital is a community-based, nonprofit hospital.

Retirement villages There are more than 10 villages in the area.

Police stations ✓

RECREATION

Cycleways There's a shared cycle path along the Torrens River and many suburban streets have bike lanes.

Bushwalking & National Parks There are a number of state reserves in the foothills to the east, with bushwalking trails and views of waterfalls. Belair National Park to the south has natural bushland and barbeque, tennis and golf facilities. Within the Burnside area, Heritage-listed Magill Stone Mine Reserve has walking trails through woodland and is especially popular in wild-flower season. Kensington Gardens has a large sports and recreational park.

Dogs The suburbs are dog friendly but dogs need to be on a leash on footpaths.

SHOPPING

The area is scattered with large shopping malls, including those at Payneham, Marden and Firle. One of Adelaide's most elegant shopping centres is Burnside Village Shopping Centre in Glenside, with designer boutiques, a Coles supermarket, speciality stores and atmospheric cafés. Adelaide Central Market is popular for fresh produce.

DINING

The eastern suburbs aren't far from Gouger Street, Adelaide's popular dining precinct.

SOCIAL ACTIVITY

• Everything

REAL ESTATE

Burnside
• Median house price: $498 000
• Median unit price: $258 000
Other Eastern Suburbs
• Houses: $340 000
• Units: $200 000

WHY LIVE HERE?

You can't get much closer to the heart of a city anywhere else in Australia – certainly not at these real estate prices.

beach suburbs
Suntanned communities

Adelaide's west coast is one long line of beaches on Holdfast Bay, with old jetties reaching over the calm water (there's no surf). They look perfect for swimming, but there are sharks out there! They say that more people die of bee stings than shark attacks, but, given the choice, I'd rather be taken by a queen-sized bee than a Great White!

The beachside suburbs around Holdfast Bay and a little further north are really very special. Brighton and Henley are the pick of the crop for retirement, with charming outdoor coffee shops overlooking wide stretches of beach. Glenelg is also appealing and is where the action is, busy with tourists ferried in from Adelaide on the city's historic trams. It is a little like Manly without the surf, and the new marina and residential development no doubt appeals to the executive set.

West Beach runs into Henley and is where the rather insignificant Torrens River meets the ocean. There are very nice beach homes all along here and further north there are a number of newish developments at West Shores, including some canal living; this waterfront style of living seems to be catching on everywhere, but I wonder if the owners continue to use their boats after their initial flurry of interest has died down. Further north still, the homes are more modest and the beachfront is more run-down. Port Adelaide in particular needs an injection of funds to preserve its many original port buildings, and a $1.2 billion redevelopment proposal to rival Melbourne's Docklands is currently under discussion. Semaphore on the beach is less appealing than the beaches to the south, but many over-sixties live here.

POPULATION

Holdfast Bay LGA
- 34 000 Est. June 2003
- 28% over sixty

West Beach, Novar Gardens and Fulham
- 28 000
- 27% over sixty

Henley Beach and Surrounds
- 13 500
- 22.5% over sixty

CLIMATE

Summer 16°C to 28.1°C
Winter 6.9°C to 14.9°C
Sunshine 89 days
Rain 121 days
Rainfall 453 mm

LOCATION & GETTING AROUND

Holdfast Bay is only 11 kilometres from Adelaide City, a driving time of 15 minutes. By the Glenelg tram it takes just 24 minutes and they run every 20 minutes.

Roads The Anzac Highway runs to the beaches from Adelaide.

Nearest airport Adelaide Airport is only minutes away.

Nearest train Brighton Station, on the Noarlunga line.

Buses ✓

Taxis ✓

INFRASTRUCTURE

Hospitals They include Glenelg Community Hospital, Flinders Private, Royal Adelaide, Queen Elizabeth, Griffith Rehabilitation and St Andrew's Hospitals, as well as Glenelg and Brighton Day Surgeries.

Retirement villages There are more than 10 in the vicinity

Police stations ✓

Local newspapers *Messenger* and *Adelaide Advertiser*

RECREATION

Beaches Seacliff, Brighton, Henley, West Beach, Glenelg and Semaphore. Glenelg Beach is Adelaide's most popular beach.

Coastguard ✓

Cycleways Cycling is encouraged; there are many bike lanes on the roads, including the Glenelg Heritage Cycle Loop.

Bushwalking & National Parks There are no national parks in the immediate vicinity but the beach is very popular and there's the Kingston Park Coast Reserve.

Dogs Dogs are allowed off-leash on the foreshore provided they are 'under effective control' and on leads between 10 a.m. and 8 p.m.

SHOPPING

Glenelg's Jetty Road has literally hundreds of shops, including a Woolworths plaza. Other shopping centres include Marion Bay and Bay Junction and along the Anzac Highway and Brighton Road. On summer weekends markets are held in Moseley Square in Glenelg.

DINING

There are many waterfront restaurants, cafés and pubs to choose from and a range of cuisines. Glenelg has mostly casual dining, while Brighton and Henley offer outdoor dining in a village atmosphere.

SOCIAL ACTIVITY

Outdoor activities include sailing, kayaking and fishing, which is popular from the jetties at Brighton and Glenelg, the rocks at Seacliff and the Glenelg breakwater. The Bay Discovery Centre in Glenelg's historic town hall has an art gallery which hosts exhibitions.

- All community organisations • All religions • Cinema
- Croquet • Fishing • Galleries • Golf • Horse racing
- Lawn bowls • Libraries • Sailing • Tennis • Yachting

REAL ESTATE

West Beach and Fulham Gardens
- Median house price: $358 000
- Median unit price: $206 000

Henley Beach
- Houses: $385 000
- Units: $236 000

Brighton
- Houses: $348 000
- Units: $255 000

Glenelg
- Houses: $420 000
- Units: $340 000

Prices on the waterfront are more expensive but still likely to be cheaper than similar positions interstate. Units are in plentiful supply and many have been newly built in high-rise complexes near or on the foreshore.

For warm seaside living, with the city only a tram ride away.

mclaren vale
Country living in Adelaide's backyard

The major wine-producing district of McLaren Vale is closer to Adelaide than the Barossa Valley, and easier to access. The town of McLaren Vale is extremely picturesque, with views of the surrounding hills and vineyards visible from the suburban streets. The region includes the neighbouring, slightly smaller town of Willunga, which is equally attractive. Plenty of retirees live in this region, and there are good aged-care facilities. This is a friendly and enjoyable community to be a part of, and the constant but manageable flow of tourists adds to the community's economy.

POPULATION

- 4500
- 23% over sixty

Both McLaren Vale and Willunga are growing steadily, the latter at a faster rate.

CLIMATE

Summer 12°C to 26.4°C
Winter 4.5°C to 12.7°C
Sunshine 61 days
Rain 147 days
Rainfall 854 mm

LOCATION & GETTING AROUND

McLaren Vale is 40 kilometres south of Adelaide on the Fleurieu Peninsula, a drive of less than 50 minutes. Willunga is 15 kilometres from McLaren Vale.

Roads Main South Road joins the Adelaide-bound M13 freeway (which changes the direction of flow according to the hour).

Nearest airport Adelaide

Nearest train Noarlunga, 10 minutes away from McLaren Vale.

Buses There are up to four coach services to and from Adelaide daily, and buses occasionally run from Noarlunga.

Taxis ✓

INFRASTRUCTURE

Hospitals McLaren Vale Southern District Community Hospital has 25 beds, and there's a major hospital at Noarlunga with public and private beds.

Retirement villages McLaren Vale Lodge and Kalyra Village (both have aged-care facilities) and IOOF Village Units.

Police stations ✓

Local newspaper *Southern Times Messenger*

RECREATION

Cycleways A shared bike and walking path runs through both McLaren Vale and Willunga. The old railway is now a bike path and there is also a bike trail from Noarlunga to Willunga. It's a great way to travel through the vineyards.

Bushwalking & National Parks There are numerous walks, some of them heritage trails through McLaren Vale and Willunga, others along the disused railway. The Kyeema, Mount Magnificent and Aldinga Scrub conservation parks are also nearby. Onkaparinga River Recreation Park has river and wetlands, bushwalking and mountain climbing, birdwatching, canoeing and fishing.

SHOPPING

McLaren Vale has an off-street shopping mall with a Bi-Lo as well as shops along the main street. Major shopping can be done at Noarlunga, 10 minutes away, or Marion, 25 minutes away.

DINING

Where there's wine, there's good food and McLaren Vale is no exception, with plenty of choices from casual to fine dining.

SOCIAL ACTIVITY

There are more than 70 vineyards to choose from, and the social stimulation of Adelaide is less than an hour away.
• Bushwalking • Fishing • Golf • Most religions
• Some community organisations

REAL ESTATE

McLaren Vale
• Median house price: $268 000
• Median unit price: $200 000
Willunga
• Median house price: $300 000
• Median unit price: $200 000

WHY LIVE HERE?

Stimulating country life in an often brisk climate, close to Adelaide.

strathalbyn
A little bit of Scotland

Established in 1839 by Scottish immigrants, this quaint village halfway between Adelaide and Victor Harbor flaunts its Caledonian heritage. It's an attractive place, with the Angas River flowing through it, some beautiful gardens and many heritage-listed buildings. Along with tourism, industries such as farming and Clipsal Electrics are helping Strathalbyn grow, and some residents commute to Adelaide to work. The scenic countryside that surrounds the town is cultivated with diversified farming, from cereal to cattle and sheep.

POPULATION

• 3220
• 25% over sixty
Another 4000 residents live in the neighbouring villages.

CLIMATE

Summer 13.6°C to 27.4°C
Winter 5.9°C to 14.8°C
Sunshine 82 days
Rain 123 days
Rainfall 493 mm

LOCATION & GETTING AROUND

Strathalbyn is 60 kilometres south-east of Adelaide, a 50-minute drive.

Roads Roads are single lane each way but outside of the holiday season they aren't very busy.
Nearest airports Adelaide
Nearest train Only the tourist train passes through on the way to Mount Barker or Goolwa.
Buses Bus to and from Adelaide on weekdays only
Taxis ✓

INFRASTRUCTURE

Hospitals Strathalbyn District Health Service
Retirement villages Two
Police station ✓
Local newspaper *Southern Argus*

RECREATION

Cycleways The roads are fairly safe and flat.
Bushwalking & National Parks The state's 1200-kilometre Heysen Trail passes west of Strathalbyn and the Kuitpo Forest is also a good hiking area. The River Angas Walkway follows the river through the town.

SHOPPING

Strathalbyn's small range of shops includes IGA and Foodland supermarkets, along with various antique and craft shops. Major shopping is in Adelaide or an hour away at Victor Harbor.

DINING

There's not a lot of choice in town but it's only 30 minutes to the restaurants at Goolwa, and less than an hour to Adelaide.

SOCIAL ACTIVITY

Activities include horse, harness and dog racing, polo, swimming in a heated pool and golf at the Ashbourne and Strathalbyn courses.

- Birdwatching • Golf • Horse racing • Horse riding
- Lawn bowls • Some community organisations
- Some religions • Swimming

REAL ESTATE

- Median house price: $246 000
- Median unit price: $175 000

WHY LIVE HERE?

Because you like country life, but don't want to be too far from city comforts, and you don't mind the sound of bagpipes.

victor harbor

Fast-growing retirees' Mecca

The former whaling station of Victor Harbor is the largest centre on the Fleurieu Peninsula. Now a popular whale-watching vantage point, the township lines the sandy beaches and rugged cliffs of Encounter Bay. It's a popular retirement locality and a thriving holiday destination, with fine colonial buildings and a wooden causeway leading to Granite Island just offshore – it's an easy walk from the town centre or you can hop on a double-decker horse-drawn tram dating from 1894. Much of the harbour is extremely shallow, but there are marinas at Goolwa and in the new development on Hindmarsh Island, which is connected by bridge to Goolwa. The huge inland waterway of Lake Alexandrina is also nearby, offering fabulous opportunities for sailing and boating.

Five kilometres north-east of Victor Harbor is the charming, historic town of Port Elliot, with cliff-top views, an excellent beach and grey kangaroos inhabiting the hills behind the coast. Further along, Goolwa Beach is popular for swimming, fishing and boating.

A household name for fresh meat and dairy products, Kangaroo Island is just 16 kilometres off the southern tip of the Fleurieu Peninsula. Kingscote is the main town on the island, which is accessible by ferry from the mainland towns of Cape Jervis and Wirrina.

POPULATION

Victor Harbor	Goolwa	Port Elliot
• 12 000 Est. June 2003	• 4345	• 1520
• 40% over sixty	• 35% over sixty	• 29% over sixty

Kingscote		
• 1650		
• 25% over sixty		

Victor Harbor has the oldest population in South Australia; the median age is 51.2, compared to the state average of 37.9. All the towns in this region are growing, Victor Harbor in particular with 22 per cent growth between censuses.

CLIMATE

Summer 15.3°C to 24.5°C
Winter 7.7°C to 15.4°C
Sunshine 57 days
Rain 127 days
Rainfall 535 mm

LOCATION & GETTING AROUND

Victor Harbor is 80 kilometres south of Adelaide, a driving time of approximately 1.5 hours via the Southern Expressway and Victor Harbor Road. Goolwa is 16 kilometres north-east of Victor Harbor and Kangaroo Island is 110 kilometres south of Adelaide.

Roads The Adelaide-bound Main South Road connects with

Victor Harbor Road, which is mostly one lane each way. The South Australian government places markers along the side of the road showing where deaths (black markers) and injuries (red markers) have occurred. There are many markers of both colours on these roads, making it a very sobering drive.

Nearest airport Adelaide

Nearest train Only the tourist trains from Victor Harbor to Mount Barker

Buses Up to four buses daily to and from Adelaide

Ferries Cape Jervis and Wirrina to Kangaroo Island

Taxis ✓

INFRASTRUCTURE

Hospitals South Coast District Hospital in Victor Harbor, a 38-bed acute public hospital, and South Coast Community Hospital (private).

Retirement villages Five in Victor Harbor and four in Goolwa

Police stations Victor Harbor and Goolwa

Local newspaper *Times*

RECREATION

Beaches Victor Harbor has calm swimming beaches and nearby surfing beaches include Middleton, Port Elliot, Goolwa and Newland Head.

Coastguard ✓

Cycleways This is an area that cyclists love for its gentle terrain and excellent views. The Encounter Bikeway covers 30 kilometres of sealed shared pathway from Victor Harbor to Goolwa. Many local roads have bike lanes.

Bushwalking & National Parks There are many reserves and parks on the peninsula and plenty of opportunities for bushwalks. Granite Island is a nature reserve for penguins and it's easy to get around on foot. The Heysen Trail begins near Victor Harbor, and ends 1200 kilometres later in the Flinders Ranges. Deep Creek Conservation Park has spectacular scenery, wildlife, camping and bushwalking, and Kangaroo Island has some excellent walks and hikes. River walks such as the Hindmarsh River Walk and the Inman River Walk are easy trails of up to eight kilometres.

Dogs Dogs must be on leashes on beaches.

SHOPPING

Victor Harbor is the retail centre, with a wide range of shopping available on Ocean Street and at the Victor Central indoor shopping mall. There are also many smaller shopping centres in the area. Produce and craft markets are held fortnightly.

DINING

The local cuisine incorporates the many regional specialities available, including wine, olives, yabbies and cockles, cheeses, venison and seafood. Dining options are varied, from seafront restaurants on Encounter Bay to vineyards set among the rolling hills.

SOCIAL ACTIVITY

There are two golf courses at Victor Harbor and fifteen on the peninsula, plus croquet and petanque clubs. The Murray River and its lower lakes accommodate yachting and river cruises, which leave from Goolwa. This area is popular for scuba diving, snorkelling and fishing from jetties, riverbanks, beaches or at trout farms. The area's many wineries are also a drawcard. Further education opportunities are available through TAFE and the University of the Third Age.

- Boating • Bushwalking • Cinema • Fishing • Golf
- Lawn bowls • Library • Most community organisations
- Most religions • Surfing • Swimming
- University of the Third Age • Yachting

REAL ESTATE

Victor Harbor
- Median house price: $273 000
- Median unit price: $213 000

Port Elliot

- Median house price: $345 000
- Median unit price: $240 000

More-expensive two-storey homes and units can be found at the new development on Hindmarsh Island.

WHY LIVE HERE?

This area is perfect for those who enjoy living near other retirees in one of Australia's most pristine environments. It's an affordable away-from-it-all location that in reality is not so far from the city.

barossa valley

Rolling hills, vineyards and lots of character

The Barossa Valley is set in gently rolling, vine-clad hills. The over-sixties tend to congregate in Tanunda, Nuriootpa and Angaston, all three of which would make perfect pictures for postcards. The towns' streets are lined with trees, gardens and buildings with character and history, dating back to 1842 and the first German settlers.

They call this the high country but it isn't so very high or so very cold in winter, though it does get hot in summer. There are plenty of interesting things to do in this area and a steady stream of tourists to add variety.

POPULATION

Tanunda	Nuriootpa	Angaston
• 3900	• 3900	• 1900
• 23.5% over sixty	• 23% over sixty	• 20.3% over sixty

The populations of all three towns are growing steadily.

CLIMATE

Summer 14.6°C to 29.7°C
Winter 5.3°C to 13.5°C
Sunshine 111 days

Rain 104 days
Rainfall 494 mm

LOCATION & GETTING AROUND

Adelaide is 75 kilometres away, a drive of around 75 minutes via the Sturt Highway, which has two lanes each way for a large part of the journey.
Roads The roads are narrow and busy with tourists.
Nearest airport Two JetRanger helicopters service the area.
Nearest train ✗
Buses The three towns are serviced by two buses daily to and from Adelaide.
Taxis ✓

INFRASTRUCTURE

Hospitals Tanunda War Memorial (with 24-hour casualty department), Angaston District (also with 24-hour casualty) and Mount Pleasant District.
Retirement villages Barossa Village (high and low care), Gawler, Mount Pleasant District Hospital Aged-Care Units and Tanunda Lutheran Home
Police stations Nurioopta, Mount Pleasant and Williamstown
Local newspaper *Barossa & Light Herald*

RECREATION

Cycleways Tanunda and Nurioopta have some off-road trails. The roads are generally narrow and tend to get a bit crowded for cycling.
Bushwalking & National Parks The Barossa is on the 1200-kilometre Heysen Walking Trail. There are many conservation parks nearby, including Kaiser Stuhl, Para Wirra (walking trails pass where gold was mined 150 years ago), Sandy Creek, Hale (for more challenging walks) and Warren. All of these parks are rich in bird and plant life.

SHOPPING

All the towns have main-street shopping strips. The off-street shopping complex at Nurioopta has an IGA supermarket and Foodland. Farmers' markets are held regularly, and there are many antique and crafts shops throughout the region.

DINING

There are plenty of great restaurants, some of them in the fabulous old vineyard buildings.

SOCIAL ACTIVITY

The highly rated 18-hole Barossa Valley Golf Club is at Kalimna near Nurioopta, surrounded by the Penfolds vineyard. There are swimming pools at Nurioopta and Tanunda, and the latter also has a recreation and fitness centre. Wineries are the attraction around here, of course, and shiraz and cab sav are the specialities of the area. The three towns host an array of social clubs, including photography, china painting, choral, gardening, conservation, dancing, dressage and darts.

• Bushwalking • Golf • Horse riding • Lawn bowls • Libraries
• Most religions • Some community organisations • Swimming

REAL ESTATE

Angaston
• Median house price: $223 000
Nuriootpa
• Median house price: $235 000
Tanunda
• Median house price: $251 000

WHY LIVE HERE?

Because it's verdant, shady and conducive to drinking fine wines.

copper coast

A triangular oasis

The Copper Coast, also known as the Copper Triangle, sits at the top of the Yorke Peninsula, isolated by a barren plain that stretches all the way to Adelaide. The Copper Triangle towns are Moonta and Wallaroo on the coast and inland Kadina. Many of the region's over-sixties have moved here from the Eyre Peninsula and areas further west.

Copper was first found in Wallaroo in 1859, leading to the area's mining and development. These days Wallaroo is a little run-down and industrialised but there are some new residential developments springing up here that are especially suited to over-sixties. Moonta is more appealing and consists of the quaint old township and newer developments at Moonta Bay. Kadina is the area's administrative centre and regional capital. The Cornish heritage in these districts is still evident today – every café sells Cornish pasties!

POPULATION

Moonta	Wallaroo	Kadina
• 3080	• 2700	• 3750
• 35% over sixty	• 32% over sixty	• 24% over sixty

The populations of all three towns are growing steadily. The population of the entire Copper Coast was estimated at 11 200 in 2003 with a median age of 44.3, well over South Australia's state average of 37.9.

CLIMATE

Summer 16.1°C to 30.5°C
Winter 6°C to 15.4°C
Sunshine 122 days
Rain 91 days
Rainfall 389 mm

LOCATION & GETTING AROUND

Kadina is approximately 150 kilometres from Adelaide, a driving time of two hours; it's 19 kilometres north-east of Moonta. Wallaroo is 10 kilometres west of Kadina and 20 kilometres north of Moonta.

Roads From Adelaide access is via the A1 which is two lanes both ways for at least half the journey.

Nearest airport ✗

Nearest train A tourist train runs from Wallaroo to Kadina and Bute (further inland).

Buses Buses run twice daily from Adelaide to the three towns.

Taxis Kadina

INFRASTRUCTURE

Hospitals Moonta Jubilee Hospital, Moonta Private Hospital and Wallaroo Hospital.

Retirement villages At least three with aged-care facilities, one in each town.

Police stations Moonta and Kadina

Local newspaper *Yorke Peninsula Country Times*

RECREATION

Beaches Moonta Bay and Port Hughes have bay beaches with very low swells, popular with families and visitors. The tiny fishing port of Port Hughes is just south of Moonta. Surfing beaches are 180 kilometres away on the south-west corner of the peninsula.

Coastguard ✓

Cycleways You can cycle anywhere you want to as the terrain is fairly flat and the roads aren't too busy.

Bushwalking & National Parks Innes National Park, on the toe of the Yorke Peninsula, has both inland and coastal walking trails. Its many attractions include wild flowers, the many species of birds, the fauna and the ocean beaches for fishing and diving. It can be quite hot and dusty in the bushland here.

Dogs Dogs must be under effective control at all times.

SHOPPING

Kadina has the most extensive and varied shopping, including a large Woolworths supermarket. Moonta has a small shopping strip and Wallaroo has a small Foodland mall.

DINING

Traditional pub counter lunches featuring Cornish pasties are the local speciality. Wallaroo is popular for fish and chips and, of course, prawns – one of the local industries is harvesting prawns. There are a number of waterfront cafés and restaurants in Wallaroo.

SOCIAL ACTIVITY

Social clubs in the area include bridge, angling, writing, gardening, crafts, quilting, woodworking and ballroom dancing. Sporting clubs include croquet, darts, tennis and sailing. There are golf courses at Kadina and Moonta, which has black gravel 'greens'. Kadina has a cinema and movies are screened in Wallaroo's town hall during holiday periods. Kadina also has a theatre which has a cultural centre and gallery, and both Wallaroo and Moonta have museums. The Cornish Festival is held every two years.

- Bushwalking • Cinema • Fishing • Gallery • Golf
- Lawn bowls • Libraries • Most community organisations
- Most religions • Museums • Sailing • Swimming • Tennis
- Theatre

REAL ESTATE

Kadina
- Median house price: $155 000

Wallaroo
- Median house price: $185 000

Moonta Bay
- Median house price: $173 000

WHY LIVE HERE?

The Copper Triangle would appeal to retirees who like to be away from the madding crowd, and who don't object to a bit of dust. Keen anglers would also be happy here.

south australia's top 10

1. **BEST RETIREMENT HOTSPOT: McLaren Vale**
   Quiet country living on Adelaide's doorstep.

2. **BEST RETIREMENT LIFESTYLE: Adelaide — Beaches**
   Good food, shopping, beaches and sporting facilities, and only a tram ride to Adelaide's CBD.

3. **BEST SMALL LOCATION: Robe/Kingston**
   Big surf and pristine beaches, bush walks and a close-knit community.

4. **BEST LARGE LOCATION: Victor Harbor**
   With half the population over fifty years of age, you would be in good company.

5. **BEST SHOPPING: Adelaide**

6. **BEST DINING: Adelaide**

7. **BEST PLACE TO CURL UP WITH A GOOD BOOK: Willunga**

8. **BEST BEACHES: Robe/Kingston**

9. **BEST OUTDOOR ACTIVITIES: Adelaide**
   Everything is close by.

10. **BEST-VALUE REAL ESTATE: Kadina — Copper Coast**

western australia

Albany 303

Augusta 306

Busselton 309

Mandurah 312

Fremantle 316

Perth 319

Yanchep 322

Kalbarri 324

Denham 327

Carnarvon 330

Exmouth 333

Western Australia's Top 10 336

Opposite: Fremantle's bull-nose verandas are a feature of the city

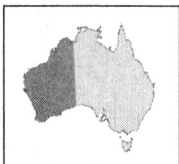

Indian
Ocean

Derby

Broome

Port Hedland

Exmouth

WESTERN

AUSTRALIA

Carnarvon

Denham

Kalbarri

Geraldton

Kalgoorlie

PERTH

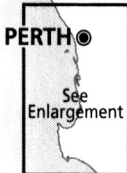

See
Enlargement

Denmark

Albany

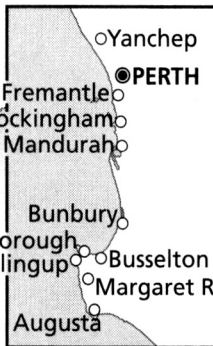

Yanchep

PERTH

Fremantle

Rockingham

Mandurah

Bunbury

Dunsborough

Yallingup

Busselton

Margaret River

Augusta

albany

Civilisation in the wild

Albany is the best coastal retirement location in Western Australia – and possibly the whole of Australia. It is simply unique. Its pristine harbour rivals Sydney's in size and beauty, and has the potential to support a population the size of Perth (although that's probably not what the locals want). The so-called CBD runs down to the harbour and features many fine old buildings in very good nick. There's no high-rise development here, so bushland or harbour is visible from every position. From many aspects the area looks uninhabited as council has managed to keep housing contained, although there's no shortage of waterfront sites at Middleton Beach and Emu Point.

Albany's harbour is made up of several waterways: Princess Royal Harbour, Oyster Harbour and King George Sound. The town is backed by Mounts Melville and Clarence; the latter is topped by a monument to the Anzacs, as this was the last port of call for many diggers who left for Gallipoli in the Great War. The only issue of note in this town is the ongoing debate as to whether and how to develop the harbour foreshore. It is probably only a matter of time before it happens and there are many fine examples elsewhere of how this can be achieved to the benefit of all parties (Townsville, Hervey Bay and Wellington, to name a few). The sleepy village of Denmark is 54 kilometres west of Albany, on an inlet and river behind the sea.

POPULATION

Albany	Denmark
• 22 250	• 2450
• 20% over sixty	• 22.5% over sixty

Albany's population grew by almost 2000 between censuses.

CLIMATE

Summer 15.3°C to 23°C
Winter 8.1°C to 15.6°C
Sunshine 44 days
Rain 178 days
Rainfall 933 mm

Albany is far cooler than the rest of WA, which is one reason why people come here.

LOCATION & GETTING AROUND

Albany is 409 kilometres south-east of Perth, a comfortable drive of 4.5 hours via the straight Albany Highway, which is in excellent condition. Despite having only a single lane each way, the road has only light traffic.

Roads The local roads are wide and well maintained, and there are no parking meters.

Nearest airport Albany, with daily flights to Perth

Nearest train ✗

Buses Daily coach services to Perth (six hours)

Taxis ✓

INFRASTRUCTURE

Hospitals Albany Hospital, reduced to 112 beds

Retirement villages Eleven; the main ones are Silverchain and Glenn-Craig, which include full care and independent living.

Police stations ✓

Local newspapers *Albany Advertiser* and *Albany Extra*

RECREATION

Beaches Middleton Beach is sensational, with white sand, calm conditions and no nasties in the harbour waters. There are also calm beaches at Emu Point. For surf you need to go to ocean beaches such as Lowlands, Perkins or the Blowholes.

Coastguard ✓

Cycleways The road to Emu Point is popular with older cyclists as it is flat. The six-kilometre Middleton Beach to CBD boardwalk is a shared pathway with the best views of the harbours and lots of animal, bird and sea life, including seals, dolphins and whales.

Bushwalking & National Parks The 1000-kilometre Bibbulmun Track terminates right in the centre of town with opportunities for long and short walks through tingle and karri forests. Several national parks are on the doorstep, including West Cape Howe and Gull Rock with choices of trails and beaches.

Dogs Dogs are allowed on the Boardwalk and Middleton Beach (leash free).

SHOPPING

Supermarkets include Woolworths, Coles, Farm Fresh Market and Foodland. There are a number of large shopping centres, including North Road, Dog Rock, Albany Plaza, Main Street and Spencer Park.

DINING

There are some excellent restaurants in town, from upmarket Leonardos to great steak meals at Russell's, and a host of casual-dining experiences in between.

SOCIAL ACTIVITY

Albany has an Over-Fifties' Club offering line dancing, cycling, exercise, ballroom dancing and walking on a weekly basis. One of the two golf clubs has views over King George Sound and boating takes place on the protected waters of Royal Princess Harbour. Horse riding is permitted on Middleton Beach. Whale watching is popular when the southern right and humpback whales arrive in the Sound. Cultural activities include the Albany Light Opera and Theatre Company, an arts centre, gallery and library.

- All community organisations • All religions • Boating
- Bushwalking • Cinema • Gallery • Golf • Horse riding
- Lawn bowls • Library • Surfing • Swimming • Tennis
- Theatre

REAL ESTATE

- Median house price: $230 000
- Median unit price: $143 000

New apartments on Middleton Beach with water views cost

between $375 000 and $400 000. Most of the housing is relatively modest and certainly not new; however, there are some very attractive older-style weatherboard homes.

WHY LIVE HERE?

Heaven would be waking up opposite Middleton Beach, going for a swim in the crystal-clear waters and then walking along the Boardwalk to town for breakfast, with views of whales cavorting offshore in spring and autumn. The climate is perfect, the locals are friendly with time to talk and there's no evidence of road rage. Albany will continue to grow, and should appeal to over-sixties from all over Australia. The one shortcoming is its somewhat remote location, but by air you could be back in Melbourne or Sydney within seven hours or so.

Robert and Diana, a couple I met, were originally from Melbourne and had moved to Albany for the climate and relaxed lifestyle. Robert told me, 'The move didn't worry us because I used to work for the bank and we moved around the country a lot. It helps if you're used to making friends in new places.'

augusta
Karri forests, turquoise waters and peace

The small, attractive town of Augusta is at the end of the road on remote Cape Leeuwin, where the Southern and Indian Oceans meet. The air is clean and the night sky glitters with stars. The locals are friendly, but other than a very active lawn bowls club and an under-utilised golf course, there's not much here. Only 40 kilometres away, however, is the appealing township of Margaret River, at the centre of the state's famous wine region. It's quite a cosmopolitan place, with many shops and eateries, including the classy restaurants that adjoin many of the vineyards. Not too far away are majestic karri forests and limestone caves in the Leeuwin Naturaliste National Park.

POPULATION

- 1128
- 39% over sixty

Margaret River's population is around 4000, with a much younger age profile.

CLIMATE

Summer 17.2°C to 23.3°C
Winter 11.1°C to 16.3°C
Sunshine 46 days
Rain 182 days
Rainfall 999 mm

LOCATION & GETTING AROUND

Augusta is 320 kilometres south-west of Perth, a driving time of just under five hours via the Busselton Highway or the more circuitous Caves Road. Margaret River is a 30-minute drive to the north.

Roads The roads in the region are sealed and well maintained, but single file.

Nearest airport Augusta, with daily services to Perth.

Nearest train Bunbury (2.5-hour journey from Perth), with coach connection to Augusta; two trains daily in both directions.

Buses Perth–Augusta (six hours)

Taxis ✓

INFRASTRUCTURE

Hospitals Augusta District Hospital with 20 beds; there's also the Margaret River District Hospital

Retirement villages Leeuwin Lodge, which is low care. Eight of the Augusta Hospital beds are for permanent care. The lack of aged-care facilities is becoming an issue.

Police stations Augusta and Margaret River

Local newspaper *Augusta–Margaret River Mail*

RECREATION

Beaches This is a harsh coastline, with strong winds, dangerous currents and big surf. The beaches in Western Australia aren't like those on the east coast – they tend to be less accessible and have barriers of fierce scrub. They look inviting, though, with white sand and turquoise-blue water. Hamelin Bay is one beach that is easily accessed, and with a crescent-shaped shoreline and calm water it's ideal for a paddle or a less-challenging swim. Remote Conto's, at the end of a corrugated dirt road, is another appealing beach.

Coastguard ✗

Cycleways There are opportunities to cycle in Margaret River on the roads leading to various vineyards or to go mountain biking on the Boranup Forest trails.

Bushwalking & National Parks Cape to Cape is a famous walk of well over 100 kilometres that runs from Cape Naturaliste to Cape Leeuwin. It can be done in stages; the inland section that winds through the Boranup Karri Forest is sublime, but it tends to be rugged and windswept along the coast. Augusta's Blackwood River has many walking tracks through wild-flower areas, forests and historical sites. The Bibbulmum Track winds through forests, river valleys and along the coast.

Dogs Permitted from Jays Beach to the caravan park.

SHOPPING

Augusta has one recently refurbished shopping strip, with a small Supa Valu supermarket. You would need to drive to Margaret River for the big monthly shop.

DINING

Dining in Augusta is limited to a Chinese restaurant and a couple of cafés. However, there are many fine restaurants in the vineyards and township of Margaret River.

SOCIAL ACTIVITY

Augusta has a small par-three golf course and an 18-hole bush course with gravel greens but fees of only 10 dollars! Clubs include spinning, weaving, art and gardening. Outdoor activities include surfing, snorkelling and canoeing; there's no marina for boating enthusiasts, which is a bit of an issue. The Civic Centre has a gym with squash courts. The area is very close to excellent vineyards, and there are many galleries and studios in the area, with an emphasis on wooden handicrafts and art. Margaret River has an open-air cinema, and the town holds an annual wine and food festival.

- Bushwalking • Diving • Fishing • Galleries • Golf
- Horse riding • Lawn bowls • Library • Swimming
- Tennis • Yachting

REAL ESTATE

- Median house price: $325 000
- Median unit price: $200 000
- Land: from $130 000

Homes on Molloy Island, on the inlet, sell from $190 000.

WHY LIVE HERE?

Augusta itself is small, but with Margaret River so close by there could be the opportunity to own your own small vineyard as a retirement folly. That could be an appealing retirement plan for some retirees, as the climate is good and beaches are close by.

busselton

A warm and peaceful haven

Busselton is more modest than its flashy neighbour Mandurah but growing equally fast, albeit from a lower population base. It is a welcoming town, with a long main street of low-rise shops leading to the shores of sheltered Geographe Bay and a jetty so long it requires a small train to take visitors out to the underwater observatory at its end. Marine and bird life abound here and whale watching is popular.

Busselton's homes are solidly built, single-storey dwellings, less pretentious than Mandurah's and realistically priced. Nearby Dunsborough is smaller than Busselton and is also a well-planned community. There are many fine beach houses hidden among the bush on the north-facing beach that runs along the bay between the two towns. Further on is Yallingup, which has no facilities and is a small holiday community on the hill overlooking the Indian Ocean. One downside of this region is its mosquitoes, which breed in the adjacent wetlands and carry the Ross River virus.

POPULATION

Busselton	Dunsborough
• 14 000	• 1635
• 21% over sixty	• 13.8% over sixty

Busselton grew by over 30 per cent between censuses, and the population of both towns doubles in tourist season.

CLIMATE

Summer 14°C to 28.5°C
Winter 7.5°C to 16.3°C
Sunshine 109 days
Rain 130 days
Rainfall 817 mm
The wettest months are May to October.

LOCATION & GETTING AROUND

Busselton is 225 kilometres from Perth, a journey of less than three hours by car.
Roads Roads are good but single lane.
Nearest airport Busselton, with regular flights to Jandakot (45 minutes) and connecting taxis to Perth.
Nearest train Bunbury. Perth to Bunbury takes 2.5 hours, followed by a 40-minute coach ride to Busselton.
Buses The trip from Perth to Busselton and Dunsborough by coach takes four hours. A local bus service operates within Busselton.
Taxis ✓

INFRASTRUCTURE

Hospitals Busselton District Hospital has 24-hour emergency services but it is in urgent need of an upgrade. Bunbury Regional Hospital is 45 minutes from Busselton.

Retirement villages Cape Care, Nova Care, Winderlup Villas, Kwelam Court and the new National Lifestyle Village for over-55s.

Police stations Busselton and Dunsborough

Local newspapers *Busselton–Dunsborough Mail* and *Capes Herald*

RECREATION

Beaches Geographe Bay's sheltered beaches face north and are great for swimming and sunbathing; Yallingup is the place for surfing. You may encounter stingers in the water from December to April, but they're not the box jellyfish variety and are more annoying than deadly.

Coastguard ✓

Cycleways There is a shared pathway along the waterfront.

Bushwalking & National Parks There are plenty of walking tracks in the Leeuwin Nationaliste National Park and the coastal walk to the Cape Naturaliste Lighthouse.

Dogs Fifteen exercise areas for dogs and two for horses.

SHOPPING

Busselton has Woolworths and Coles supermarkets and plenty of other shops. Dunsborough has a well-planned mall with a large Coles supermarket.

DINING

Busselton has several ethnic restaurants and a little further afield there are upmarket restaurants along Caves Road, some of them attached to vineyards.

SOCIAL ACTIVITY

The Geographe Leisure Centre has both indoor and outdoor swimming pools and a fitness centre, and the Naturaliste Centre runs leisure courses and workshops. There are a number of seniors groups, including the Gadabouts, Healthy Lifestyle Group and Seniors Forum; the Weld Theatre has a repertory club. There are many wineries close by, particularly in the Margaret River region. Dunsborough Lakes is an 18-hole championship golf course surrounded by resort-style housing. Busselton has two courses, one of which is a par three.

• Bushwalking • Golf • Horse riding • Leisure centre • Library
• Most community organisations • Most religions • Surfing
• Swimming • Theatre

REAL ESTATE

• Median house price: $310 000
• Median unit price: $241 000

WHY LIVE HERE?

For the casual, stress-free lifestyle and peaceful surroundings – the beach between Busselton and Dunsborough in particular would be a great location for a beach shack. This is a go-ahead place which has clearly represented a good investment for residents.

mandurah
Boom town

In all my travels around Australia I have not seen so much development in one place – I came across twenty new land releases and countless new estates in various stages of completion in and around Mandurah. At this rate, the area will be another Queensland Gold Coast in a few years. Fortunately, there is plenty of space to grow.

The city of Mandurah is well planned, and its progressive council appears to be coping well with the sea-change phenomenon that has caused such massive growth. The ocean frontage and natural attributes of the Peel Inlet have been enhanced with an adventurous harbour marina development, and a system of artificial canals and channels links the massive inland lakes to the sea.

Indeed, there is water, water everywhere. The city's contemporary Performing Arts Centre and War Memorial exemplify the council's dedication to creating cutting-edge public spaces.

There is a wide choice of residential styles here, from super-extravagant canal-side mansions and clusters of seaside apartment buildings on the marina to more modest homes away from the water. Other location choices within Mandurah include small beachside communities such as Dawesville and Melros Beach. The region is such a popular retirement hotspot that a UK television programme recently (unofficially) rated it as the place where most Brits would choose to retire within WA.

POPULATION

- 54 600 Est. June 2003
- 22.9% over sixty

This is one of the fastest growing areas in Australia. In 1996 the population was 36 000, in 2001 it was over 46 000 and by June 2003 it had leaped to 54 600. I would not be at all surprised if the 2006 census reveals a population for Mandurah in excess of 70 000. Rockingham, just 30 kilometres away on the coast, had a population of 78 700 in 2003 – it has a much younger age profile but it is feasible that these two areas will merge into one.

CLIMATE

Summer 17°C to 29.5°C
Winter 8.6°C to 17.3°C
Sunshine 136 days
Rain 103 days
Rainfall 875 mm
The climate is Mediterranean, hot in summer but low in humidity.

LOCATION & GETTING AROUND

Mandurah is 70 kilometres south of Perth via the modern Kwinana Freeway, a driving time of approximately 50 minutes.
Roads The roads are very good and a large proportion of funds are allocated to road enhancement.

Nearest airport Perth, 80 kilometres away and a travelling time of 75 minutes.

Nearest train Rail services are planned to commence in December 2006 with an expected travel time of 50 minutes to Perth.

Buses Regular connections to Perth (under 1.5 hours) and there are also extensive local services

Taxis ✓

INFRASTRUCTURE

Hospitals Mandurah District Hospital with 130 beds, Peel Health Campus and Private Hospital and 14 medical surgeries.

Retirement villages More than 15, ranging from full care to independent living.

Police stations ✓

Local newspapers *Mandurah Coastal Times*, *Mandurah Mail* and *Mandurah Telegraph*

RECREATION

Beaches There are numerous beaches, but access is often hampered by scrub.

Coastguard ✓

Cycleways There are six excellent dedicated cycle and walking paths with scenic views.

Bushwalking & National Parks There are numerous reserves on the Peel Inlet and ocean front in Mandurah. Yalgorup National Park, just south of Mandurah, has 10 lakes, dunes and walking trails.

Dogs This is a dog-friendly area, with seven off-leash beaches and 11 reserves for leashfree activities.

SHOPPING

There is an abundance of shopping centres, particularly between Smart Street Mall and Mandurah Forum. The shopping area adjacent to the inlet is well contained and pedestrian friendly, and the road into town is lined with a huge, warehouse-style shopping precinct.

DINING

Outdoor dining is a feature of Mandurah, particularly on Mandurah Terrace and the boardwalk overlooking the estuary.

SOCIAL ACTIVITY

Fishing, prawning and crabbing are popular activities in the estuary, and there are plenty of areas for swimming plus indoor heated pools and saunas in the Aquatic Recreation Centre. There are three internationally renowned golf courses to choose from: Kennedy Bay, Secret Harbour and Meadow Springs Country Club. There is also a very active and comprehensive Senior Citizens Centre and a new Performing Arts Centre overlooking Mandjar Bay which hosts many productions and contains a gallery and theatre. Further education is available at the new university and Peel Education Campus.

• All community organisations • All religions
• Aquatic centre • Bushwalking • Cinema • Croquet
• Fishing • Golf • Lawn bowls • Library • Museum
• Swimming • Tennis • Theatre

REAL ESTATE

• Median house price: $272 000
• Median unit price: $200 000
Waterfront views start from $700 000 and drop-dead gorgeous homes on the canals or beachfront average $1.2 million. The North and South Boat Harbours offer new two-bed apartments for $600 000 to $900 000.

WHY LIVE HERE?

The council is progressive and the infrastructure appears to be keeping pace with growth. The town and waterfront are very appealing, although the many new developments in the back-blocks are less tempting.

fremantle

Charming olde-worlde port

Visiting 'Freo' is like stepping back in time. The hard-working port city on the mouth of the Swan River and Indian Ocean has retained its 100-year-old bond stores, civic buildings, retail outlets and pubs, and maintained them beautifully. There are no structures over two storeys in this pedestrian-friendly city. The *QE2* and cruising super liners provide a constant flow of affluent visitors to keep the economy buoyant and local restaurant and retail standards high. The veranda-shaded streets bustle with locals and tourists and are lined with outdoor cafés. A fleet of ferries take daytrippers to and from Rottnest Island, which is closest to the mainland at Fremantle.

North Fremantle is separated from the city by Fremantle Harbour and tends to be very industrialised. There is a wide choice of housing, which overlaps into Perth's southern suburbs such as Cottesloe.

POPULATION

- 31 000
- 20% over sixty

CLIMATE

Summer 18.1°C to 27.9°C
Winter 10°C to 17.1°C
Sunshine 126 days
Rain 122 days
Rainfall 769 mm
It gets quite warm in summer but humidity is low.

LOCATION & GETTING AROUND

Fremantle is 20 kilometres south-west of Perth, a driving time of approximately 25 minutes.
Roads The Stirling Highway connects Fremantle to Perth.
Nearest airport Perth Airport is 26 kilometres away, a driving time of 35 minutes.
Nearest train Fremantle, a 30-minute journey from Perth.

Buses The bus trip from Perth takes just under an hour. This is a very public-transport friendly town – a free bus runs around the city every 10 minutes, and even the car parks are cheap.

Taxis ✓

INFRASTRUCTURE

Hospitals Fremantle Hospital and Kaleeya Hospital, a 95-bed public and private hospital

Retirement villages Seven, including full care and independent living: St Francis Aged Care, Freemasons Nursing Home, Garden Parklands (with 64 strata apartments), Southern Cross Care for the Aged, Tapper Street, Rex Beall Independent Unit and F. Wright Independent Living.

Police stations ✓

Local newspapers *Fremantle Herald*, *Fremantle Community Gazette* and *Rooster*

RECREATION

Beaches The best beaches are on Rottnest Island.

Coastguard ✓

Cycleways Fremantle's cycleways are well established and extensive, particularly along the river and foreshore, with links to Perth. There are also forest nature trails that are appropriate for cycling.

Bushwalking & National Parks Rottnest Island, visible from Fremantle's foreshore, is only 25 minutes away by ferry. The island is 11 kilometres long and 4.5 kilometres wide, and is serviced by a free shuttle bus. It's a popular destination for cycling, fishing, golf, swimming, surfing and snorkelling.

Dogs A dog-friendly area with 17 dog exercise areas, including five foreshore locations.

SHOPPING

The Fremantle markets have over 150 stalls of fresh produce and craft items. E-Shed Markets, in a restored warehouse on

Fremantle's wharf, has an international food court, arts, crafts and gifts. Rather than being concentrated in huge shopping centres, Fremantle's shops tend to be specialist outlets located in tree-lined streets and malls such as King's Square, Essex, Market and High Streets. Shopping hours are also more extensive, usually extending from 8 a.m. to 7 p.m. Apart from the markets, you can also find Coles, Woolworths, Action and Dewsons supermarkets.

DINING

Because of the constant flow of tourists, especially from cruise ships, there are numerous restaurants and cafés to choose from and standards are high. People come from all over Perth to dine in Fremantle. Fishing Boat Harbour is particularly popular (it was where the America's Cup was centred), with a variety of restaurants and cafés. The café strip on South Terrace features cuisines from many different cultures.

SOCIAL ACTIVITY

Culturally based facilities include the Fremantle Arts Centre which runs a diverse programme of exhibitions, courses and workshops. There are four theatres, three cinema complexes, one art-house cinema, a library and over a dozen music venues. The Fremantle Leisure Centre has a health club and swimming pool, aqua fitness and yoga. The Stan Reilly Social Centre provides activities and meals for the over-sixties. There is a large yacht club and several golf courses, and for further education the University of Notre Dame is located in Fremantle.
• All community organisations • All religions • Aquatic centre
• Cinema • Fishing • Galleries • Golf • Lawn bowls • Library
• Museums • Surfing • Swimming • Tennis • Theatre
• Yachting

REAL ESTATE

• Median house price: $453 000
• Median unit price: $275 000

WHY LIVE HERE?

For lifestyle, facilities and proximity to the capital city, this is an excellent retirement choice.

perth
Modern metropolis

Perth is arguably the most beautiful city in Australia. The Swan River is not just any old river – it's a wide expanse of water that's more like a huge lake, with the impressive CBD on one side and wealthy suburbs and parklands on the other. The streets and parks are immaculately cared for; the public transport is new, highly efficient and frequent; and the roads are exceptionally good, with numerous dual-carriageway freeways.

Perth is a very dry, hot city and it suffers from water shortages and restrictions. The humidity is low, fortunately, but some over-sixties spend the hot summer months further south to avoid the heat. Popular retiree suburbs include the beach suburbs of City Beach, Floreat and Cottesloe; the nearby suburbs of Swanbourne or Mount Claremont; and suburbs overlooking the Swan, such as Dalkeith and West Perth. Much of the housing is extravagant to the extreme; as gardening is not an easy pastime here (don't even think about English cottage gardens – only native gardens do well), the houses often take up the whole block. Mindarie, 30 kilometres north of City Beach, is a popular alternative, where townhouses overlook the marina and canals.

POPULATION

Approximately 20 per cent of the population in Perth's popular retiree suburbs is aged over sixty.

CLIMATE

Summer 18.1°C to 30°C
Winter 8.4°C to 17.5°C
Sunshine 131 days
Rain 114 days
Rainfall 821 mm

LOCATION & GETTING AROUND

The beach suburbs are only 15 minutes from the Perth CBD, as Hay Street runs straight from the centre of town to City Beach. The road is lined with trees and low-rise shops before passing through the newish estate of Mount Claremont and Bold Park.

Roads Local roads are good and freeways also run through the area.

Nearest airport Perth Airport is 20 kilometres from City Beach, about 25 minutes to drive.

Nearest train Shenton Park, on the Perth-to-Fremantle line, is nine minutes from Perth CBD. The train passes through some popular retirement suburbs but not all of them.

Buses Less than 20 minutes from Perth CBD

Taxis ✓

INFRASTRUCTURE

Hospitals Sir Charles Gairdner Hospital (Charlie Gairdner's) and Royal Perth, both of which are large hospitals.

Retirement villages Many, ranging from independent villas to full care. Other retirement villages are located at Applecross, Swanbourne, Subiaco and Scarborough.

Police stations Nedlands

Local newspaper *West Australian*

RECREATION

Beaches Cottesloe Beach has a stylish pavilion and lawns, and is very popular for swimming, surfing, fishing and picnicking. City Beach and Floreat Beach are also easily accessed.

Coastguard ✓

Cycleways A shared pathway runs along the foreshore through City and Floreat Beaches. Bold Park and Kings Park also have shared pathways.

Bushwalking & National Parks You could walk away many hours in Kings Park overlooking the Perth CBD – it's the most interesting park and botanic gardens in Australia. Bold Park is a huge expanse of bush between the city and the beach suburbs and has many walking and horse-riding trails.

Dogs Many on- and off-leash areas including the foreshore and Bold Park.

SHOPPING

This is the city, so there are numerous shopping centres. The Forum and Boulevard centres are near City Beach.

DINING

The Swan River and beachfront are home to a large range of restaurants and cafés, and Cottesloe Beach also has some good places to dine. Fremantle, not far down the road, is known for its vibrant nightlife.

SOCIAL ACTIVITY

• Everything

REAL ESTATE

• Median house price: $775 000
• Median unit price: $288 000

Units at Ocean Gardens retirement village in City Beach sell for around $220 000. In Mindarie townhouses with views are priced at $430 000. I could happily live in a luxury apartment or townhouse in West Perth looking down on the CBD with the magnificent Kings Park as my backyard. The price would be about $1.5 million, or over $2 million less than the equivalent would cost in Sydney or Melbourne.

WHY LIVE HERE?

All the amenities of a modern metropolis but without the crush, on the brilliant Swan River.

yanchep
Sandswept

Alan Bond was a master entrepreneur, creating something out of nothing. In the 1980s, he took the sand and spindly scrub of this dry, hot and barren (not to mention unattractive) countryside and developed Yanchep and neighbouring Two Rocks. The beaches here are separated by a no-go zone of brown scrub, making access to the water not always easy. There are some expensive houses here, though, next to but rarely overlooking the Indian Ocean and scattered through the bush.

Yanchep doesn't have any shops; you'll find them at Two Rocks where neat homes sit side by side on the ordered, treeless streets. There's a marina here, where Bondy's boys trained for the America's Cup Challenge. Sand and low scrub is ever present, preventing any real foliage from growing, and water is fed into four or five large tanks from a bore and distributed to the residents.

POPULATION

Yanchep
- 2000
- 22.4% over sixty

Two Rocks
- 1500
- 25.2% over sixty

Both places grew 10 per cent between censuses.

CLIMATE

Similar to Perth.

LOCATION & GETTING AROUND

Yanchep is 50 kilometres north of Perth, which takes around 50 minutes to drive. The Mitchell Freeway is excellent, at times four lanes each way. Two Rocks is six kilometres north of Yanchep.

Roads Average to poor
Nearest Airport Perth
Nearest train Clarkson, 20 minutes away
Buses Six per day to Perth
Taxis ✗

INFRASTRUCTURE

Hospitals Joondalup, 30 kilometres away
Retirement villages One is rumoured to be planned for completion in 2006.
Police stations Two Rocks
Local newspapers *Sun City News* and *Two Rocks Gazette*

RECREATION

Beaches The sea is a beautiful turquoise blue. Yanchep's main beach, which is protected by a small reef, looks very inviting and is patrolled in season.
Coastguard ✓
Cycleways There are no cycleways but the terrain is flat.
Bushwalking & National Parks Yanchep National Park features a combination of caves, walking trails and lakes. Unfortunately, half the park was burnt out in an intentionally lit fire in December 2004.
Dogs Two beaches permit dogs.

SHOPPING

Two Rocks has a small mall with basic shops, including a small supermarket and pharmacy but no bank.

DINING

Eating options are very limited; there's a restaurant in the Cape Capricorn Resort and at the Marina Tavern.

SOCIAL ACTIVITY

The Sun City Country Club has an 18-hole golf course, complete with emus. The Recreation Centre has a writers' group, library, carpet bowls and cards as well as arts and crafts. There's no swimming pool and no cinema.
• Golf • Lawn bowls • Library • Swimming

REAL ESTATE

• Median house price: $248 000

There are many architect-designed houses here; those close to the ocean are priced at over $800 000. The houses are solid and attractive but I wonder if they are over-capitalised in this environment.

WHY LIVE HERE?

In the words of one of the locals, 'There are no break-ins, and you can walk the streets safely. The community is extremely close and looks out for each other. We had some illness in the house a while ago and next thing you know there's a neighbour with a pot of soup at the front door.'

kalbarri
Isolated seaside beauty

The isolated resort town of Kalbarri is 580 kilometres north of Perth and 150 kilometres north of Geraldton, on the Coral Coast. It's set on a protected estuary at the mouth of the Murchison River, and is home to a thriving fishing industry. The landscape is spectacular, particularly at sunset, with Kalbarri National Park, the steep gorges of the picturesque Murchison River and the craggy, windswept cliffs overlooking the ocean. Offshore, the marine life includes dolphins, sharks and whales.

Geraldton is Kalbarri's larger neighbour, although at 150 kilometres away it's not a close neighbour! Formerly a convict settlement, it is an old town with a history and old buildings to prove it. Geraldton is renowned for the quality of its lobster fishing and it has many pristine beaches. There are wineries nearby in the Chapman Valley.

POPULATION

Kalbarri	Geraldton
• 2150	• 25 500
• 33% over sixty	

Kalbarri's population is growing, while Geraldton's is stagnating.

CLIMATE

Summer 20.6°C to 34.2°C
Winter 9.8°C to 21.4°C
Sunshine 185 days
Rain 65 days
Rainfall 369 mm

LOCATION & GETTING AROUND

Kalbarri is 580 kilometres (seven hours) north of Perth and 160 kilometres (1.5 hours) north of Geraldton.

Roads The Brand Highway heads north from Perth to Geraldton, and the route further north to Kalbarri is via the North West Coastal Highway and Port Gregory Road. All these roads are sealed, but roads in national parks are unsealed.

Nearest airports There are three flights to Perth per week, and the flight takes up to two hours. There is also an airport at Geraldton, with 55-minute flights to Perth.

Nearest train ✗

Buses Bus services three days a week; the trip to Perth takes eight hours.

Taxis ✓

INFRASTRUCTURE

Hospitals Geraldton Regional Hospital and St John of God Hospital, also in Geraldton. The Kalbarri Health Centre is open 24 hours and has a resident doctor, physiotherapist and visiting dentist. An ambulance is available.

Retirement villages ✗

Police stations Geraldton and Kalbarri

Local newspapers *Geraldton Guardian*, *Midwest Times* and *Kalbarri Town Talk*

RECREATION

Beaches Kalbarri's calm estuary and crescent-shaped sandy beach is great for swimming, and surfing is popular at Jake's Point. To the south of Kalbarri there is a beautiful fishing beach with good access at Eagle Gorge. Lucky Bay can be accessed by 4WD. There are many beaches near Geraldton (Sunset, Town, Pages, Greys, St Georges, Back, Champion Bay) and all the beaches in this area are free of stingers, sea snakes and poisonous fish.

Coastguard ✓

Cycleways Chapman River mountain bike trail, Geraldton. At Kalbarri, there is a cycle path along the coastline and cliff tops with spectacular views.

Bushwalking & National Parks Kalbarri National Park, 57 kilometres east of the township, has fantastic red-and-white banded rock formations and deep gorges carved into the cliffs overlooking the Murchison River. There are plenty of walking trails to lookouts and rock pools, and over 800 species of wild flowers in the park as well as kangaroos, emus, ospreys and wedge-tailed eagles. Along the coast there are walks along the majestic cliff tops.

SHOPPING

There are two supermarkets in Kalbarri and a range of grocery shops, and most shops are open seven days a week. There is also a pharmacy and post office.

DINING

Perhaps predictably, the speciality is seafood, particularly lobster. There are a few restaurants and cafés, and some of them overlook the Murchison River.

SOCIAL ACTIVITY

Water sports are what Kalbarri is about: aquascooters, canoeing and fishing from the beach and ocean. There is a nine-hole golf course and swimming pool, plus an oceanarium, wild-flower centre and seahorse sanctuary. The Rainbow Jungle houses 350 birds and is the largest walk-in parrot aviary in Australia. At Geraldton there are two golf courses, a marina, museum, race course, library and art gallery. The city hosts the Sunshine Festival in the last two weeks of October.

- Bushwalking • Fishing • Gallery • Golf • Horse racing
- Horse riding • Lawn bowls • Library • Snorkelling
- Surfing • Swimming • Tennis

REAL ESTATE

- Median house price: $250 000
- Median unit price: $150 000
Few homes are available for sale.

WHY LIVE HERE?

To enjoy a life free of pollution and pressure, and to never feel cold.

denham
Dolphins, dugongs and pearly shells

Located on the Peron Peninsula on the shores of Shark Bay, the remote marine paradise of Denham is the most westerly town in Australia. It's a small but charming place where tourists tend to stop over on their way to interact with the dolphins at Monkey Mia, 28 kilometres away on the other side of the peninsula. Dolphins swim to the water's edge to be fed by hand, thousands of dugongs live in the bay and ancient stromatolites grow in the shallows.

Denham was historically a pearling port but it now thrives on fishing and tourism. It has a beautiful beach and jetty and two of its buildings, St Andrew's Church and the Old Pearlers Restaurant, have been built entirely from shell aggregate taken from Shell Beach. The town's power is largely provided by wind turbines. I thought the stars in the Margaret River were bright but up here they are amazing. It is hot, of course, too hot for many retirees, who prefer to live south of Kalbarri, and some locals head south during the summer months. Anywhere north of here is going to be even hotter.

POPULATION

- 1430
- 37% over sixty

CLIMATE

Summer 21.2°C to 36.9°C
Winter 9.2°C to 20.7°C
Sunshine 210 days
Rain 38 days
Rainfall 212 mm
Denham is cyclone prone and very hot, but not too humid.

LOCATION & GETTING AROUND

Denham is 826 kilometres from Perth on the shores of Shark Bay, approximately a nine-hour drive.

Roads Travel from Perth is via the North West Coastal Highway and Shark Bay Road, both of which are sealed.

Nearest airport Monkey Mia (Denham) Airport. There are flights to and from Perth five days a week (just over two hours).

Nearest train ✗
Buses ✓
Taxis ✓

INFRASTRUCTURE

Hospitals Shark Bay Silver Chain Health Centre and Nursing Post at Denham. The closest hospital is Carnarvon Regional Hospital, which is 331 kilometres away.

Retirement villages ✗
Police stations ✓
Local newspapers *Midwest Times* and *Northern Guardian*

RECREATION

Beaches Denham's beautiful beach has calm water and safe swimming. Dolphin Beach at Monkey Mia is picturesque and popular for interaction with dolphins. Fifty kilometres to the south of Denham is Shell Beach, made up of millions of tiny white seashells; at low tide you can walk hundreds of metres into the bay. Nanga Bay Beach offers superb swimming and fishing.

Coastguard ✓

Cycleways Shared pathways from Denham to Little Lagoon
Bushwalking & National Parks Shark Bay is a World Heritage area with plenty of pristine beaches, inlets and bays. The Hamelin Pool stromatolites can be viewed from a boardwalk. The Francois Peron National Park is accessible by 4WD vehicles.

SHOPPING

Denham has two supermarkets, a Foodland and a Tradewinds.

DINING

Denham specialises in seafood and is particularly known for its prawns and fresh snapper. There are a couple of hotel/motel and resort restaurants and cafés. The Old Pearler Restaurant is probably the area's most popular dining option.

SOCIAL ACTIVITY

There are many water-based activities such as fishing (jetty, beach and deep sea), sailing and snorkelling. There are several boat charter services (including self charter) and cruises such as trips to Dirk Hartog Island to see turtles and on glass-bottomed boats to view a pearl farm.

- Boating • Diving • Fishing • Golf • Lawn bowls • Library
- Museum • Sailing • Snorkelling • Swimming • Tennis

REAL ESTATE

- Median house price: $260 000
There aren't a lot of houses for sale in Denham.

WHY LIVE HERE?

I can't think of a more remote, more beautiful place to be if you love nature, fishing or diving, are happy to be cut off from the rest of the world and don't mind the heat.

carnarvon
Sunny and remote

Carnarvon is a thriving town at the mouth of the Gascoyne River. It is like a small oasis, backed by a vast dry land, with bananas, grapes, mangoes and tomatoes growing in riverside plantations. Carnarvon is the commercial centre for the district: a large fishing industry provides prawns, crabs and snapper, and to the north salt is mined for export. The town's features include One Mile Jetty on Babbage Island, its wide main street (typical of many country towns) and the Big Dish, once used for communications and now providing extensive views of the landscape. The social centre of the town seems to be Fascine Bay, formed by the southern arm of the Gascoyne River, where people gather for picnics, swimming, fishing and walking on the landscaped shores.

POPULATION

- 7275
- 24% over sixty

CLIMATE

Summer 22.2°C to 31.5°C
Winter 10.5°C to 22.5°C
Sunshine 163 days
Rain 32 days
Rainfall 230 mm
Cyclone prone but not as humid as other tropical locations.

LOCATION & GETTING AROUND

Carnarvon is 905 kilometres north of Perth via the Brand and North West Coastal Highways, a driving time of just under 11 hours. Geraldton is 480 kilometres to the south.

Roads Carnarvon is on the North West Coastal Highway, which heads both south and north of the city. Some of the coastal roads are unsealed.

Nearest airport Carnarvon; two-hour flights to Perth are available daily.

Nearest train ✗
Buses Daily coaches to Perth (12 hours) and a local bus service
Taxis ✓

INFRASTRUCTURE

Hospitals Carnarvon Regional Hospital
Retirement villages ✗
Police stations ✓
Local newspaper *Northern Guardian*

RECREATION

Beaches Town Beach is a popular swimming beach with coarse white sand. Fascine Bay at the mouth of the Gascoyne River is also good for all water sports and picnics. The beaches to the north, such as Bush Bay, New Beach and Three Mile Beach, are all excellent for surfing but there are signs warning of treacherous king tides. This is a magnificent stretch of coastline, with high cliffs yielding spectacular ocean views. Point Quobba has a protected lagoon that's ideal for swimming and Pelican Point is popular for swimming and fishing. Oysters, fish and crayfish can be found at the beach next to the Blowholes.

Coastguard ✗
Cycleways There are some shared-use pathways
Bushwalking & National Parks The Kennedy Range National Park, 150 kilometres due west of Carnarvon, is a spectacular wilderness area with views of gorges and colourful rock faces; after rain it can be lush with wild flowers. The former pastoral station of Francois Peron National Park has an old pearling camp site, lovely beaches and dolphins. Rocky Pool and Chinaman's Pool are popular fresh-water swimming holes along the river which attract many varieties of bird life.

Dogs There are dog exercise areas at Small Boat Harbour, Wise Park and on the town's beachfront.

SHOPPING

Carnarvon is a regional shopping centre and has most well-known chain stores and supermarkets.

DINING

Most restaurants are found in the hotels and motels, offering a variety of cuisines, and there are also cafés and seafood eateries.

SOCIAL ACTIVITY

Water activities include swimming, sailing, surfing, windsurfing, snorkelling, fishing in the Facine inlet and whale watching in winter. For cultural and educational activities there is a museum of local artefacts plus a lighthouse museum and a TAFE for ongoing education. Carnarvon hosts a rodeo, annual rock concert and yachting regatta.
- Boating • Fishing • Golf • Lawn bowls • Museums
- Sailing • Snorkelling • Some community organisations
- Some religions • Surfing • Swimming • Waterskiing

REAL ESTATE

- Median house price: $139 000
- Median unit price: $100 000

WHY LIVE HERE?

For its relaxed, tropical lifestyle and dry climate. Conveniently located between the Shark Bay World Heritage area and the pristine Ningaloo Reef, this is a spectacular coastal area with solid residential and tourism growth.

exmouth
Hot and sunny nature reserve

Exmouth has a very dry, hot climate which the locals list as one of its best assets; the other is the sheer beauty of the place. The remote town is situated on the North West Cape, just a kilometre from the ocean on the Exmouth Gulf. The road stops here, so there is no passing traffic, but there is plenty to see and do. The famous Ningaloo Marine Park protects an accessible coral reef that offers magnificent diving and snorkelling, and the Cape Range National Park has opportunities for bushwalks and 4WD touring.

Exmouth was established in the 1960s as a service town for the US naval station that was based here; the US navy left in 1992, leaving the pristine environment to be enjoyed by locals and tourists alike. With the funds from the sale of the land formerly occupied by the navy, the community has funded a modern airport and marina facilities. Exmouth is self-sufficient, with a range of facilities and services usually only found in towns twice its size.

POPULATION

- 3140
- 28% over sixty

CLIMATE

Summer 24°C to 33.6°C
Winter 14.6°C to 22.9°C
Sunshine 230 days
Rain 22 days
Rainfall 294 mm
The area is prone to cyclones.

LOCATION & GETTING AROUND

Exmouth is 1250 kilometres north of Perth, a drive of around 13.5 hours via the North West Coastal Highway. It is 370 kilometres from Carnarvon, which takes 4.5 hours to drive.
Roads The Learmonth–Minilya Road runs 180 kilometres from

the North West Coastal Highway into Exmouth. Many roads in the area are unsealed.

Nearest airport Learmonth Airport, 35 kilometres south of Exmouth (accessible via shuttle bus), has daily flights to Perth.

Nearest train ✗

Buses Three services a week to Perth

Taxis ✓

INFRASTRUCTURE

Hospitals Exmouth District Hospital; Community Health Service, four doctors, a dentist and a physiotherapist.

Retirement villages ✗

Police stations ✓

Local newspapers *Northern Guardian* and *Exmouth Expression*

RECREATION

Beaches Exmouth's Town Beach has safe swimming, windsurfing and sailing, with a yacht club and boat ramp. Pebble Beach and Bundegi Beach, to the north, are good for swimming, snorkelling and fishing. The Ningaloo Marine Park begins at Bundegi and boats leave from the beach for coral viewings. The Tamarisks, 30 kilometres south, is a shady picnic spot with safe swimming.

Coastguard ✓

Cycleways All footpaths have dual pathways for cyclists and pedestrians. A walk/bike trail circumnavigates the town and runs to the naval base.

Bushwalking & National Parks The Cape Range National Park has panoramic coastal views, particularly of Ningaloo Reef, plus sandy beaches, walking tracks, good snorkelling and swimming. Shothole Canyon, south of Exmouth, has some spectacular scenery along its walking trails, with views of gorges, colourful rocks and canyons; it's advised not to walk here in the heat of summer and to be careful of loose rocks. Ningaloo Reef is over 260 kilometres long, making it one of the largest fringing reefs in the world. The reef is particularly close to the coast and contains many species of coral and fish – ideal for snorkelling.

Dogs There are plenty of open spaces and beach areas for exercising dogs but they are not allowed on ovals and recreation grounds.

SHOPPING

There is a mall on Ross Street, two supermarkets and the usual hardware, pharmacy, newsagent and local craft shops.

DINING

Exmouth has three reasonable restaurants: Whalers, Exmouth Bar and Grill, and Rock Cod Café.

SOCIAL ACTIVITY

Many of Exmouth's social activities focus on outdoor pursuits such as swimming, snorkelling, diving and kayaking. Game fishing is a popular pastime in the Exmouth Gulf, as are coral cruises, and turtle rookeries can be visited during the summer months. Exmouth's golf club has 18 holes and greens of sand. There are five tennis courts and a 50-metre public swimming pool, a starlight cinema, library and TAFE. The small harbour has public boating facilities.

- Bushwalking • Boating • Cinema • Diving • Fishing • Golf
- Lawn bowls • Library • Sailing • Snorkelling • Swimming
- Tennis • Windsurfing • Yachting

REAL ESTATE

- Median house price: $270 000
- Median unit price: $134 000

WHY LIVE HERE?

To live close to nature in a beautifully remote location, and enjoy the ocean and bushland.

western australia's top 10

1. BEST RETIREMENT HOTSPOT: Albany
An old-fashioned town with an air of independence, set on a magical harbour.

2. BEST RETIREMENT LIFESTYLE: Fremantle
All the benefits of city living in an olde-world atmosphere.

3. BEST SMALL LOCATION: Busselton
It may not be small for long, as Busselton is in the process of being discovered.

4. BEST LARGE LOCATION: Mandurah
It's no wonder the population is exploding.

5. BEST SHOPPING: Perth

6. BEST DINING: Perth

7. BEST PLACE TO CURL UP WITH A GOOD BOOK: Margaret River

8. BEST BEACHES: Kalbarri

9. BEST OUTDOOR ACTIVITIES: Fremantle
For Rottnest Island's swimming, surfing, snorkelling, diving, boating, golf and bushwalking.

10. BEST-VALUE REAL ESTATE: Carnarvon

new zealand

North Island 341

  Bay of Plenty 341

  Kapiti Coast 345

South Island 349

  Marlborough Region 349

  Nelson 352

  Christchurch 355

New Zealand's Top 10 359

Opposite: High above the native forest,
Nelson's Skywire reaches speeds of 100 km/h
(Photograph courtesy Latitude Nelson)

Auckland

Kātikati
Tauranga
Rotorua

Bay of Plenty

BAY OF PLENTY

N E W

North Island

Z E A L A N D

Picton
Paraparaumu
Nelson
◉WELLINGTON
Marlborough Sounds
Blenheim

South Island
Christchurch

Pacific Ocean

There are many good reasons to consider New Zealand as a retirement option. Firstly, it is a lot closer to Australia than you might think. It takes only three hours to fly there – less time than it takes to fly from the east to the west coast of Australia. The flights are relatively cheap, too; one-way fares can be as low as $250 plus taxes, sometimes even less. Secondly, it is almost in our time zone. Thirdly, Aussie dollars are worth more than Kiwi dollars, and the cost of living and housing are cheaper than in Australia (real estate prices quoted in this chapter are expressed in Australian dollars). Fourth, the cities are modern but more laid-back than Sydney or Melbourne; the architecture is innovative; and, of course, there's also its world-class wines and great dining. The fifth reason is New Zealand's lack of poisonous spiders, snakes, crocodiles, stingers and nasty fish, plus there are fewer mozzies . . . okay, there are some sandflies. The climate is wetter and cooler than most Aussies experience, but the flip side is the ability to have colourful English gardens which don't die when you leave them for a week. Despite the weather, New Zealanders are outdoor folk who enjoy fishing in streams and the ocean, kayaking, rafting, bushwalking, sailing, golf and a host of death-defying action sports.

Finally, New Zealanders speak the same language as us – well, almost. There are a few terms you will need to master: an Esky is a Chilli Bin, a bubbler a water fountain, bushwalking is tramping and a weekender is a bach (pronounced 'batch').

north island
bay of plenty
Plenty of everything on the Sunshine Coast

It is not surprising that New Zealanders are flocking to live in the Bay of Plenty, in the North Island's north-east. With its beautiful beaches and unspoilt rainforests, plus the infrastructure of a commercial port, it has the appeal of a holiday resort. The area's key retirement magnets are Tauranga, Katikati, Papomoa Beach and Te Puke. Picturesque Tauranga is the country's fifth-largest city, with historic buildings and harbour views. Just five minutes away at the entrance to the harbour is Mount Maunganui, which has popular thermal salt pools, outdoor cafés and bustling shopping strips.

The Bay of Plenty area is known for its produce, particularly kiwi fruit. The housing throughout ranges from modest to highly appealing beach houses, plus there are high-rise apartments at Mount Maunganui.

POPULATION

Tauranga	Te Puke	Katikati
• 100 000	• 7000	• 3000
• 22.5% over sixty	• 24% over sixty	• 33% over sixty

This is one of the fastest-growing locations in the country.

CLIMATE

Summer 14.6°C to 23.9°C
Winter 5.0°C to 14.3°C
Sunshine 2257 hours
Rain 110 days
Rainfall 1202 mm

LOCATION & GETTING AROUND

Tauranga is 200 kilometres from Auckland, around a 2.5-hour drive, and it's only a few hours from the nearest ski fields.

Roads The A2 road from Auckland is in good condition but unfortunately single file for much of the way. The local roads become very congested in holiday and peak periods.

Nearest airports Tauranga Airport has daily domestic flights only. Hamilton Airport is 75 minutes away, with direct flights to Australia.

Nearest train ✗
Buses Intercity and local buses
Taxis ✓

INFRASTRUCTURE

Hospitals Tauranga Hospital has 300 beds and a 24-hour emergency department

Retirement villages There are many excellent villages and resorts appealing to over-55s and up, some on golf courses. New ones are currently under construction in all towns in this region.

Police stations Tauranga, Katikati, Mount Maunganui and Te Puke

Local newspapers *Daily Bay of Plenty Times* and *Bay News*

RECREATION

Beaches Mount Maunganui's patrolled beach is very popular and there are lovely long stretches of beach at Papamoa and Maxwells Road Beach on the harbour.

Coastguard ✓

Cycleways Many streets and footpaths have dedicated bike and mobility-scooter lanes, and there are cycle paths on the foreshore.

Bushwalking & National Parks Mount Maunganui has a number of walks with views of the sea and harbour. A booklet detailing 15 walks is available from the town's council, taking in the ocean, harbour foreshores, wetlands and McLaren Falls Park.

Dogs There are no specific dog exercise areas. No dogs are permitted on the beaches at Katikati or Mount Maunganui.

SHOPPING

Tauranga's shopping strip stretches for twelve blocks along busy Cameron Road, as well as the less busy web of streets in the town centre. Pak'nSave is a great value-for-money supermarket warehouse. Mount Maunganui has an extensive shopping strip, where the accent is on holiday wear and fare, plus there's the Bayfair Shopping Centre, reputedly one of the most successful retail complexes in New Zealand.

DINING

The dining is first-rate, with a choice of many fine restaurants as well as cafés. There are healthy alternatives, with sushi a popular choice, and outdoor dining is pleasant at Tauranga and Mount Maunganui.

SOCIAL ACTIVITY

There is plenty to entertain the over-sixties in the Bay of Plenty, and this is one of New Zealand's warmer locations (hence its nickname, the Sunshine Coast). There are plenty of water sports and fishing is popular in the harbour and ocean, as is sailing at Tauranga and Mount Maunganui. There are eight golf courses in the area, plus a large bridge club and a very arty community in Katikati. The Tauranga Arts Festival presents a biannual programme of dance, theatre, music, workshops and exhibitions. For further education, the University of Waikato is at Tauranga.

• All community organisations • All religions • Bushwalking
• Croquet • Fishing • Golf • Horse racing • Lawn bowls
• Libraries • Sailing • Swimming • Theatre

REAL ESTATE

• Median house price: $250 000
• Median unit price: $400 000

There are many fine homes in this area, a number of them with older-style character.

WHY LIVE HERE?

A safe, friendly environment where the dollar goes further than in Australia, the sun shines more than in the rest of New Zealand and the quality of life is good. A local told me: 'We refer to it as the Sunshine Coast rather than the Gold Coast because it is a lot more laid-back than the Gold Coast in Oz.'

kapiti coast
Sea change close to Wellington

The Kapiti Coast starts at Paekakariki, only thirty minutes from Wellington, and stretches north through Raumati Beach, Paraparaumu, Waikanae Beach, Te Horo and Otaki. This is one long stretch of beach, overlooking the Tasman Sea and the protected nature reserve of Kapiti Island. Originally, the houses here were baches (weekenders) but that is changing and there are some fine examples of innovative beach homes, many in the Mexican style. It is still possible to purchase an old bach with water views but if you're expecting golden beaches you'll be disappointed as the sand is the volcanic black variety, and after rain the beach is frequently littered with debris from the forests.

Paraparaumu is the commercial hub, with a large retail shopping centre. Retirees tend to move here from Wellington as the temperature is a degree or so warmer. One of the most appealing aspects of this region is its proximity to the capital, one of the most beautiful cities in the world. Surrounded by green hills and a large harbour, the compact city of Wellington is rich in shopping, cafés, restaurants and entertainment, plus it has some sensational architecture.

There are three problems on the Kapiti Coast which need to be addressed before you might be comfortable moving here. There is a shortage of water – otherwise unheard of in this country; the local hospital is inadequate and needs to be upgraded; and the fire brigade is run mostly by volunteers. Given the number of residents who are moving into this area, however, it is surely only a matter of time before improvements are made.

POPULATION

- 40 000
- 28% over sixty

Wellington is a very young area with a total population of over 400 000.

CLIMATE

Summer 13.2°C to 21.5°C
Winter 4.4°C to 12.4°C

Sunshine 2065 hours
Rain 113 days
Rainfall 1036 mm

LOCATION & GETTING AROUND

The Kapiti Coast is 50 kilometres north of Wellington.

Roads The roads are in good condition and State Highway One runs along the coast. New Zealand's roads are quite dangerous as they tend to be narrow and mostly single file, with few overtaking opportunities despite 100 km/h speed limits. Highway One is sometimes closed for hours at a time due to accidents.

Nearest airports Paraparaumu Airport, with local flights only. Wellington's international airport is only 40 minutes away, with direct flights to Australia.

Nearest train Efficient services between the Kapiti Coast and Wellington.

Buses Local buses plus coaches to Wellington

Taxis ✓

INFRASTRUCTURE

Hospitals Paraparaumu Hospital and the large Wellington Hospital

Retirement villages There are 10 in the area and the number is growing to meet demand. They are well presented, and many offer full care.

Police stations There are police stations in all six towns.

Local newspapers *Dominion Post*, *Kapiti Observer* and *Otaki Mail*

RECREATION

Beaches Swimming is safe as the water is extremely shallow and calm. There is only one surf club – I suspect the method they use to save swimmers in distress is to simply walk out and get them.

Coastguard ✓

Cycleways The area is flat and there are cycleways along the foreshore. The 18-kilometre Rimutaki Rail Trail is a shared pathway across streams and through old tunnels.

Bushwalking & National Parks Kapiti Island is a nature reserve and bird sanctuary crisscrossed with walking trails – it's relatively quiet as only 50 visitor permits are issued daily. The numerous walks on the mainland include the large coastal reserve of Queen Elizabeth Park and the Waikanae River path, shaded by willows.

Dogs The beaches and riverbanks are popular walking areas, and rules are pretty relaxed.

SHOPPING

The Coastlands Shopping Town at Paraparaumu is the largest shopping centre, with a variety of major department stores and a Pak'nSave supermarket. Raumati has a boutique shopping centre.

DINING

Good cafés and restaurants are sprinkled along the coast, especially at Raumati.

SOCIAL ACTIVITY

The area has four golf courses, one of which is amongst New Zealand's best. Other activities include trout fishing, rafting, kayaking and horse riding (even on the beach). There is not a lot of boating as it is too shallow for a marina and boats need to be trailored out to deeper water by tractor. You would need to drive to Plimmerton or Wellington for ocean fishing or sailing. Clubs include an aero club, car club, chess, bridge, music society, model planes and trains, Rotary and an arts and crafts society.

- Cinema • Croquet • Fishing • Golf • Horse riding
- Lawn bowls • Libraries • Most community organisations
- Most religions • Museum • Sailing • Swimming • Tennis

REAL ESTATE

- Median house price: $200 000
- Median unit price: $180 000

There is only one high-rise apartment block on the coast – its construction caused such an uproar that no more than four storeys are now permitted under the District Plan. There are only a few apartment blocks, as most of the accommodation consists of free-standing dwellings. Some very innovative architecture on the foreshores starts from $750 000. At Waikanae there are some large blocks with beautiful older-style homes and lush gardens. It could be feasible to pick up a small cottage for $150 000.

WHY LIVE HERE?

Currently the Kapiti Coast suits retirees from Wellington who want to remain close to family and friends. However, I doubt you will find better value for money anywhere and it really is only a few hours from Australia's east coast. Of course, it does have a somewhat colder climate than many Aussies are used to.

south island
marlborough region
Picture-perfect isolation

World renowned for its wine, the picture-postcard Marlborough Region is on the north-eastern tip of the South Island, overlooking waterways and surrounded by steep, forested hills. The largest centre is Blenheim and it's popular with over-sixties, as is the smaller but highly picturesque port of Picton from where the ferries cross Queen Charlotte Sound and Cook Strait to Wellington. Scattered throughout the region are small fishing and rural hamlets such as Havelock and Seddon. The sunken valleys, steep mountains and bays and inlets of Queen Charlotte Sound are home to wonderful bird and sea life and ideal for serious bushwalking. The only drawback to the region is that it's occasionally subject to flooding.

POPULATION

- 40 000
- 20.5% over sixty

Blenheim has the largest population, with almost 27 000 citizens; Picton's population is 4000. The region is growing slowly overall.

CLIMATE

Summer 12.6°C to 23.6°C
Winter 2.1°C to 12.7°C
Sunshine 2459 hours
Rain 78 days
Rainfall 689 mm

LOCATION & GETTING AROUND

Blenheim is almost 300 kilometres north of Christchurch, a five-hour drive. It is over 100 kilometres from Nelson and accessible to Wellington via a ferry from Picton, which takes around three hours.

Roads Highway One runs through the region and down the east coast to Christchurch.

Nearest airport Blenheim

Nearest train Picton–Christchurch

Buses ✓

Taxis ✓

INFRASTRUCTURE

Hospitals Wairau Hospital in Blenheim and a Community Health Centre in Picton.

Retirement villages At least eight in Blenheim and Picton

Police stations Blenheim, Picton and Havelock

Local newspaper *Marlborough Express*

RECREATION

Beaches The bays and beaches of the Marlborough Sounds are mostly accessible by boat and walking tracks. Many of the bays are steep-sided with sandy beaches, and those in Picton, Shelly Beach and Bobs Bay are particularly good for swimming and boating. There are also the quiet beaches of Port Underwood and the Waikawa Foreshore.

Coastguard ✓

Cycleways There are dedicated trails within reserves and the towns. Bicycle tours operate throughout the area, using the narrow roads. It is advisable to fix a flag to the side of your bike to keep the traffic just that little bit further away.

Bushwalking & National Parks The world-famous Queen Charlotte Track winds for 70 kilometres through lush coastal forest, along ridges and around coves and bays. The track can be done in sections, with ferries as transport, and there are spectacular views of the Queen Charlotte and Kenepuru Sounds. There are also many other walks to choose from in this region.

Dogs There is an exercise area in Taylor River Reserve in Blenheim and one in Picton at the Auckland Street Reserve.

SHOPPING

There are supermarkets in Blenheim, Picton and Havelock, and grocery stores in all townships. Blenheim has a full range of shopping and department stores, and craft and gifts shops are found throughout the region.

DINING

Excellent restaurants are scattered throughout the Sounds and the vineyard areas. The restaurants overlooking the harbour at Picton are especially pleasant. Green-lipped mussels, available throughout the South Island and a New Zealand delicacy, are very popular in this region.

SOCIAL ACTIVITY

Along with tramping (bushwalking), other popular outdoor activities include exploring the Sounds by boat, trout fishing in the many rivers, beach and deep-sea fishing, rafting, sea kayaking, river cruises and horse trekking in the high country. Major events include the annual food, wine and beer festival, various garden festivals and the biennial Classic Airshow. Flying and gliding are popular here, as aviation engineering is one of the main industries and many retirees are ex-Air Force. The area is home to one of the largest collections of pre-WWII airplanes in the world, and there are also large collections of vintage machinery and classic cars.

• Boating • Bushwalking • Diving • Fishing • Galleries
• Horse riding • Libraries • Most community organisations
• Most religions • Museums • Sailing • Swimming

REAL ESTATE

• Median house price: $350 000
The quality of real estate here is variable but there are some very nicely presented homes and limited opportunities to purchase apartments.

WHY LIVE HERE?

If you enjoy nature and bushwalking, you may never tire of this area. It best suits outdoor types, although an interest in wine would also be an advantage.

nelson
At one with nature

Nelson overlooks Tasman Bay, just south of Marlborough Sounds, set amongst some of New Zealand's most popular national parks. Nelson is the name of both the city and the region. The city is small, sheltered by hills and flanked by sea and golden beaches. It's reputedly Australasia's largest fishing port, and tour boats make their way from here to secluded bays and pretty inlets. Nelson's compact retail centre has plenty of cafés and restaurants to cater to the many tourists who visit, lending the town a cosmopolitan feel which belies it size. The Nelson region's economy is based on fishing, horticulture (largely vineyards, stone fruit orchards and hops), tourism and forestry. It's also an area with a very vibrant arts community, which is reflected in its range of arts activities and festivals.

POPULATION

City of Nelson
- 41 600
- 20% over sixty

Nelson is growing slowly but at a slightly faster rate than neighbouring Marlborough.

CLIMATE

Summer 13.0°C to 22.3°C
Winter 1.5°C to 12.2°C
Sunshine 2407 hours
Rain 94 days
Rainfall 985 mm

LOCATION & GETTING AROUND

Nelson is 423 kilometres from Christchurch, a driving time of just over six hours. It is 109 kilometres from Picton, just over two hours by car. There are ferry connections to Wellington from Picton.

Roads State highways run west to Motueka and Golden Bay, East to Blenheim and Picton, and south through Murchison to the Lewis Pass and the west coast.

Nearest airport Nelson Airport operates daily internal flights but there are no international flights.

Nearest train ✗

Buses ✓

Taxis ✓

INFRASTRUCTURE

Hospitals Nelson Hospital and Alexandra Hospital, Richmond

Retirement villages Six in Nelson

Police stations Nelson and Motueka

Local newspaper *Nelson Mail*

RECREATION

Beaches The most central beach is Tahunanui, popular for swimming, windsurfing and kiteboarding. Cable Bay Reserve, 13 kilometres outside Nelson, has safe swimming, great kayaking, picnic grounds and a walkway. The Glen, Boulder Bank Reserve and Monaco Reserve also have swimming and good picnic areas. Slightly further away are the beautiful golden beaches of Abel Tasman National Park and Golden Bay.

Coastguard ✓

Cycleways There is an extensive network of cycleways throughout Nelson City and off-street cycling on the Stoke Railway Reserve, Whakatu Drive and Tahunanui Beach Reserve.

Bushwalking & National Parks Nelson is well known for the three national parks on its doorstep. The Abel Tasman National Park, with its golden sandy beaches and turquoise waters, has a coastal track skirting inlets and bays. Kayaking is good here and it is possible to swim with seals at some of the beaches. Kahurangi National Park has native forest with a range of tracks stretching from the mountains to the coast. The rugged mountains of Nelson Lakes National Park have plenty of plant and bird life, and lakeside tracks and trails winding through beech forests.

Dogs Nelson has numerous exercise areas, including some near beaches and rivers.

SHOPPING

Nelson's shopping is compact but varied, and it has a number of supermarkets. There are shopping centres throughout the area, with Richmond's the largest outside the city of Nelson. Nelson is renowned for arts and crafts, including pottery, jewellery, woodworking, weaving, glassworks and painting; there are galleries in the old coolstores on Mapua Wharf. The Saturday outdoor markets sell food, jewellery and crafts. The ring which featured in the *Lord of the Rings* trilogy was created by local Nelson jeweller Jens Hansen.

DINING

Restaurants can be found in the vineyards and along the waterfront, along with pubs and cafés. The most common cuisine is fresh local seafood, served with local wines. A Hooked on Seafood Festival is celebrated in March. Mapua Wharf has fabulous restaurants housed in old boatsheds, and Richmond also has a restaurant/café strip.

SOCIAL ACTIVITY

Plenty of outdoor activities are available, including sailing, diving, sea kayaking, horse riding, golf, skiing, caving, and trout and sea fishing. There are arts, crafts and garden trails, and plenty of art galleries, studios, theatres and cinemas. The region holds the annual Nelson Arts Festival, Summer Festival and biannual Chamber of Music Festival.

• Arts & crafts • Bushwalking • Cinema • Diving

- Fishing • Galleries • Golf • Horse riding
- Most community organisations • Most religions
- Sailing • Swimming • Theatre • Windsurfing

REAL ESTATE

- Median house price: $350 000
- Median unit price: $275 000

There are some very attractive homes in this area, many with views.

WHY LIVE HERE?

The location is a little remote but there's a constant stream of visitors passing through. You could either be part of it or just opt to do your own thing.

christchurch
An English country garden

Christchurch is like an English village on a large scale – the river is even named the Avon and it looks like its namesake, right down to the flat-bottomed boats punting along its length. Known as the Garden City, Christchurch has expansive parks and gardens, and the river meanders across town to the botanic gardens in stunning Hagley Park. It's also a pedestrian-friendly city, with wide footpaths, the large central Cathedral Square at its heart and trams doing a loop of the city, from the gardens to the square.

The city's Pacific coastline features beaches and rocky inlets; inland and to the west are farmlands, rivers, forested foothills and lakes, followed by villages and ski areas such as Mount Hutt in the Southern Alps. To the south are rivers popular for rafting, fishing and kayaking, while to the north there's the whale-watching centre of Kaikoura.

POPULATION

- 335 000
- 18.5% over sixty

CLIMATE

Summer 12.2°C to 22.5°C
Winter 1.9°C to 11.3°C
Sunshine 2102 hours
Rain 85 days
Rainfall 648 mm

LOCATION & GETTING AROUND

Christchurch is the South Island's biggest city, located on the east coast on Pegasus Bay in the Canterbury region.
Roads Highway One runs north to south and Highway 73 is the main road heading west.
Nearest airport Christchurch, with international flights
Nearest train Christchurch. The *TranzAlpine* runs daily to Greymouth. The *TransCoastal* train to Picton via Kaikoura and Blenheim connects with the Interislander ferry to Wellington and the North Island.
Buses ✓
Taxis ✓

INFRASTRUCTURE

Hospitals Christchurch, Burwood and Princess Margaret are public hospitals, although the latter two tend to be specialist hospitals. Private hospitals are St George's and Southern Cross.
Retirement villages Over 20 in the area
Police stations ✓
Local newspapers *Ashburton Guardian* and *Press*

RECREATION

Beaches Christchurch's long stretches of sandy beach are patrolled in summer; they include Spencer Park, Waimairi, New Brighton, the Pier, the popular Sumner Beach and Taylors Mistake (which is good for surfing). There's also swimming in the estuary of the Avon and Heathcote Rivers.
Coastguard ✓

Cycleways With its flat topography and cycle network (which is being expanded), Christchurch is bicycle-friendly. There are also some off-road paths.

Bushwalking & National Parks Arthurs Pass National Park is directly west of the city on Highway 73. The Hanmer Forest National Park is within easy reach of Christchurch to the north, and offers walks through forests of native and exotic trees, rafting, horse trekking and swimming in thermal pools. The Mount Cook National Park between Christchurch and Queenstown is home to New Zealand's highest mountain and longest glacier, and as well as being a favourite for mountaineering and skiing it also has some easy family walks. Within Christchurch's surrounds is the Bexley Wetland with expansive views and abundant bird life. Foreshore tracks include Southern Pegasus Bay Track, heading north to Spencer's Park, and there are also more-urban City Heritage Trails. The beach at Taylors Mistake has walks around Godley Head.

Dogs There are many parks and foreshore areas available for dog exercising, including Groynes Dog Park and agility course, Victoria Dog Park, Horseshoe Lake Reserve, Radley Dog Park and agility course, Styx Mill Reserve and Bottle Lake Reserve.

SHOPPING

As can be expected in any large city, there are plenty of shopping malls, including Eastgate Mall, Riccarton, South City, South City Centre and New Brighton Pier Mall. There are also many arts and crafts stores, and the Art Centre has a collection of handicraft outlets and workshops and hosts weekend markets.

DINING

The range of dining is vast, with all varieties of international cuisines available. In the city centre there are many popular restaurants in Colombo, Cashel, Manchester and High Streets. Oxford Terrace, overlooking the Avon River, has a strip of outdoor restaurants, cafés and wine bars. Sumner and New Brighton Beaches have good seafood restaurants.

SOCIAL ACTIVITY

The many outdoor activities include boating, rafting, kayaking, ballooning, gondola rides, skiing and mountain biking. There are a wealth of cultural centres, theatres, art and craft exhibitions, galleries, a maritime museum, military museum and the Canterbury Museum. There are also various gardens and wineries to explore, and the Floral and Romance Festival takes place annually in February.

- All community organisations • All religions • Arts & crafts
- Boating • Bushwalking • Galleries • Golf • Horse riding
- Museums • Surfing • Swimming • Theatre • Walking

REAL ESTATE

- Median house price: $210 000

WHY LIVE HERE?

This is a special place, which will appeal to all anglophiles who love gardens and to anyone who would like to live in a small city close enough to the great outdoors of the South Island.

new zealand's top 10

1. **BEST RETIREMENT HOTSPOT: Nelson**
   Picturesque, peaceful and upwardly mobile.

2. **BEST RETIREMENT LIFESTYLE: Bay of Plenty**
   New Zealand's Sunshine Coast.

3. **BEST SMALL LOCATION: Picton**
   Historic fishing port surrounded by nature's beauty.

4. **BEST LARGE LOCATION: Christchurch**
   City of parks and gardens.

5. **BEST SHOPPING: Wellington**

6. **BEST DINING: Christchurch**

7. **BEST PLACE TO CURL UP WITH A GOOD BOOK: Picton**

8. **BEST BEACHES: Tauranga**

9. **BEST OUTDOOR ACTIVITIES: Marlborough Region**
   A tramper's paradise.

10. **BEST-VALUE REAL ESTATE: Kapiti Coast**

appendix 1: the statistics

Identifying the retirement hotspots featured in this book was not an easy task. My first port of call was the Australian Bureau of Statistics (ABS), which gave me a list ranking the percentage of people who were aged over sixty-five in urban centres at the time of the last census (August 2001).

In order to ascertain where the over-sixties were concentrated, I examined the ABS statistics for each urban centre in detail. In the case of capital cities, I studied each area by postcode in order to obtain the potential nominees for retirement hotspots. The list I was developing provided some false leads; for example, some places showed a leaning towards over-sixties because the younger people were leaving town. If the total population of a location is shrinking, it's hardly a retirement magnet. By comparing the 1996 census data with that taken in 2001, I was able to eliminate places where the population was declining.

In addition to the census data, I used the June 2003 Estimated Resident Populations by Local Government Area and June 2002 Median Age Data by Local Government Area reports to help identify hotspot locations. Unless otherwise specified, the population figures used in this book were drawn from the August 2001 census, the details of which were released in 2003.

It's interesting to note that, according to the ABS, in June 2002 the national median age was approximately thirty-six. This means that half the population of Australia was younger than thirty-six and half the population was older. At the time of the last census, 16.8 per cent of the Australian population were aged over sixty and 12.6 per cent were over sixty-five years old.

appendix 2: tips for selecting your ideal retirement location

Are you prepared to up sticks and move away from your familiar neighbourhood with all its baggage? Inevitably, it will be a balancing act because, no matter how you look at it, there are always compromises to be made.

Many people believe the ideal retirement solution is to retain their home in the city or town where they have lived for a large part of their lives and to buy a second property in one of their favourite places. For example, in the colder months a sojourn to Far North Queensland for four to six months during the dry season may suit a retired Taswegian better than being in either place year-round. For retirees looking for a second home, this book provides all the available options to explore.

But having two homes is expensive. If you like the idea of having two homes but are unable to afford them, there are alternatives. One is to downsize, buying a small bolthole in your hometown and a more substantial home in your chosen retirement location. Another is not to sell or buy at all, but to let out the family home and rent in the chosen location. This is an excellent way to test the concept and have an escape plan should it not work out.

If you don't want to spend your time permanently in one place, and prefer to experience everything on offer, perhaps you need to consider purchasing a mobile home. Australia's Grey Nomads are estimated to number around 80 000 – that's the size of a large city – and sales of mobile homes are booming. Many retirees have sold their homes and now live on the road, spending just a few days or even several months in each location, without any fixed plan or deadline. Perhaps, like me, they have been searching for the one perfect location before setting up a permanent new home. This nomadic population can only increase as Baby Boomers join the numbers of Grey Nomads travelling around Australia.

Whichever strategy you choose, you will need to do your homework before you cut the umbilical cord with your old ties. Here are four steps to help you make the right choice.

1. Think about what you want before you start looking. Write down a list of what is important to you, and if there are two of you make sure you both agree with the list.
2. Go through all the retirement locations in this book that meet your requirements. Select a number of possible locations – the more the merrier.
3. Do some further desk research on your short list. Many councils can mail you a New Residents Kit which contains useful advice, and the Internet is also a useful tool to gather information.
4. Spend time in the chosen area before you buy, ideally a full year so you can experience each season.

Once you've narrowed the field, the following checklist of points to consider should help you make your decision.

- How will you keep in contact with your family and friends?
- The location may be suitable now, but will it be suitable when you are older?
- Are there medical considerations to take into account?
- Are there sufficient shops, restaurants and cafés in the area, and can you walk to any of them?
- Can you afford the home and lifestyle you want?
- If you intend to move into a unit, will you miss the garden? Will you be happy sharing decisions with others in the body corporate? Will you mind having neighbours living on the other side of a common wall?
- Will you be able to take your pets along with you?
- Is there sufficient mental, cultural and physical stimulation in the new location?

- Is the climate acceptable to you, year-round?
- What are the local community issues and problems?
- Can you test out the idea without fully committing?
- Do you have an escape plan in case it doesn't work out?

THE COSTS

Most older people who live in a capital city and who own their own homes believe that by selling up they can move to a similar standard of home and have a bit of money left over to help fund their retirement. However, because of the costs associated with buying and selling there may not be quite as much money left over as they first thought. In addition, prices in some retirement hotspots have risen considerably and the differential may not be large. It is therefore important that you prepare a thorough budget that covers all the moving costs and your day-to-day spending requirements.

The cost of selling and buying a home is significant. Firstly, unless you sell privately, you will have to pay a hefty commission to a real estate agent. Commission is normally around 2 per cent, although agents are competitive and open to negotiation; there is no commission payable to the agent when purchasing. Don't forget to ensure that the GST is included and not added after a commission rate is agreed. Another selling cost will be the price of any advertising for the sale or auction, which may include additional items for photography, drafting floor plans, printing leaflets and a website entry.

Depending upon the circumstances, vendors may be liable for tax applied to the sale price; check the situation with your accountant. Legal fees apply to both the sale and purchase of a home and are typically a couple of thousand dollars. A cheaper alternative to using a solicitor is to use a conveyancer. One of the largest costs for purchasers will be stamp duty, and again it depends upon the state in which you are purchasing. On average, the stamp duty on a $500 000 purchase will be $20 000, varying from around $12 000 in Queensland to $26 000 in Victoria. In

Queensland investment properties attract a higher scale of stamp duty than homes purchased by owner-occupiers. Finally, there are the moving costs, including the cost of freighting furniture intrastate or interstate.

Selling your family home for, say, $700 000 and buying one for $500 000 could therefore involve the following costs:

Sale costs

Agent's commission	$14 000
Advertising costs	$5000
Legal costs	$2000
Removalist costs	$4000

Purchase costs

Stamp duty on purchase	$13 000
Legal costs	$2000

Total moving costs   **$40 000**

Instead of having $200 000 left over after the purchase of your new home, you have only $160 000.

The next aspect to consider is what to do with the $160 000 you now have in your pocket. If you are planning to invest the money rather than spend it on a boat, you will need to seek professional advice. As a rule of thumb, $100 000 invested conservatively should return 5 per cent per annum after tax. Our theoretical $160 000 should return around $8000 every year after tax.

If you have a superannuation fund you should have your financial affairs reviewed annually. To find a financial adviser in your area you can contact the Financial Planning Association or visit your local bank.

YOUR RETIREMENT LIFESTYLE

The above simplified example shows that saving money should not be your primary reason for moving. The main reason to move is to enjoy a better and more relaxed lifestyle. This includes a better climate, moving away from the frenetic bustle and pollution of the city and being closer to the pleasures which you now have time to enjoy.

I believe that lifestyle preference is the only valid reason for relocating. The reason for this is simple: money doesn't buy happiness. Choose your location because you really want to be there.

COMMUNICATIONS

Wherever you retire in Australia, chances are you will have access to modern communications. Pay TV and the Internet may be accessed via satellite or phone line with delays, there may be imperfections in television reception and black holes in mobile phone coverage, but services are improving every day. Even Karumba in the Gulf Savannah region now has television reception. You can with reasonable certainty assume that your chosen area has coverage, but if you want to be absolutely positive you should check with the relevant provider.

RETIREMENT VILLAGES

Where possible, I have identified where retirement villages are located. The number of retirement villages in capital cities is considered to be adequate and growing to meet future needs. However, in many coastal locations outside the metropolitan areas they are in short supply and there are waiting lists. The presence of a retirement village may not be something you consider when you first retire but it could become an issue in later years. If this is a concern for you, check the availability of suitable retirement villages in the area before committing and make sure you ask about the extent of waiting lists and plans to open new villages.

By 2025, one in three Australian citizens will be aged over fifty-five. State and federal governments recognise that existing facilities will not be able to cope with future demand and that they must rethink their approach to the ageing community. Greater emphasis on the concept of 'ageing in place', with services coming to the elderly rather than the reverse, will be necessary to supplement the supply of dedicated retirement villages.

PRESSURE ON INFRASTRUCTURE & SERVICES

Another issue to keep in mind is that infrastructure and services in some country areas may not meet your expectations. Our population is on the move but the infrastructure of newly popular locations may not be meeting requirements. Residents are continually pushing local governments for facilities such as hospitals and other important infrastructure and the situation can only worsen. In recognition of this problem, seventy coastal councils have formed a National Seachange Taskforce to consider funding alternatives.

Increased populations also create pressure on the local environment – the beaches and national parks which we love so dearly. These pressures can only worsen as the Baby Boomers start to retire. At the last census there were over 3 150 000 people aged over sixty in Australia; by 2010 that figure will reach over 4 500 000. Areas that appeal to retirees today are going to become even more popular and more congested. More-remote areas, such as 1770 and Agnes Water, are emerging as new retirement destinations, which in turn will place pressure on their infrastructure.

An example is Queensland's Sunshine and Gold Coasts. A few years ago the roads feeding the Sunshine Coast were perfectly adequate; they are now bumper to bumper for a part of every day. The Queensland Government is so concerned about development on the Gold Coast that it has announced a plan designed to switch development to Ipswich, which is not on the coast and has a poor public image.

Before moving to a growth area, it is important to check exactly how the council plans to cope with the increasing population.

BABY BOOMER RETIREES

Currently, retirement in Australia revolves around golf courses, lawn bowls and fishing. I can't recall a location which doesn't have the first two, and the latter is a prominent pastime even in most inland retirement locations. I have also noticed the high dependency on clubs for food and entertainment. It's likely that the Baby Boomers will require more choice, which can only be a good thing. There are already signs of change in some of the locations; for example, an increase in architect-designed housing, in the standards of service and quality of dining. Perhaps we will see a cosmopolitan revolution of sorts, as more country areas become citified. It's more likely that we will see increased options emerging, with more locations breaking the stereotype and doing their own thing like Byron, going more upmarket like Noosa, more gentrified like Berrima, more arty like Mudgee or more pampering like Daylesford.

It will be interesting to see how the retirement magnets adapt to the Baby Boomers or whether the Baby Boomers will simply adapt to their new environment.

These are exciting times, and more and more of us are realising that there are lifestyle options in retirement beyond the horizons of our own backyards. I hope this book will help readers make choices that will enhance their retirement and make these the most enjoyable years.

appendix 3: notes

POPULATION

Unless otherwise noted, population sizes and approximate percentages of over-sixties are based on the August 2001 census. The 2003 figures are estimates provided by the Australian Bureau of Statistics, rather than hard data.

CLIMATE

Temperature statistics indicate the mean daily minimum and maximum temperatures in peak summer and winter. 'Sunshine days' are the mean number of clear days per annum; the Bureau of Meteorology's definition of 'clear days' is 'free from cloud, fog, mist or dust haze'. 'Rain days' are the average number of days on which rain fell per annum. Rainfall is the mean annual rainfall. All Australian climate information is from the Australian Bureau of Meteorology website.

New Zealand information comes from council and MetService sources. 'Sunshine hours' are the mean average number of hours of sunshine per year.

REAL ESTATE

Prices are based on the twelve-month median prices quoted on real estate websites such as domain.com.au, where available, for 2005. Prices quoted in the New Zealand chapter are in Australian dollars.

acknowledgements

The information included in this book relies heavily on a number of people and a number of sources.

Sources included the Australian Bureau of Statistics, the Australian Bureau of Meteorology, the domain.com.au real estate website and what seemed like every tourist bureau in Australia and every council website in Australia. The willingness of volunteers in tourist offices to provide information and discuss retirement in their area was outstanding. In many cases I needed to follow up with councils for more information, and was always given the utmost help and support in providing the information I needed.

My sister Susan Labutis conducted much of the early desk research and I am deeply indebted to her thoroughness and ability to cut through the Internet to the facts which are not always easy to find. My son Antony accompanied me to numerous Queensland locations and I appreciated his company as well as his input. On many of the field trips I would have been lost without my partner Judy. She had a natural affinity for the project and was able to speedily unearth relevant information and ask probing questions of locals.

I would also like to thank Penguin Books for their support and guidance. I dealt with a number of publishers at Penguin, partly because they tended to go off on maternity leave as soon as they became involved in my project! Specifically, my thanks go to Julie Gibbs, Ali Watts, Kirsten Abbott and senior editor Janet Austin.

Finally, I would like to thank the hundreds of Australians and quite a few New Zealanders we spoke to on our travels and who all took the time to talk to us. It is amazing that, despite the distances, we are all pretty much the same. Australians and New Zealanders laugh easily, are very friendly and don't take themselves too seriously. And every one of them reckons their particular spot is the best place on the planet.

index

1770, Qld   31–3, 85

Adelaide, SA   279–85, 299
Agnes Water, Qld   31–3
Albany, WA   303–06, 336
Albury, NSW   234
Alexander Beach, Qld   44
Alstonville, NSW   97, 98
Amity Point, Qld   66–9
Angaston, SA   293
Anna Bay, NSW   127, 129
Ansons Bay, Tas.   258
Apollo Bay, Vic.   225–7, 243
Applecross, WA   319
Arrawarra, NSW   106
Atherton, Qld   17–20
Augusta, WA   306–09
Avalon, NSW   147
Avoca, NSW   140, 142
Ayr, Qld   25

Babinda, Qld   22
Bairnsdale, Vic.   201
Ballina, NSW   94, 95, 97–100
Balmoral, NSW   150–2
Balnarring, Vic.   211
Bangalow, NSW   93, 95, 96
Bargara, Qld   34–7, 85
Barham, NSW   234
Barossa Valley, SA   293–5
Barwon Heads, Vic.   221
Bateau Bay, NSW   135
Batehaven, NSW   171
Batemans Bay, NSW   171–5
Battery Point, Tas.   264
Bay of Fires, Tas.   258
Bay of Plenty, NZ   341–4, 359
Bayview, NSW   147
Beaumaris, Tas.   258
Bega Valley, NSW   175–9
Bellara, Qld   56
Bellarine Peninsula, Vic.   221–4, 243
Bellarine, Vic.   221
Bellevue Hill, NSW   153–5
Belmont, NSW   131–4
Benalla, Vic.   234
Bermagui, NSW   175–9
Berrima, NSW   189–93
Berry, NSW   159, 162
Biggera Waters, Qld   70, 74, 77
Binalong Bay, Tas.   258
Bingal Bay, Qld   20
Black Rock, Vic.   216

Blackheath, NSW   185–8
Blenheim, NZ   349–51
Blue Mountains, NSW   185–8, 194
Blueys Beach, NSW   123, 125, 126
Bogangar, NSW   89
Bold Park, WA   319
Bomaderry   159, 161
Bongaree, Qld   54, 56
Bonny Hills, NSW   115
Bowral, NSW   189–93
Breamlea, Vic.   221
Bribie Island, Qld   54–7
Bridport, Tas.   254–7, 269
Brighton, SA   281–5
Brighton, Vic.   216–19
Broadbeach Waters, Qld   78
Broadbeach, Qld   71, 74, 75, 81
Broadwater, Qld   70, 77–9
Brook Hill, NSW   139
Broulee, NSW   171
Brunswick Heads, NSW   93
Buderim, Qld   46–7
Bundaberg, Qld   34–7
Bundanoon, NSW   189–93
Bungan Beach, NSW   147, 148
Burleigh Heads, Qld   71, 73, 83, 85
Burleigh Waters, Qld 79
Burnett Heads, Qld   34
Burnie, Tas.   248
Burnside, SA   279
Burrawang, NSW   189–93
Burrill Lake, NSW   167
Busselton, WA   309–12, 336
Byron Bay, NSW   93–6, 194

Caboolture, Qld   55, 57–60
Cairns, Qld   14–17, 85
Callala Bay, NSW   163
Caloundra, Qld   51–3
Camden Haven, NSW   115
Camperdown, Vic.   228
Cape Woolamai, Vic.   208–10
Capricorn Coast, Qld   27–31
Cardwell, Qld   21–3
Carnarvon, WA   330–2, 336
Cassowary Coast, Qld   20–4
Castlemaine, Vic.   231
Chevron Island, Qld   79
Christchurch, NZ   355–8, 359
City Beach, WA   319–21
Clear Island Waters, Qld   79
Cleveland, Qld   67
Clifton Springs, Vic.   221

Clunes, Vic. 230
Coal Point, NSW 131
Cobargo, NSW 175
Cobden, Vic. 228
Cobram, Vic. 234–7
Coffs Harbour, NSW 106–09, 194
Colac, Vic. 228–30
Collaroy, NSW 147
Connewarre, Vic. 221
Coolangatta, Qld 70, 75, 83–4
Coolum Beach, Qld 45–6, 85
Copper Coast, SA 296–8, 299
Coral Coast, Qld 34–7
Corlette, NSW 127, 128
Corowa, NSW 234
Cottesloe, WA 319–21
Cowes, Vic. 208–10
Cremorne Point, NSW 150–2
Creswick, Vic. 230, 231
Crowdy Head, NSW 119
Cudmirrah, NSW 168
Curlewis, Vic. 221
Currumbin Waters, Qld 79
Currumbin, Qld 71, 83–4
Cypress Gardens, Qld 79

Dalkeith, WA 319
Dalmeny, NSW 171
Darling Point, NSW 153–5
Dawesville, WA 313
Daylesford, Vic. 230–3, 243
Dee Why, NSW 147
Denham, WA 327–9
Denhams Beach, NSW 171
Denmark, WA 303
Devonport, Tas. 248
Dimboola, Vic. 237
Dooralong Valley, NSW 135, 139
Dora Creek, NSW 131–4
Double Bay, NSW 153–5
Dover Heights, NSW 153–5
Dromana, Vic. 211
Drysdale, Vic. 221
Dunsborough, WA 310
Dunwich, Qld 66–9

Echuca, Vic. 234
Eden, NSW 175–9
Edgecliff, NSW 153–5
Elanora, Qld 79
Elizabeth Beach, NSW 123
Elliott Heads, Qld 34
Emerald, NSW 106
Emu Park, Qld 27–31
Emu Point, WA 303
Ephraim Island, Qld 77
Erina, NSW 141
Erowal Bay, NSW 163
Ettalong, NSW 140
Euroa, Vic. 234
Evans Head, NSW 97
Exeter, NSW 189–93
Exmouth, WA 333–5

Federal, NSW 93

Felixstow, SA 279
Fingal Bay, NSW 127–30
Fingal, NSW 89, 90
Fingal, Tas. 258
Firle, SA 279
Floreat, WA 319
Florida Gardens, Qld 78
Forster, NSW 123–7
Frankston, Vic. 211–14
Fraser Coast, Qld 37–41
Fraser Island, Qld 37, 38, 39–40
Fremantle, WA 316–19, 336
Fulham, SA 282

Gatakers Bay, Qld 38
Geelong, Vic. 221
Geraldton, WA 324–7
Gerringong, NSW 156, 157
Gerroa, NSW 156
Glen Eira, Vic. 216
Glenelg, SA 281–5
Glynde, SA 279
Gold Coast, Qld 70, 84, 85
Goolwa, SA 289–93
Gordon, NSW 144–5
Gordonvale, Qld 22
Gorokan, NSW 135
Gosford, NSW 139–43
Grafton, NSW 103–05, 194
Great Lakes, NSW 123–7
Green Point, NSW 131
Gulgong, NSW 183

Hampton, Vic. 216–19
Harrington Waters, NSW 119
Harrington, NSW 119
Hastings Valley, NSW 115, 116
Hastings, Vic. 211
Havelock, NZ 349
Hawks Nest, NSW 127
Henley, SA 281–5
Hepburn Springs, Vic. 230–3, 243
Herberton, Qld 19
Hervey Bay, Qld 37–41, 85
Hinchinbrook Island, Qld 21, 23
Hindmarsh Island, SA 289
Hobart, Tas. 264–8, 269
Holdfast Bay, SA 281–5
Hollywell, Qld 70, 77
Hope Island, Qld 70, 74, 75–7
Horsham, Vic. 237–9, 243
Huskisson, NSW 163–7
Hyams Beach, NSW 163

Iluka, NSW 100, 101
Indented Head, Vic. 221
Innisfail, Qld 21, 23
Inverloch, Vic. 205–07
Irymple, Vic. 239
Isle of Capri, Qld 78

Jervis Bay, NSW 163–7, 194
Joslin, SA 279

Kadina, SA 296–8

Kalbarri, WA 324–7, 336
Kangaroo Valley, NSW 159–60
Kapiti Coast, NZ 345–8, 359
Kapiti Island, NZ 345, 347
Karuah, NSW 127
Karumba, Qld 11–13
Katikati, NZ 341–4
Katoomba, NSW 185–8
Kensington Gardens, SA 279
Kiama, NSW 156–9
Killara, NSW 144–5
Kincumber, NSW 141
Kingscliff, NSW 89, 90, 91, 92
Kingscote, SA 290
Kingston, SA 273–6, 299
Kingston, Tas. 264
Kirribilli, NSW 150–2
Korora, NSW 106
Kuranda, Qld 18
Ku-ring-gai, NSW 144–6

Labrador, Qld 70, 78
Lake Cathie, NSW 115, 118
Lake Conjola, NSW 167
Lake Macquarie, NSW 131–4
Lake Tinaroo, Qld 19, 20
Lakes Entrance, Vic. 201–05
Launceston, Tas. 261–4, 269
Laurieton, NSW 115, 118
Lavender Bay, NSW 150–2
Lemon Tree Passage, NSW 127
Lennox Head, NSW 95, 97, 98, 99
Leopold, Vic. 221
Leura, NSW 185–8
Lighthouse Beach, NSW 115
Lilli Pilli, NSW 171
Lindfield, NSW 144–5
Long Jetty, NSW 135
Lorne, Vic. 225–7, 243

Macksville, NSW 110
Maclean, NSW 100, 102
Magnetic Island, Qld 24
Main Beach, Qld 71, 74
Mallacoota, Vic. 199–201, 243
Malua Bay, NSW 171
Mandurah, WA 312–15, 336
Manly, NSW 147–50, 194
Mannerim, Vic. 221
Marcus Hill, Vic. 221
Marden, SA 279
Margaret River, WA 306–09, 336
Marlborough, NZ 349–52, 359
Maroochydore, Qld 48–50
Maryborough, Qld 39
Matcham, NSW 139, 142
McLaren Vale, SA 285–7, 299
Melbourne, Vic. 216–21, 243
Melbourne – by the bay, Vic. 216–19, 243
Melros Beach, WA 313
Mentone, Vic. 216
Merbein, Vic. 239
Merimbula, NSW 175–9
Mermaid Beach, Qld 71, 73, 83
Mermaid Waters, Qld 79

Metung, Vic. 201–05
Miami Keys, Qld 79
Miami, Qld 71, 73, 83
Middleton Beach, WA 303
Midway Point, Tas. 264
Mildura, Vic. 239–42
Milton, NSW 167–70
Mindarie, WA 319
Mission Beach, Qld 20–4
Mittagong, NSW 189–93
Mollymook, NSW 167–70
Mona Vale, NSW 147–9
Monkey Mia, WA 327, 328
Mooloolaba, Qld 48–50
Moonta, SA 296–8
Moore Park, Qld 34
Moreton Bay, Qld 55, 61
Moreton Island, Qld 54, 61
Morisset, NSW 131–4
Mornington Peninsula, Vic. 210–15, 243
Mornington, Vic. 211–14
Moruya, NSW 171–5
Mosman, NSW 150–2
Moss Vale, NSW 189–93
Mossy Point, NSW 171
Mount Eliza, Vic. 211–14
Mount Maunganui, NZ 341, 343, 344
Mount Victoria, NSW 185–8
Mount Wilson, NSW 185–8
Mount Claremont, WA 319
Mount Martha, Vic. 211–14
Mudgee, NSW 182–4
Mullumbimby, NSW 93, 96
Mulwala, NSW 234
Murray Bridge, SA 276–8
Murwillumbah, NSW 89, 90, 91, 92
Myall Lake, NSW 123

Nambour, Qld 46–7
Nambucca Heads, NSW 110–13
Narooma, NSW 171–5
Narrabeen, NSW 147
Narrawallee, NSW 168
Nelson Bay, NSW 127–30
Nelson, NZ 352–5, 359
Nerang, Qld 71, 72, 73, 74, 80
Neutral Bay, NSW 150–2
Newcastle, NSW 131
Newhaven, Vic. 208–10
Newport, NSW 147
Nhill, Vic. 237
Noarlunga, SA 285
Noosa Heads, Qld 42, 43
Noosa, Qld 42–5, 85
Noosaville, Qld 42, 44, 45
Norah Head, NSW 135
Normanton, Qld 11, 12, 13
North Haven, NSW 115
North Stradbroke Island, Qld 66–9
Novar Gardens, SA 282
Nowra, NSW 159–63
Numurkah, Vic. 234
Nuriootpa, SA 293

Ocean Grove, Vic. 221

Ocean Shores, NSW 93
Old Bar, NSW 119
Opal Cove, NSW 106
Otaki, NZ 345
Ouyen, Vic. 239–42

Pacific Harbour, Qld 54
Paekakariki, NZ 345
Palm Beach, NSW 147–50
Palm Beach, Qld 71, 73, 83
Palm Cove, Qld 16
Pambula, NSW 175, 176
Papomoa Beach, NZ 341
Paradise Point, Qld 70, 74, 77, 78
Paradise Waters, Qld 79
Paraparaumu, NZ 345–8
Payneham, SA 279
Paynesville, Vic. 201–05
Pearl Beach, NSW 140
Peregian Beach, Qld 42, 46
Perth, WA 319–21, 336
Phillip Island, Vic. 208–10
Pialba, Qld 38
Picton, NZ 349–51, 359
Pittwater, NSW 147–50
Point Lonsdale, Vic. 221
Point Lookout, Qld 66–9
Point Piper, NSW 153–5
Point Vernon, Qld 38
Port Adelaide, SA 282
Port Douglas, Qld 14–17
Port Elliot, SA 290
Port Hinchinbrook, Qld 21
Port Macquarie, NSW 115–19
Port Sorell, Tas. 251–4
Port Stephens, NSW 127–30
Portarlington, Vic. 221
Portsea, Vic. 211–14
Possum Creek, NSW 93
Pottsville Beach, NSW 89, 92
Pretty Beach, NSW 140
Pumicestone Passage, Qld 54
Pymble, NSW 144–5

Queen Charlotte Sound, NZ 349, 350
Queenscliff, Vic. 221–4, 243

Rainbow Bay, Qld 38
Raumati Beach, NZ 345
Ravenshoe, Qld 18, 19
Red Cliffs, Vic. 239–42
Red Hill, Vic. 211
Redcliffe, Qld 60–3
Rhyll, Vic. 208–10
Rialto, Qld 78
Rio Vista, Qld 78
Robe, SA 273–6, 299
Robertson, NSW 189–93
Robina, Qld 71, 72, 73, 74, 80
Rochester, Vic. 234
Rockhampton, Qld 27–31, 85
Rose Bay, NSW 153–5
Rosebud, Vic. 211
Roseville, NSW 144–6
Rottnest Island, WA 316, 317, 336

Royston Park, SA 279
Runaway Bay, Qld 70, 78
Russell and Macleay Islands, Qld 66–9
Rye, Vic. 211

Salamander Bay, NSW 127
Salt, NSW 89
San Remo, Vic. 208–10
Sanctuary Cove, Qld 70, 75–7
Sanctuary Point, NSW 163
Sandringham, Vic. 216–19
Sandstone Point, Qld 54
Sandy Bay, Tas. 264
Sapphire, NSW 106
Sapphire Coast, NSW 175–9
Sawtell, NSW 106, 107, 108
Scamander, Tas. 258
Scarborough, Qld 60
Scarborough, WA 319
Scarness, Qld 38
Scottsdale, Tas. 254–7
Seal Rocks, NSW 123
Seddon, NZ 349
Semaphore, SA 282
Seven Mile Beach, NSW 158, 161
Shearwater, Tas. 251
Shelly Beach, NSW 135
Shepparton, Vic. 234
Shoal Bay, NSW 127–30
Shoalhaven Heads, NSW 159, 161
Shoalhaven, NSW 159–63
Smiths Lake, NSW 123
Soldiers Point, NSW 127
Somerset, Tas. 248
Sorell, Tas. 264
Sorrento, Qld 78
Sorrento, Vic. 211–14
South Mission Beach, Qld 20
South West Rocks, NSW 113–15
Southern Highlands, NSW 189–93, 194
Southport, Qld 70, 73, 74
Sovereign Island, Qld 70, 75–7
Speers Point, NSW 131
St Georges Basin, NSW 163
St Helens, Tas. 258–61, 269
St Huberts Island, NSW 140
St Ives, NSW 145
St Leonards, Vic. 222
St Marys, Tas. 258
Stieglitz, Tas. 258
Strathalbyn, SA 287–9
Subiaco, WA 319
Sunrise Beach, Qld 42
Sunshine Beach, Qld 42
Sunshine Coast, Qld 42–53
Surfers Paradise, Qld 71, 72, 74, 75, 81–2
Sussex Inlet, NSW 169, 171
Swanbourne, WA 319
Swansea, NSW 131–4
Sydney, NSW 144–55, 194

Tamworth, NSW 179–81
Tanunda, SA 293
Taree, NSW 119–23
Taroona, Tas. 264

Tathra, NSW   175–9
Tauranga, NZ   341–4, 359
Te Horo, NZ   345
Te Puke, NZ   341
Tea Gardens, NSW   127
Terang, Vic.   228–30
Terrigal, NSW   140
Tewantin, Qld   42, 44, 45
The Entrance, NSW   135
Tin Can Bay, Qld   38
Tinderbox, Tas.   264
Tocumwal, NSW   234
Tongala, Vic.   234
Toorak, Vic.   219–21
Tootgarook, Vic.   211
Toowoomba, Qld   63–6
Toowoon Bay, NSW   135, 136
Toronto, NSW   131–4
Torquay, Qld   38
Toukley, NSW   135, 137
Townsville, Qld   24–7, 85
Trentham, Vic.   232
Trinity Gardens, SA   279
Tuggerah, NSW   135–9
Tugun, Qld   83
Tully, Qld   21, 22
Tuncurry, NSW   123–7
Tuross Heads, NSW   171
Turramurra, NSW   144
Tweed Heads, NSW   89–92
Tweed Valley, NSW   89–92
Two Rocks, WA   322–3
Twofold Bay, NSW   175
Tyabb, Vic.   211

Ulladulla, NSW   167–70
Umina, NSW   140
Urangan, Qld   38
Urunga, NSW   110

Valentine, NSW   131
Varsity Lakes, Qld   71
Vaucluse, NSW   153–5

Ventnor, Vic.   208–10
Victor Harbor, SA   289–93, 299
Vincentia, NSW   163–7

Wahroonga, NSW   144–5
Waikanae Beach, NZ   345
Wallaroo, SA   296–8
Wallington, Vic.   221
Wallis Lake, NSW   123
Wamberal, NSW   139
Wangaratta, Vic.   234–7, 243
Warners Bay, NSW   131–4
Warracknabeal, Vic.   237
Warrawee, NSW   145
Warriewood, NSW   147
Watsons Bay, NSW   153–5
Wauchope, NSW   116
Wellington, NZ   345–8, 359
Wentworth Falls, NSW   185–8
West Beach, SA   282
West Perth, WA   319
West Shores, SA   282
Whale Beach, NSW   147, 148
Willunga, SA   285–7, 299
Winchelsea, Vic.v228
Wingham, NSW   119
Wongaling Beach, Qld   20
Wonthaggi, Vic.   205, 206, 207
Woolgoolga, NSW   106, 107, 108
Woorim, Qld   54, 56
Woy Woy, NSW   140, 142
Wynyard, Tas.   248–51, 269
Wyong, NSW   135–9

Yallingup, WA   310
Yamba, NSW   100–05
Yanchep, WA   322–4
Yankalilla, SA   289
Yarramalong Valley, NSW   135, 139
Yarrawonga, Vic.   234–7, 243
Yeppoon, Qld   27–31
Yorkeys Knob, Qld   15, 17
Yungaburra, Qld   18, 19